D0783884

DIS/CONNECTED

DIS/CONNECTED

Why our kids are turning their backs on everything we thought we knew

Nick Barham

First published in Great Britain in 2004

10 9 8 7 6 5 4 3 2 1

First published by
Ebury Press
Random House, 20 Vauxhall Bridge Road, London SW1V 2SA

Random House Australia (Pty) Limited
20 Alfred Street, Milsons Point, Sydney, New South Wales 2061, Australia

Random House New Zealand Limited
18 Poland Road, Glenfield, Auckland 10, New Zealand

Random House South Africa (Pty) Limited
Endulini, 5A Jubilee Road, Parktown 2193, South Africa

The Random House Group Limited Reg. No. 954009

www.randomhouse.co.uk

A CIP catalogue record for this book is available from the British Library.

Cover Design by Two Associates
Text design and typesetting by Perfect Bound Ltd

ISBN 0091895863

Papers used by Ebury Press are natural, recyclable products made from wood grown in sustainable forests.

Printed and bound in Great Britain by Mackays of Chatham Plc

Thanks to all the people I spoke to.

You gave up your time and opinions.

Whether you're in here or not, you told me great stories.

Special thanks to Amanda, Anthea, Ben, Ivan, Jake, Leah, Martha, Martin and Nick K.

For reading fragments and keeping me connected.

Contents

Ready to party, then shot

LAST PHOTO

THE SUN, Saturday, January 4, 2003

Ghet

TWO MILLION WEAPONS ON UK'S STREET

Expert Roger Gray — a former Met police firearms officer — said: "Major UK cities are awash with illegal weapons...

Dangerous

UP to two million guns are on the streets of Britain, official estimates say.

Weapons ranging from 22 rifles to machine guns are freely available on the black market.

Many are smuggled in from ex-Soviet states.

Others are made from replica guns and air rifles, which can be converted with basic skills.

He added: "Hand guns are now a fashion accessory in the drug trade, along with black BMWs.

"You find that World War

Violen...s gan

CRAZED CULTURE

Happiness before horror . . . from left, injured Cheryl, Charlene who died, injured Sophie and Latisha who was also killed

Girls cut down in drug gangs' hail of bullets

By ANDREW PARKER

Teenage twin sisters were among the victims of a terrifying gun battle at a New Year's party yesterday.

Last night 18-year-old Charlene Ellis lay dead — while her sister Sophie was having surgery for bullet wounds.

GUN CARNAGE

TERROR

By MIKE SULLIVAN
Crime Editor

COP BLAMES BANDS FOR GUN PLAGUE

A POLICE chief yesterday slammed bands like So Solid Crew for fuelling Britain's rising gun culture.

Scotland Yard Commander Alan Brown warned that violent lyrics were turning youngsters on to firearms.

And groups like So Solid — whose saw band member Ashley "Asher D" Walters jailed last year for 18 months for having a gun were setting a bad example.

said: "It is all about face and respect. If someone disses you and you've got a firearm then people are shot.

"These people have no understanding of the consequences of using a firearm in this way.

A darker generation?

The idea for this book came in January 2003. At the time I was working in a large London ad agency, reading magazines, surfing websites, watching movies, checking out gigs and shops on behalf of trend-conscious clients. They were interested in what young people were up to, and part of my job was to tell them.

On New Year's Eve 2002, in Birmingham, two teenage girls, Charlene Ellis and Letisha Shakespeare, were shot dead as they stepped outside a party for some fresh air. They were the victims of a gun battle between two rival gangs.

This shocking and violent incident was disturbing enough in itself. But what surprised me was that it provided the impetus for a deep, anguished debate about contemporary British culture. Over the next few days the UK media focused as much on what they believed 'caused' this tragedy as on the tragedy itself. In the *Sun*, Scotland Yard Commander Alan Brown blamed violent lyrics for 'turning youngsters on to firearms'; elsewhere, Mr Blunkett led several attacks on 'appalling' rap lyrics, and Neil Fraser, a music producer known as the Mad Professor, stated in a letter to the *Telegraph* that 'the producers of BBC Radio 1's ragga and hip-hop shows should share some of the guilt every time a black youth dies from a gun in Britain'.

But the most sweeping criticisms and finger-pointing came from the minister for tourism, film and broadcasting, Kim Howells. 'For years I have been very worried about these hateful lyrics that these boasting macho idiot rappers come out with. It is a big cultural problem. Lyrics don't kill people but they don't half enhance the fare we get from videos and films. It has created a culture where killing is almost a fashion accessory.'

And he didn't stop there. A week later he was criticising video games and movies for simply being 'blood-spattered entertainment' and bemoaning the 'pornography of violence' that was infecting a generation of kids. In February he went further on Radio 4, denying that economics and poverty had any effect on crime, and again isolating rap music as a key factor in rising gun violence.

As someone who worked on the fringes of young British culture, I was struck by the ferocity of some of these attacks. Of course a similar debate surfaces every few years. But this particular moral panic trundled on long after the media had forgotten Charlene and Letisha, and it was always about the same thing: the extent to which fictitious things (songs, films, games, etc) bleed into the 'real' world, and make people behave differently. The attacks against the music industry, and more broadly most elements of youth entertainment, coupled with a refusal to acknowledge that real world conditions like education, poverty or the family might play a role in antisocial behaviour, disturbed me. It seemed to represent a new level of something I'd noticed over the years: kid-bashing, and general criticisms of many elements of contemporary culture: film, video, games, graffiti, music, clubs, drugs and so on.

It reminded me of similar reactions to other pieces of entertainment: the panic over violent video games like Quake in the mid-nineties; the hysteria over video nasties in the eighties, the outrage at the Sex Pistols, Frankie Goes To Hollywood, Ozzy Osbourne and, before my time but singing the same song, the fear of rock and roll, or the prophecies of reefer madness. This time, however, it seemed that people were getting more worked up than ever.

Picturing the bat-eating antics of Ozzy or Holly's leather cap made me realise how quickly these images of shock and cultural dissolution became harmless, even quaint – embraced by the society that once saw them as evil, stored fondly in its collective entertainment memory. Ozzy is now lauded as a parental role model, and the antics of his dysfunctional family and crucifix-infested mansion are seen as bizarre, but never dangerous. The Sex Pistols, once arrested for playing 'God Save the Queen', are recognised as musical visionaries, part of a tradition stretching through Jim Morrison, Kurt Cobain, Marilyn Manson: artists who had the courage to stir things up. On the mainstream TV reality show *I'm a Celebrity* ... Johnny Rotten is described as a perfect gent, the best character on the show, despite calling the public 'fucking cunts' for not voting him off.

As with all aspects of modern culture, the amount of time between fear and acceptance has been compressed. These days things change more quickly. In 2001, George Bush described Eminem as 'the most dangerous threat to American children since polio'; 22 March 2003, and he wins an Oscar. In the acceptance speech, the star's co-writer, Luis Resto, describes him in a very different way: 'He has symphonies in his head that I'm privileged to put on the tape. He's a good man, good heart. Here's to you, Marshall. Thank you so much.'

So why, this time, had the shooting ignited such a widespread and passionate debate?

I thought about my own experiences: childhood brushes with the obscene and the horrific. I remembered watching *The Evil Dead* at a family barbecue when I was twelve, hanging out in the TV room with the other kids while parents drank outside: half scared, half exhilarated ... seeing that pencil go into the girl's leg and knowing it was fake, even as it looked so painful.

I remembered sitting with my best friend when I was eleven, watching *The Omen*, rewinding and slo-moing again and again the scene where the pane of glass slices off some guy's head. Even without the slo mo, I think I knew it wasn't real.

I remembered watching my first porn film with a bunch of friends one sunny afternoon, and laughing, half embarrassed, half curious. I wondered if it had affected me. Or how it had affected me.

More broadly I wondered how accurate the current swipes at modern culture were. And I got curious about that culture itself. (I wondered how much Kim Howells really knew about hip hop, and where he'd picked up that knowledge. Is it part of a briefing session he receives? From whom? A civil servant? Someone from the music industry?)

I wanted to know if things were different now from when I was younger, or if it was the same shit but a different culprit. Were younger people really darker, more violent, more doomed than before, or was entertainment once again being blamed for deeper social problems? Were the actions of a few being mistaken for the reactions of a generation? Was it the same old kid-bashing, an older generation unable to recognise and accept the new values and creativity of its youth?

Because of course young people have always had a hard time from their elders. Possibly it's a jealousy thing, revolving around those age-old themes: beauty, health, opportunity, energy, idealism. Hope.

Describing the ways that the younger generation are less moral, more selfish, than previous, more responsible generations is a game that has been handed down over the centuries. And yet, in an age when youth culture is almost worshipped and seen by many as the source for all culture; where 15- to 24-year-olds are courted by brands and entertainers, it seems odd that the myth of their inherent corruptness continues.

That's where this all started. And it took me much further than I originally had planned. I was not looking for an explanation for Charlene and Letisha's deaths – they are inexcusable – but I wanted to understand why they became the catalyst for a large-scale critique of so much of modern Britain's entertainment. I wanted to discover and describe a more rounded picture of what young people are up to. To hear their voices. To get an idea of what they are watching, playing, wearing, listening to. What they are thinking. To see how far they've come. And where they think they're going.

I was particularly interested in the instances where the actions of kids seemed most inexplicable and dangerous to older groups; because it was these activities and beliefs which seemed to generate the most passion from the people involved in them. It wasn't hard to find the negative areas; the charges against this generation. Here is a selection of quotes from the media that shouted out to me around the time I started thinking about this book. Reading them certainly suggested that Britain's inheritors were going to drag the country down into a mire of ignorant sexual and narcotic abandon.

'Judging from my own kitchen table, intelligent speech does sometimes seem to be to be at a premium among youngsters these days,' said linguistic expert Professor Robin Dunbar of Liverpool University. It is a worrying trend, not just for those who lose an ability to use language, but for the fate of the planet.

Observer, **January 2003**

Modelling themselves on gangsters in films such as *Scarface*, the seven youths carried out 28 attacks armed with handguns and knives 'for kicks' ... The carjackers spent their days watching every available gangster film on video and DVD, with the mobster hit *Scarface*, starring Al Pacino, a particular favourite. They acted out scenes of carjacking from these movies and also from computer games, including Grand Theft Auto. The seven even acted out their fantasies by posing for black and white Bugsy Malone-style photographs, clad in gangster garb and waving guns.

Evening Standard, **December 2002**

Since getting digital TV, my children have had access to the Hits, a TV channel that simply shows pop videos. Without exception, they are soft, and sometimes not so soft porn ... The extraordinary sexualisation of society is eating away at childhood ... At middle age, I find myself shocked, disturbed − and paradoxically, somewhat bored − by the drowning of the world in flesh and cursing.

Evening Standard, **December 2002**

Investigators have detailed the sex habits of almost 1,000 men and women aged 18–30 let loose on the Greek islands. One in four slept with at least two people within 24 hours. Thirty-four per cent of men had sex without protection while 79% of girls and 82% of men had oral sex at least once during a two-week holiday.

News of the World, **January 2003**

A woman claimed yesterday she pulled out 18 of her own teeth while high on the rave drug GHB. Samantha Courts, 25, was found by a pal 'in a trance' with the teeth in a bowl on the floor ... Samantha told Bolton

Crown Court: 'It was me who pulled them out. I thought I was getting a witch out of my throat.'

Sun, **November 2002**

Kylie Minogue has attacked reality TV shows such as *Pop Idol* and *Popstars*, saying they encourage children to develop a 'frightening' obsession with fame. Speaking on BBC Radio 1's Jo Whiley show, she said youngsters just wanted to become famous, without giving thought to developing any specific talent.

BBCi News, **November 2002**

Clearly these representations are not fictitious, but their aims are limited: to demonstrate how shallow, violent, stupid and self-deluded British youth is. How more comprehensively fucked up than any previous generation. Violence, drunkenness, prejudice and irresponsibility do exist within this group of people, as they do in all age groups and in all countries. But to use these examples to represent an entire generation is rather like looking to our prison population, the stars of *Britain's Worst Driver*, the government or the royal family in order to understand Britain.

Yet these are the visions that abound in the media, to the horror of parents, teachers, the government, and, perhaps more worryingly, the people they claim to be about. Visions of a violent, oversexed and idiotic generation. A world of confused values, perverse morality and over-stimulation. But most importantly a world that is not understood. A different world.

During 2003 I spoke to kids dressed as tigers who had dropped 5 Es, I spoke to ten-year-olds who were making short films, and teenage girls who travel the country trying to catch a glimpse of Busted. I chatted with 'hard to reach' kids in colleges, and a sixteen-year-old who was selling T-shirts via his own website. I spoke to cybers, skaters, charvas, goths and boy racers. I also spoke to Kim Howells, the minister who had been responsible for me starting off on this journey in the first place, and Beverley Thomas, mother of one of the two girls shot over New Year.

I visited clubs, festivals, skateparks, protests and shopping malls: the hubs of young Britain. And of course their bedrooms, those crammed, messy centres of their personalities.

Dis/connected is not meant to be a comprehensive or representative study of British youth. This story will not be told by bar graphs, pie charts or statistics. It will be told by people.

It will not attempt to reduce the variety and contradictions of British youth cultures into a neat soundbite. This is not a book about average youth, or mainstream Britain. I was not looking for Basildon kid. In averages and statistics we lose the individuality that gives culture its significance and its power.

However, nor was I looking for the tales of disaster. They are easy to find and well chronicled. The junkies, the crackheads, the car thieves, the bullies. All of these exist in Britain. And are often connected to many of the subjects covered here. But I questioned whether they represented the inevitable contact with drugs, sex, computer games and hip hop. Or if people who do or use all these things could emerge undamaged. Even enhanced.

This was what interested me. Whether contact with the books, the music, the clubs, the clothes, the games – the things that are often identified as signs of a criminal, wasted, selfish, oversexed and undereducated destructive generation – could have a different, less problematic ending. Inevitably, then, I spent most of my time with kids in their free time, away from the influence or restrictions of schools, parents, jobs, and so on. All of these play a part in young people's lives, but I felt that their leisure time offered the purest example of their expressiveness, and the times and places when their passions were most evident.

In these places I spoke with people aged between ten and their early twenties. I believed that the late teens would be most revealing because it's a period of more freedom and independence. But I was less interested in age than attitude and behaviour.

I was not looking for a universal theory or even a clear logic. Today's world is fragmented, contradictory, multiple, disjointed. This book reflects that. Although I have ordered the chapters according to the various accusations levelled at British youth, most of the people I spoke to could have appeared in most of the chapters. That is, most of them are multiply guilty as charged: they take drugs, love fashion, spend hours in unreal worlds and break many of the nation's laws. Quite often all at the same time.

This book is a collection of conversations – with graffiti artists, fetish models, wannabe pop stars, black-clad goths. I was keen to hear what they had to say, and to present their voices. I also turned to the stuff that surrounds them for insight and understanding. The brands, the music, the celebs, the clothes often speak as brightly and dynamically as they do. So, this book is also a contemporary archaeology … looking towards an environment for clues about its inhabitants.

I had ideas about where to look and what I was going to find. I used the most common criticisms – dumbed down, promiscuous, criminal, superficial, drug abusers – as starting points and saw where they took me. Certainly what I found out changed the way I felt about Britain and its inhabitants.

2003 was the year that saw the largest march for peace ever ignored by a prime minister, who came to power as one of the most popular PMs ever and completed his second term being accused of 'pottiness', murder and lapdoggery.

It saw those venerable British institutions – the government and the BBC, both paid for by and therefore meant to represent the British public – lose the trust of the nation as they became entangled in the suicide of Dr Kelly. Which in turn seemed to have arisen as a desperate Labour government tried to find some evidence for its occupation of Iraq.

2003 was the year when a comedian dressed as a transvestite Osama Bin Laden managed to stroll into Prince William's 21st birthday party, and plant a kiss on the heir's cheek, as his grandmother allegedly giggled, mistaking Aaron Barschak for a mischievous Prince Harry.

When Prince Charles had to issue a denial that he was the 'senior member of the royal family' involved in a scandal that the papers weren't allowed to mention.

When the temperature busted the 100 degrees mark and Britain became continental. And heated up a succession of hedonistic festivals and promiscuous late nights.

And when the term 'spit roast' lost any associations of Sunday lunch, following revelations about Premiership players' habit of sharing young girls.

A year when mobile ringtones made more money for record labels than singles did; when Robbie Williams established himself as Britain's biggest entertainer, when 50 Cent dominated the MOBO awards and Kylie's butt became the most desirable body part in the world, leading J-Lo to try to headhunt her bum make-up artist.

When David Blaine spent forty-four days starving himself in public, swinging above the Thames in a transparent box. So even though he was there in the flesh, it looked like you were watching him through a screen.

For most of the people I spoke to there was nothing strange about a government that lied to its people; a royal family that were little more than a posh soap opera, or a global star whose fame came from his past as a crack dealer and surviving being shot nine times.

In Britain 2003, this was normality. And it was a wonderful year to travel the country to try to understand its inhabitants better.

'We are the government'

'*Big Brother* viewers tend to say they are good at judging people; political junkies are the opposite – they are good at analysis, but their emotional intelligence is low. The political class has fallen into the trap of understanding itself but not those outside it.'

Professor Coleman, Oxford University, April 2003

A gang for every area

Birmingham looks like one of Britain's more multicultural cities. And Soho Road in Handsworth seems to contain all of those cultures. The school signs are in several languages. Vegetable stores spill out onto the street, offering more colour and variety than any Sainsbury's or Tesco's. A Caribbean Kitchen sits next to KFC in a row of restaurants. Across the road, Beauty Queens Cosmetics promotes itself as a specialist in Afro and Euro human hair. Vibrant weaves and colourful hair decorations hang from the doorways. DTF – Asian Books and Musicals displays a range of curved drums and plump guitars in the windows. On the security grille for the Bollywood Connection someone has scrawled 'Lions of Panjab'. Fly-posters for the Bhangra Knights rub shoulders with those for Gilles Peterson and Rathayatra 2003, and one advertising an Asian Atkins diet. Half a mile up the road is Birmingham's biggest Sikh temple: Gurdwara Nishkam Sewak Jatha.

I'd originally travelled to Birmingham to speak to Beverley Thomas, the mother of Charlene Ellis. On that trip I'd also sat in on a social services' Introduction to Youth Work session, and been struck by the sense of division – both between different races, and between different gangs – as the young black, Asian and white trainees shared experiences. I'd got talking to one of the participants called Modasar, who'd promised to show me around and to introduce me to some Birmingham teens, and so a couple of weeks later I'm strolling along Soho Road, checking out what appears to me to be a truly multicultural street.

When Modasar arrives, though, he tells me a different story. He describes Soho Road as the front line, separating the areas of Birmingham that are associated with the Burger Bar Crew and the Johnson Boys – the two gangs implicated in the deaths of Charlene Ellis and Letisha Shakespeare at New Year. And as we drive to a college in East Birmingham, he points out other territories and zones. His presentation of Birmingham is a fragmented one. He talks of whole schools being associated with one gang, and how there are different no-go areas for people of certain races. We drive past a sign for Cholmsley Wood, a district he describes as verging on Combat 18. While Modasar emphasises the tribal nature of much of young Birmingham, he is also keen to point out that when he talks about gangs, he's not referring to organised crime, or the kind of scenarios we might see in documentaries about Compton in Los Angeles. The gangs here are often just collections of friends, doing some robbing and fighting. There are guns, of course, but it's not quite the lawless jungle that the media described following the deaths of Charlene and Letisha.

I wanted to talk to the kids here about living in such a fragmented and disconnected city, both with regard to other kids, but also with regard to Britain and the various contacts they have with its institutions – its schools, the government, the police. One of the common criticisms of young people is their lack of respect for such organisations and the people who run them, and I wanted to discover how deep-seated it was.

Modasar arranges for me to talk with some pupils from a bridge course: under-sixteens who have dropped out of school and are studying at a sixth-form college instead. At the front desk, a burly security guard makes me sign in and wait in the hall while Modasar locates our class. There are about fifteen people in the room, but only a couple sitting at the computer-equipped desks. The rest are hanging out, and there's a lot of noise and banter. One of the students is running around the room; another is accusing a third of being a terrorist.

First off I speak with Charlotte, Majahid and Amanda. We're in a small study next to their classroom. Majahid sits between the two girls, impassive in his NY cap and hoodie. Charlotte has long brown hair and a serious expression, while Amanda is more playful. She wears a blue fleece and lots of gold-ish jewellery: big hooped earrings, fingers crammed with rings.

'There is a gang for every area,' says Majahid when I ask him about the city. 'There is a gang for different parts like Stechford. If you go to a different area, there is a gang for there. Because of colour, yeah, people think differently. Because they are Asian or black, people think: look at that Asian, they want to pick on the Asian people you see, or they want to pick on a different colour.'

Charlotte ('I'm the ginger') tells me about being called a white honky recently because she was in the wrong area, and continues with a more disturbing story. She mentions that she used to hang out with the Yardley Massive.

'I went out with a half-caste and he got his head kicked in because I went out with him. I was walking down the road with him back to my house and then my mate's brother, the gang's leader, has seen me with him and because he's older he can't hit him, because he's only like fifteen. So what he does, he goes back and tells someone that is my age to kick the shit out of this lad I was going out with, so he got battered.'

I'm surprised at her matter-of-fact manner as she describes her boyfriend getting his head kicked in.

'Weren't you upset by what happened?'

'Yes, just the fact that that shouldn't go on, I'm allowed to go out with whoever I like. It's none of their business.'

Despite this assertion, and the fact that she stopped hanging with the Yardley Massive, the kicking signalled the end of her relationship.

'So, how do things like that make you feel about living here? What's it like growing up in Britain today?' I'm expecting more local stories, but immediately the conversation turns general.

'I can't stand Tony Blair,' Charlotte states bluntly, looking at me half challengingly as if I'm going to leap to his defence. I don't.

'Why not?'

'I've met him, he's a div. I met him down the Swan, it's like this thing at the back where no one else can go, and he was there because my mate's mum is part of Labour and I met John Prescott and ... he doesn't really care about anyone, bar himself. He's going on about joining in with America, to like bomb people and whatever, he doesn't realise he's got a little safe house, but none of us have. I can't stand him.'

'He doesn't care about other people,' adds Majahid. 'He cares about himself.'

And then Charlotte accuses the PM of the same prejudice that is dividing Birmingham. 'He's racist, you can tell he's racist.'

'He is racist,' agrees Majahid. 'Because he is picking on other colours instead of his own, you see. Why does he attack Iraq? Because he is picking on one colour, not his own colour. Maybe tomorrow he will bomb a black country. He's a two-minded person you see, he ain't trustable.'

'What about the rest of the government?'

'They haven't got our interests,' continues Majahid. 'They think about themselves. The government doesn't think nothing about the public, it's always Tony Blair.'

Local hooligans

I walk back to the classroom to see if anyone else wants to come and talk. Some more jostling and bitching at each other and Shaqib, Shayne and Laurine join me. Shaqib, who likes to be called Gismo, has a provocative smile; Shayne is quieter and nervously picks at scabs on his arm when we're talking. Laurine has the presence and the opinions. She's wearing a pale blue Funky knitted top, slender black trousers and knee-high boots. Her hair is scraped tight back to show a tough, smart face. When I take a picture of them she puts her arms on the two guys' shoulders, half protectively, half to show she's in control. Again, they're friendly and thoughtful as we talk. The conversation quickly moves on to their city.

'Birmingham is horrible,' Shayne tells me. 'Where I live it's all kind of crimey: drugs, alcoholics. It just ain't worth living there. It's all car crimes and stabbings.'

With a similar matter-of-fact tone to Charlotte, Laurine tells him, 'That is natural, man, I'm sorry.'

I ask Shayne who's doing all the crime and he looks at Laurine and smiles.

'Local hooligans, like Laurine.'

'Excuse me!' Laurine fires back, and then elaborates. 'Where I live they range from the age of about five onwards. I live in Castle Vale and it's not very nice, but I don't talk to them because they are stupid. To be honest with you, I used to be one of them, I used to be in there, in the drugs and everything, I used to be in everything.'

'And what does being in everything mean?'

'Basically what it is, you sit in the park or you sit on the corners of the street or sit in the shop and then you are bored, so you think let's rob this place, so you go in there. If you've got no money we'll go, let's go on the raids, and then you go out there and rob people for their stuff, their phones for their money to sell, to get money to buy drugs.'

'You must have heard of PSA,' says Shaqib.

'You must have heard of the Burgers and the Johnsons,' adds Laurine.

I tell them I've heard of the Burgers and Johnsons but not the PSA.

'That's my family, man,' Laurine tells me proudly.

'It's a crew, isn't it? It's my age lads and that but they are rough for their age. They do razes and stuff.'

'What's a raze?' I ask.

'When you go out there and rob people just to get money for yourself.'

'But they just do it in broad daylight.'

'Yes, they just go on, like one day you are walking down the street, it could happen to you. It's like say you see someone, say it's me and a couple of friends down there, it's like, oh I want them pair of shoes, you've got no money, let's go on a raze. Then by the end of the day you've got your pair of shoes and more. That's how it is.'

Smirking, Shayne tells me how he currently can't go down the Yardley area. 'Because they've got a couple of crews looking for me. I keep having a fight with the wrong people and now a lot of people are after me.' He's smiling and the other two are laughing outright. I ask them what's so funny. It sounds terrifying.

'Because it's funny, it is really funny,' smiles Laurine. 'It's like anyone could put a crew together and say, right we are going to go out there and batter this person.'

'Aren't you bothered by the violence or the threats?'

'I'm not bothered,' says Laurine.

'Me I've got beef, yeah with people but I just don't bother going there,' adds Shaqib. 'I see them now because one person, I was in town, he tried to stab me up and that and I know the guy very well, but sometimes he's there and sometimes he can be like a little dickhead. But at the end of the day I told feds and the police ... '

'But you can't do that in this day and age, you can't go to the police,' Laurine tells me. 'You would be called a conspirer. Once you are called a conspirer and an informer, everyone is looking for you. It's like if someone was to rough me now and there was a police station just across the road and I run over there and tell them, I've got all of them, their family, their friends, their friends' friends and their friends' friends' friends all after me. And there is no point. So I just say, in this day and age you have to deal with it in your own way. The police can't do nothing.'

I'm struck by Laurine's insistence that the police would be unable to help a fifteen-year-old girl about to be roughed. I ask her what she thinks of the systems and structures that are meant to be there to support and help them if they have difficulties.

'They are rubbish man,' she tells me. 'You don't feel connections with them.'

'Social services are a load of bullshit,' continues Shayne. 'My aunt died because of them. She died when she was about ten. Social services were meant to be looking after her. Social services saw her from head to foot in bruises and they didn't do nothing.'

Laurine reveals a similar lack of respect.

'My mum used to hit me a lot and I went to social services about it. And they didn't do nothing. My mum left my dad and I stayed with my dad and they are just pathetic. They think they know what they are talking about, they think they know how you feel and they don't, they don't know nothing. They try to put you on this track that you have to go and the track they are leading you is bullshit, it's complete bullshit. At the end of the day, the police, the social services, the government, they can all fuck off because in this society we are the government. They don't do nothing for us.'

'So where do you go if you are in trouble or whatever, who do you look to?'

'To your mates.'

'Your family, friends, that's the only place I go now,' agrees Shaqib. 'I don't go to the police no more.'

By now, Laurine is on a roll and the media is her next target.

'The newspapers tell so much shit, I swear. Basically they get the story off someone and they twist it, completely twist it.'

'And that story probably isn't even true in the first place,' Shayne tells me, nodding his head emphatically. 'I don't believe stuff I read in the newspapers.'

'I don't believe none of it. The only place I look at is when I go in the newspapers to see what's on TV and my star signs.'

'And the sport.'

'All I read is the football scores.'

'And the comic strips.'

'Do you know what?' Laurine interjects. 'I went to church the other day, yeah, because I go to church and I had to be a spokesperson for something. We were all like in this stand and people were asking us questions about how the media influenced young people today and I said to them at the end of the day when it comes to music you are your own person. If like 2Pac, 50 Cent, they are telling you about their life story, they are not telling you to go out there, get a gun and shoot people. They are not telling you, it is up to you. It is up to you.'

'I agree,' adds Gismo.

'At the end of the day everyone has got their own mind.'

'If I shoot down the street and shoot a thousand people then that is up to me.' Shayne smiles, making a gun gesture with his hand. 'Not anyone else.'

Laurine nods fiercely in agreement, and is off again.

'I listen to my music because I think what they are talking about is important. It's like Eminem, everyone says Eminem fuck this, fuck that, but Eminem speaks absolute truth. If you watch the film *8 Mile*, it's his life, it's his own life. This is how he's trying to put across how he's been in his life and for us not to go that way. All this shit they say about Eminem is a bad influence, he's not. My dad and my mum used to think Eminem is a bad influence and I sat my dad down, I sat my mum down and said, listen to what he's talking about, don't just listen to the foul language, just listen to what he's talking about. I made them sit down and listen to the whole album. And now my dad sits there in his car listening to Eminem saying fuck you this and fuck you that and my dad loves it.'

As I speak to other groups of kids in Birmingham similar themes recur: the presence of violence and a sense of racial and cultural separation. The dislike for and distrust of the government and the importance of friends and family to support and direct you. A fierce independence, almost an individual disconnection, best expressed by Laurine's war cry, 'We are the government.' But it is perhaps Irfan, a big, good-looking sixteen-year-old at another college, who sums up the disconnections from Britain most simply.

'I don't really call myself British. I'm a Muslim, that is it.'

While his religion might offer a clear reason for difference and disagreement, his sentiments are echoed by the majority of teens and twenty-somethings I speak to over the course of the year. For Muslim, substitute whatever passion or belief system the kids hold. From boxing to Busted. Ketamine to Kylie. But rarely do they identify with their nation, their schools or the government. The passion and energy is saved for other people, other places.

Make tea not war

Nowhere is the sign of the British public's distance from the forces that govern it clearer than at February's anti-war march. The weather is amazing after a long shitty winter: a completely clear sky and crisp air. I stand beneath Nelson's Column and watch the crowds move past. They appear to be endless. As far as I can see, it's people and a plenitude of placards: 'Gulf Sale', 'Peace not War', 'Save the Humans', and the rallying call for the whole march: 'Not in my name'. A public declaration to Tony that if he does invade Iraq, he does it without the support of millions of his countrymen. But the poster of the day, the one that gets all the headlines in the Sunday newspapers, is the curiously effective yellow one, featuring our Tony with a teapot on his head and an AK under his arm, with the legend: 'Make Tea Not War'.

My favourite is more complex: 'Talk to the palm, because you ain't the bomb'. Two different phrases, taken from disposable TV culture and repurposed to make an anti-war statement. I like the way that two things which could be seen to be in opposition – day-time chat shows and anti-war sentiments – have been merged.

Strangely enough, the enormous truck belonging to the flamboyant and fame-hungry boxer Chris Eubank is parked up here as well. He sits in the cab, waving at crowds and every now and then giving the klaxon a good pull. The engine is running. I wonder if he makes any connection between the West's hunger for oil and his own frivolous consumption.

Today there is a very different feeling from other marches I have attended. Little anger or sense of violence, just lots of people walking slowly: families, prams, kids, grandparents. The police are friendly and helpful, a change from the suppressed brutality that often bubbles under at protests. The whole thing is positive – as if the marchers believe they can affect policy – and it is incredibly well behaved. As one person I get talking to says sardonically: 'It's a middle England thing: middle-aged, middle-class people unite.'

Certainly the younger protestors I speak to are noticeably white middle class. Less sportswear and gold than the kids in Birmingham. More bright colours and hippy or punk outfits. But the sentiment and attitude towards Blair and his government are remarkably similar.

A group of fourteen-year-old girls is sitting on the steps of Nelson's Column. They are smoking cigarettes quickly, taking a few drags each and passing them on. Waving 'No Blood for Oil' posters, they are singing Bob Marley's 'Redemption Song' when I get talking to them. They wear combat jackets, massive trousers and skate shoes. I speak with two Hannahs. They don't know who Hans Blix is, or what Resolution 1441 means, but they know what they feel about the war.

'It is an excuse to bomb a country for no particular reason. Other than the rise in oil prices.'

'Anything that Bush says, it feels like Tony Blair will do exactly the same. He is not a proper leader.'

They say they have little faith in British politics, and then tell me, laughing, about their song.

'I would just like to say: Yellow Cat says Don't Bomb Iraq. We made up a song, called "Yellow Cat" – and it is to do with not bombing Iraq.'

And with that, the group bursts into song again.

Okay … 1, 2, 3, 4
We don't want no fucking war
5, 6, 7, 8
Don't let Bush decide our fate
9, 10, 11, 12
Don't let war destroy our world!

I give them a small clap and move on, smiling.

Wearing a 'Oi George, NO!' sweatshirt, Jordan is less playful. When I ask him what he thinks about Blair, he's quick to reply.

'A cunt.'

'Yes, he is a Bush arse-licker,' adds Camilla, his girlfriend. 'And he is not our leader.'

'And is there is anyone in government or in politics who you think of as your leader?'

They both start laughing.

'Basically, if there is, their voices aren't being heard.'

Aman, aged eleven, on his first march with his dad and younger brother, agrees.

'We don't want America to bomb Iraq because they are just bombing Iraq for oil.'

'What do you think about Tony Blair?'

'Selfish and I don't really like him.'

I get one of the most passionate rants from Hugh and Jack. They're both wearing punkish leather jackets, covered in paint and band names. Jack's got a respectable Mohawk, standing a good six inches off his skull, and Hugh's wearing a padlock and chain round his neck. He carries a very home-made sign reading: 'No war between nations. No peace between classes.' I'm tempted to ask him what class he represents and who he's at war with.

Hugh's obviously the spokesperson. He answers most of my questions while the larger Jack looks benignly on.

'I think it is complete bollocks, it is just another fucking war in the name of oil, just more fucking capitalism, globalisation in business. I think that more people should be alert as to the reasons why we are going to war, this has absolutely fucking nothing to do with terrorism, stopping terrorism, and it is a fucking sham that we are stopping the Iraqi regime, and it is true that it is fucked up, and harsh, but we have been supporting it for years, and it is hypocritical.'

'There are much worse regimes,' adds Jack. 'Like South Africa. It is exactly the same, but Iraq is floating on oil. So it is a bit of a coincidence.'

'Yes. What about fucking Columbia and places? We are supporting their death squads and shit, well what about that? You have got some fucking priorities. It is bollocks.'

Like everyone else, there is no sense of the government or Tony representing what they believe in.

'I think he is just another fucking politician. How many of them are going to voice our opinions? None. That is what history shows. There is no point in representative politics, because it's not going to represent you.'

So, lots of kids don't like the government or politicians. I shouldn't be surprised, I suppose. I never liked Thatcher much when I was a kid. Although I didn't make it on to my first march until I was eighteen or nineteen. With Hugh's call to revolution ringing in my ears, I leave the crowds and cut through the streets of Soho, heading for Hyde Park. By Carnaby Street, only a couple of hundred metres away from the main march, a group of teenage girls are waiting with nervous excitement outside a nondescript office.

I ask Rosanna, thirteen, and Georgia, fourteen, what they're up to.

'We are basically …' Rosanna is so excited that she muddles her words. She giggles and starts again. 'We entered this competition with *Cosmo Girl* and what it is we want to get a photo shoot with Blue. And you have to explain why you are the bigger fan, and we didn't get through, but we had a go.'

'We are their biggest fans.'

'We have been around, we came here about what time … seven thirty this morning.'

It's now about two in the afternoon.

'What about the march,' I ask. 'Did you think about going on that?'

'The anti-war, yes, I have heard – that is why we came up so early,' explains Rosanna.

'To miss the march?'

'Yes,' they reply in unison.

'So, what do you think about the war?'

'We are neutral,' says Rosanna, sounding like Switzerland. 'But at the march, I am not really that bothered. Because whatever happens, I don't think it is going to change anything. But Blue is like here, we have been supporting them for ages. Like quite a few years. So; there's no choice where we'd be.'

As I'm waiting, Blue turns up in a blacked-out Chrysler people carrier. The girls go wild as the vehicle drives into the office's car park. There is far more passion in that five minutes of hysteria, crying and pushing than anything I see during the march. One of the girls gets kissed by Lee, and when she comes back her hands are shaking. This is Lee Ryan, known as the Clown Prince of Pop to the tabloids due to a sequence of highly public and brainless antics, and yet he can inspire more emotion and support than our country's leaders, or even the march against them.

Later on, as Britain rolls into war, I can't help thinking that Rosanna and the girls had a more productive day than Hugh, Jack, the two Hannahs, and the rest of the marchers. Blair didn't listen to a million marchers, while at least Lee stopped for a kiss. As Rosanna prophesied, the march – the largest in peacetime Britain – didn't change anything. Whereas waiting around the back of Carnaby Street delivered much more of a result.

Nobody listens

As I move across Britain, on marches, at parties and cruises, in bedrooms and in skateparks, there is a powerful sense of disconnection from British society. Nobody I speak to feels strongly attached to a British way of life – as represented by its laws, its governments, its elders. As an age group, as a bunch of people, they feel that they have very little representation or understanding in the traditional corridors of power. That's probably been the case for decades of young people.

This disconnection is often presented in the media as apathy, as indolence, and as lack of interest in everything. But the energy and passion of the Blue fans got me wondering about such general criticisms.

I meet Gemma at a Legalise Cannabis festival, and am struck by her energy so arrange to go and talk with her at her south London flat. She lives on the Kingswood Estate. The first car I see as I turn in has no tyres. A group of children play on the swings. When I ask them how to get to Gemma's block, they point in three different directions and laugh. Not sure who to believe, I take advice from the eldest.

I recognise the estate name because of an attempted rape I'd read about there in March, when a catsuited intruder had been fought off by a 78-year-old woman. It is wide rather than high, a sprawling mix of four- to six-storey blocks and rows of houses. As I turn a corner, the Crystal Palace TV aerial appears, and more surprisingly I catch a glimpse of a stone castle, encircled by brick buildings.

As I drive past identical estate blocks, I see a group of elderly women tending a magnificent flower bed. On the ground, the place feels urban, but as I climb the stairs to Gemma's one-room flat – the oldest kid was telling the truth – there is a great view towards central London. Trees, sunlight and Foster's gherkin glinting magically in the distance.

So among the knackered cars, the trash in the streets, the graffiti and the concrete primary school that has the air of a prison camp to it, there are jewels. Gemma, I discover, is one of these. Her parents were both heroin addicts. Her father died when she was three. She has lived alone since she was sixteen. Now nineteen, she's currently on benefits, and gets £42 a week, of which £30 has to go on arrears and court costs from a time when her social worker didn't turn up.

Her flat contains a bed, some shelves for her decks and stereo, and an assortment of fliers from various clubs on the wall. The curtains are drawn closed, even though it's a beautiful evening, so we sit in a gloomy twilight. On the inside of the front door she's attached some industrial sign so that the second half of it is concealed and it makes a cheap drugs gag: 'Warning! You are in danger of wasting.' There's a sticker for Vagabond music and, above it, she's stencilled: 'I only attract what I project. Pleasant thoughts make a pleasant day.' Gemma is tough yet sentimental, damaged yet able to laugh about it. She wears all black with a silver design on her sleeveless T-shirt. A small gold cross hangs round her neck.

'My parents lied to me a lot. I have no doubt that my parents did love me, but at that time, you know, and obviously cos of the drugs, you know, there's only one main thing to them, which is the heroin, so they could never really give me the time, or the support or the love that I actually needed, so growing up it kinda, it did affect me, I was ill for a while. I was depressed and I had to go to a hospital, an adolescent unit a few times. I've actually been in a couple of hospitals. I started counselling when I was twelve – when I say I've done it, I've done it you know. I've spoke to counsellors and therapists, I've done art therapy, and voice therapy, and Childline and psychiatrists and psychologists. And it was all crap. It was, it was. That's one thing I have a lot of anger about, the support and the system, like social services and that, was complete and utter crap.'

Gemma continues for a solid five minutes, eyes glinting, hands pointing beyond the curtains.

'They don't listen, the politicians, everything, it's bollocks. It's all absolute crap. You know this is where I was raised in England, and I'm proud to come from England but there's a lot of a shame there too, cos I think this country's a bit fucked up to be honest with you.

'Look at it, look at the state of the place. I don't know what it would take to get this country in order but it would take a lot of work, and a lot of the right people. I mean for example the Millennium Dome, that could have re-homed every homeless person in London, yeah? Instead build a shit fucking marshmallow building, yeah that got bankrupt and still loaning, with an extra fuck knows how many million dollars afterwards because it was so crap. It's disgusting. It is disgusting. That is my word, disgusting. It's a strong word but I feel it's appropriate. There are people out there that care, and there are people out there that are doing their bit to make England better, but there's not enough of them, do you know what I mean?'

Gemma's anger abates rapidly when we start talking about something she does care about: her music. Suddenly she's all smiles and bright eyes, enthusiastically tapping my arm to make a point and jumping up to play fragments of tracks.

'Yeah, DJing! Where can I start? I mean throughout my life music has always been a big thing to me. It was like my way of escaping what was really going on around me and just indulging in my music and you know music it never lets you down, do you know what I mean, it doesn't lie to you, it doesn't go away, it's always there and I found that I did have certain talents within music. I started mixing and my first mix was absolutely unbelievable. The buzz that I got, it's basically mixing one tune into the other to make a song out of one tune, and I heard the soundwaves and everything going through your ears. It was like this feeling all the way up from my body and from that moment on I wanted to be a DJ and that's it.

'There's a lot of feeling and emotion inside there that I wanna put across through the music that needs releasing. And the way I thought I could release that is through my mixing, but when I went to college and started studying music production the feeling was absolutely amazing. It was the same feeling of being able to mix, but being able to put them sounds down on a computer and hear them back, them sounds that you've got in your head are inside you, and you can hear it being played back to you. It's the most incredible feeling.'

Going into more detail about her music making – Inspirational Recordings: 'People are going to be blown away by it' – she talks happily about music software Pro Tools, Cubase, Reason, Acid Pro as she plays her first song to me. Not finished, she tells me, but it's a start. The girl who has been talking to me sounds like a woman when she sings. She says that when her mum heard the song, she couldn't believe it was her daughter.

'Nothing is ever easy, do you know what I mean? Nothing ever comes handed on a plate, so there is a lotta hard work but you know it is about determination, at the end of the day, and really wanting it, and I do. I do. And I do believe in myself a hundred per cent and that's one thing I have learnt as well is believing in yourself.'

As I leave, she gives me a book called *Notes from a Friend* by Anthony Robbins: 'A quick and simple guide to taking charge of your life'. Normally it's the kind of book I'd run a mile from, but given what she has told me tonight, I take it with me. Transformation is possible. She hands it over with the words – 'Thinking ain't enough, you've got to do it.' I don't know if she's talking about me or her.

Charva or goth, skater or boy racer?

I was more surprised by the separation between the different areas in Birmingham than I was by the anti-government sentiments I found everywhere. Early on in the year, I learnt that although the media might like to talk about teenagers as if they form one homogeneous group, kids see things very differently.

Most people I talked with were very clear about what they were, and what they were not. People differentiated themselves from each other in terms of what drugs they took – drinkers vs pill heads vs GHB junkies – what part of town they came from, the music they were into, the clothes they wore or the kind of car they drove.

Conversations are shot through with descriptors and shorthands, means of indicating whether or not people were your sort of people. My introduction to the nuances of young divisions comes from eleven-year-old Heathcote, who I find in a skatepark. I'm taking pictures, and when I turn round I spot him filming me. Unruly blond hair, a T-shirt that reads 'Skateboarding is not a crime', a grubby plaster cast on his left wrist covered in tags, and a flurry of bright plastic bangles on his right.

A few days later, we're in his kitchen. He's talking with animation about skateboarding and about the films he puts together before he says, with a mock-serious expression:

'But there is a downside to skating. At school, there are lots of anti-skateboarders.'

'What do you mean, anti-skateboarders?'

'Well, generally they don't really call themselves this, but they are called townies and they are sort of MCs, like the sort of people that call themselves bad man or rude boy, wear tracksuits and that sort of gear. Skateboarding is a sort of rebellion against the townies.'

'And what are townies?'

'They're like chavs. But they don't call themselves that. They call themselves normal people, or some of them call themselves MCs. They are not an individual, they are just sort of all grouped together. One of the things about townies, they have to have a brand name. If you wear like something which has no brand, they will be like: ah, that is fake. The thing is, it is not really fake, because it is still a jumper. But I wouldn't see it like that if I was a townie, cos they see us the same. And townies don't call skateboarders, skateboarders, or rollerbladers, rollerbladers; they just call them grungers. They're like: you grungers, you worship the devil, or you look like a Bee Gee, or you're from the eighties.'

'So are you a grunger?'

'Grungers are kind of punks, but I am a semi-grunger, but like I am not really a grunger, because I don't like heavy metal, but that is also quite stereotypical, because I have a bunch of grunger friends which don't like heavy metal and mainly if a grunger is a rollerblader, they are a rollerblader. And if a grunger is a skateboarder, they are a skateboarder. For grungers, if they are a BMXer, they are a BMXer.'

I'm feeling slightly confused by this point, wondering if grunger is simply a term for anyone who isn't a townie.

'Are they the main groups?' I ask carefully.

'Well, then there is the sort of more extreme of grungers, which is goths. Which sort of have dark clothing, eye shadow, stuff like that.'

'And they don't skateboard, right?'

I know exactly what goths are, and I can't imagine them taking their black skirts and buckle-laden shoes down the skatepark.

'Some of them do. But like, goths are almost like a religion. I mean they don't believe in personal items. I don't know much about goths. But I have I think two goth friends.'

'And are the different groups friendly to each other?'

'Not always, no.'

'Does it ever get nasty?'

'I wouldn't say very, but townies take grunger as a cuss. And skateboarders cuss each other, just because it is fun. I mean townies are very sort of sensitive in that they have a lot of pride. For skateboarders, townie is the most popular cuss, it is like "your mum" or something, cussing each other's mums.'

'And does everyone belong to one of these groups? What if someone doesn't want to be labelled? Is that all right?'

'Some people just say I am not going to say slang, I am not going to skateboard, I just want to be who I am, and I want to be a person. I am not like that, but I definitely respect it. I mean my best friend is like that. He has actually labelled himself a scownie: skateboarder and a townie.'

Scownie, chav, grunger. Despite his best efforts, I leave Heathcote's flat less than clear about the differences between the groups. Looking for more answers, I find a godsend: urbandictionary.com. Its strapline is 'Define your world' and it invites you to submit your own definition for words. On this site I get a greater sense of the disdain that particular groups feel for one another.

Charvas, or charvs: a race of lower-class, pathetic life forms who for some reason think they are better than everyone else. They especially show dislike towards goths, punks, skaters, grungies, etc (they group them together as 'hippies'). They wear ugly burbury caps that hang off the back of their heads, stripy jumpers, a pair of stupidly priced boots with tracksuit bottoms. They also wear too many rings, sometimes with a matching kinder egg chain.

Goth: A misnomer for a follower of bands such as Marilyn Manson, Tool, Korn, Slipnot, etc. Generally, bands like these were part of the reason why 'goths' kept seeming whinier and whinier. Now not only are there bands trying to portray themselves as goth when goth is effectively dead, but now mass marketing has decided to reshape the subculture to cater to a very lucrative demographic: rebellious teenagers of middle- to upper-class families.

Skater: Some stupid kid who thinks they're a punk and insists that pop sucks, but Good Charlotte are the best band in the world, even though Good Charlotte are blatantly pop. They also like to think they can skate but usually this just involves owning a skateboard and falling off it after 30 seconds of trying. They also write in their own language, which is a very incoherent form of English. Examples include 'u sk8? das gay if u don sk8'.

This attitude is repeated in conversations I have throughout the year. A trio of Busted fans tells me about the kind of boys they like.

'There's all garage boys round here and we're into skater boys and there's none round here.'

'Cos they're all like what we call rude boys and that's what Busted aren't.'

'Busted are punky skater rock.'

'Does it make a difference?'

'Yeah it does.'

A bunch of kids in Newcastle talk me through their downloaded Spanish techno.

'This is what the charvas like.'

'Two types of people in Newcastle: charvas and goths.'

'I'm not a charva … '

'But we listen to charva music … and people think that the clothes that we like look like charva clothes. Check shirts. Stripes and all that.'

'What's the difference between charvas and everything else. Is it style?'

'It's everything. It's who you listen to. If you're a goth you wear baggy clothes and listen to different music.'

'It's about what you like.'

I chat with two kids at Homelands, a huge dance music festival. Izzy is wearing a plastic choker round her neck, while 'Major' Tom is in full military gear and camo face paint.

'A couple of years ago when I started going clubbing everyone was wearing cyber stuff and it was cool, and the townies, total dickheads, were like: "Ugh, they're like freaks", and now they're wearing it and it's not original any more, you're like desperately trying to find something original, that's why he's wearing that.' Izzy laughs, pointing towards Tom, who smiles proudly and gives a salute.

'Before, when you dress up cyber, it was a way of saying, come talk to me, I'm really friendly and I don't mind chatting to strangers, but now townie people have taken it over, and sometimes when you're out clubbing you see people who if you go over to chat to them they give you attitude, and they've got the townie kind of attitude: "Look at me", you know, strut around. Especially the girls. With little hot pants. It looks good; it's just the attitudes: they think they're all it.'

The detail and passion with which most kids could define themselves suggested a level of intolerance that I had not been expecting to find. Almost a conservatism that didn't want to accept people's different lifestyle and fashion choices. There wasn't the rigidity or direct confrontation as with the original youth tribes – those balmy evenings when Mods and Rockers would kick the shit out of each other on Brighton beach – but the number of different groups and number of people involved in those groups seemed much greater.

'Songs about guns'

'Children come out of school talking about guns,' says Paul Simpson, a church youth worker on the Stonebridge estate in north London. 'The mentality is so much more vicious now. They don't talk about beating each other up, they talk about killing each other. The simple fact is that with a gun, you are someone; you can hold your own. Without one, you are a dead man.'

British-born Ryan, 26, now retired from crime, agrees. 'Most of the time you don't feel safe without a gun because you know everyone else has one. And if you want to deal, you need a gun to stop yourself getting robbed, or to rob others, or just to stop people who want to diss [show disrespect to] you. Most of the time it's OK, but every now and then you pick the wrong person and that's when wars start.'

Observer, September 2003

Blood and laughter

The diagram shows you how to kill somebody. It features a man's torso, drawn in anatomical style so you can see the organs, the muscle tissue and skeleton. Standing out from the black on faded yellow, the major arteries are in bright red. Next to various body sections are tips, delivered in a casual, jokey tone.

'Stomach. Exposed element of the lower digestive tract. No amount of sixpack action will withstand rigorous laceration. Neck. A vital region containing thick bundles of veins and arteries. Severing these will often prove fatal.'

At the bottom of the page, the prophecy: 'Heads will roll. Limbs will fly. Blood will splatter.'

This is an ad for The Mark of Kri, a PlayStation game set in medieval Japan, which couples Disney-like animation with luscious gory action as Rau moves through the game, finishing off people with swords, arrows and his bare fists. It's not the most violent of games, but the ad does its best to suggest its nastiness, signing off with: 'The Brutal Place. The Bloody Place. The Barbaric Place. The Third Place.'

Certainly Britain likes these kind of places. Violent entertainment is everywhere. And often, as in the ad for Kri, it's not treated very seriously.

Examples of entertainment that celebrate violence abound. From the Backyard Wrestling videos which advertise themselves by showing an unconscious, blood-covered teen and the legend 'Warning: This violent videotape will shock you', to the game of the same name which promises to let you 'punish your opponent by implementing instruments of pain like thumbtacks, barbed wire, light bulbs, stop signs, baseball bats, tables, fire … '

This sense of exaggeration and near absurdity surfaces in movies as well. Kill Bill, Tarantino's fourth movie, and certainly his most gory, features Uma Thurman on a revenge mission, slashing her way through legions of Yakuza gangsters, leaving a trail of limbs, ears, feet and intestines behind her. The first part ends with her slicing the top of her target's head off. For a second the woman looks straight to camera and we see her brain through the top of her head before she slumps to the ground. It's a funny scene.

If you want something a little more real, then the internet's your best bet. Rotten.com has been offering 'pure evil since 1996'. Its speciality is pictures of gruesome deaths and unfortunate accidents. So the aftermath of a shotgun to the head, showing a neck stump, a chin and then a flower of unrecognisable flesh. Or a boy with his arm tangled in a meat grinder with the fingers clearly protruding from the other end. As well as the random – 'Decapitation by helicopter' or 'Suicide jumper lands on car' – there is a whole area devoted to celebrity corpses, and, of course, weird porn, under the title Fetish Maximus. It is extreme, unpleasant and strangely amusing.

Violent is certainly an aesthetic choice. A fashion shoot in *Vice* magazine, set in south London, features a selection of moody black youth posing with pistols, shotguns, knives and mottos.

'I got the name Blade from certain incidents that have gone down on road, ya get me? I need tools to deal with the drama. Boy, there are a couple of people walking around with scars right now. I didn't really want to be talking to some magazine bout I'm so gangsta but I'm sorry, that's how I keep it blood.'

Brands like Levi's and Reebok are complicit in the glamour of tough, getting street association in a way that traditional advertising could never deliver.

That violent imagery and lyrics abound in today's Britain is undeniable. What is less clear, though, is how this level of violence seeps through to our real lives. One of the old arguments that surfaces again and again is that violent entertainment endorses and encourages violent behaviour. In May, the *Sun* runs a story about 'The Matrix Murders', describing four cases where the crime appears to be influenced by the movie. And in December 2002, the *Evening Standard* writes about carjack mobsters who looked to movies for style cues. The accompanying photo shows them dressed as twenties gangsters, carrying guns and sporting trilbies.

Stories like these, which focus on extreme individual cases, become the evidence for critics of vast swathes of modern entertainment, and lead to the type of headlines that sparked my curiosity. 'Minister calls for a halt to violent games and TV shows' reads one headline a couple of weeks after the murders of Charlene and Letisha, and goes on to present Kim Howells's views on the heartlessness at the centre of so many films and games.

Surely this blanket criticism of entire entertainment genres was an overreaction. Could the experiences of the kids in Birmingham be down to their entertainment tastes? Was Shayne being entirely honest with himself when he said it was his decision and his only to murder people in the street? Or were other, more disturbing forces at work?

There was only one place to begin.

Ministry of Sound Bites

Last time I was in Trafalgar Square there were hordes of riot police, kids smoking skunk underneath Nelson's Column and a guy cycling around with a sound system strapped to his bike. But now I'm on official business to visit a minister in the Department for Culture, Media and Sport. Ministry of Culture. Stupidly, I can't help thinking of the Ministry of Sound. Certainly in recent months, Kim Howells has been the minister for sound bites, with his criticisms of gangster rap ('macho idiot rappers'), computer games ('pornography of violence') and contemporary art ('cold, mechanical, conceptual bullshit'). Here was a man who had clearly stated that the wrong kind of entertainment could have more effect on crime than poverty.

The Ministry of Culture is next to Trafalgar Square. I wait in the lobby until Kim's assistant greets me: a neat man, black suit, tidy black quiff. He takes me into the ministerial office. There's a big table, covered in newspapers, some slightly shabby green sofas. Unexceptional art on the walls. It certainly doesn't feel like a modern-day cultural hub. More ministry than culture.

We sit on sofas, the sprawl of news between us. Kim is friendly and expansive. He gives the impression of someone who loves his job, and loves to talk. Throughout our conversation neat man in black looks at his watch, and tries to get Kim to hurry up, but Kim seems happy to let our interview stretch well beyond the allotted time. He begins by explaining the origin of his ministry (originally, disparagingly named the Department of Fun by its critics) and underlining the importance of entertainment to Britain.

'We've never understood fully as a nation the part that entertainment plays in the economy. Forget for a moment whether it's good culture or bad culture, whether it's spiritually fulfilling or detrimental, it is huge business. A few bands in south Wales – the Stereophonics, the Manics (forget Tom Jones, he's in a class of his own) – they've probably generated as much money as one big steel plant did, and maybe more. To understand that is critical.'

Kim sees two main roles for his ministry: to 'prod culture along', and to make sure it makes some money for the UK. Sitting back in his sofa, drinking coffee that has been brought in on a silver tray, he becomes more and more passionate.

'We're particularly cursed in this country by the notion that cleverness equals academic excellence in a very narrow range of subjects. As education minister I remember being quite shocked that everyone assumed that the important subjects that kids should study were mathematics and English. Now they are fantastically important, but the notion that they are more important to a child than music, arts, drama is a very curious one and says a lot about the kind of society we live in. Very few civilisations are remembered for their economists or their accountants. They're remembered for their artists. And that's not an accident. Artists and architects, engineers: they make the world that we live in. We don't really understand the significance of what it is that artists and musicians do. What they produce is incredibly powerful.'

As he talks I wonder at the gap between Kim Howells the critic of gaming and hip hop, and Kim Howells the passionate advocate of entertainment. He claims that the DCMS is 'culture neutral. It is important that it doesn't reflect the likes and dislikes of individuals. Otherwise you create a salon of great experts who decide what is good art and what is bad art.'

'Isn't that what you've been doing?' I ask him. 'You've criticised whole genres of entertainment.'

'The reason I'm so critical is because I believe that entertainment is so influential on behaviour. It has always had tremendous power over me. I can define my life in many ways in terms of music and pictures and I think a lot of people feel like that.'

To underline this point he embarks on a story about a get-together in a south London pub before Labour came into power. Rather than following the thread of this vital meeting, he became distracted by the jukebox, which happened to be belting out 'Save All Your Kisses'. I don't know if this says more about the power of entertainment or the quality of the meeting he was attending but I let it go as he makes a broader point, suggesting that we let much modern entertainment flow over us, without understanding what it is signifying.

'I find it absolutely impossible not to listen to words. I always listen to the lyrics.'

And from Kim's point of view, the reason he is so critical of certain types of entertainment is because he cares.

'If you happen to care then you have to say something about it. In my book anyway. Otherwise what are you?'

'Tell me what's behind your comments about gaming and hip hop,' I ask him. He goes on to express an exasperation with what he sees as a show-off culture.

'For me it's part of something bigger. If you try and understand the current fascination with glamour, if you think about the role that all this plays in people's lives, it's a hugely important role, and if it doesn't matter to you then I wonder why. I can't stand it when footballers punch the air. I can't stand the triumphalism, that braggart culture, that look-at-me-I'm-great, and the worst expression I've heard of that is the image of some gun-toting "I'm the greatest thing that ever walked the earth, hey bitch". That is the ultimate turn-off for me. When that sort of phoney, hard-man look-at-me-I'm-a-gangster crap is used as a fashion accessory and to sell records then I think it's a bit sick. If people want to do it, let them do it. I don't believe in censorship, but it's a kind of infantile culture which I don't have to live with.

'I think record producers, artists, distributors should think about it a bit more. I wouldn't want any government or any regime to try and say you can't do it, but because culture is important it should be talked about. I was shocked and upset by the murder of the two girls in Birmingham, and I just said that people ought to be thinking about what the hell we are trying to do with this stuff. What was interesting about the debate that followed was that it hadn't been taking place. That's the important thing really. It does form such a massive part of people's lives. Everybody's saying the population's disconnected from politics. I just think that the politics of culture are probably the most important of any.'

Which is why he's so personally passionate about it being the right type of culture, however contradictory he sounds to me.

'In the end people have got to make choices. They have to decide if they want to live in a society that's ridden with gangsters and people who carry knives and guns … or they don't. It's as simple as that.'

I wonder what Shayne would make of that, and figure he'd probably agree.

'Great artists may have been anarchists but I sense that at the heart of every artist is the desire to make society a better place, sometimes a fairer place, sometimes a more interesting place, but never to destroy that commonality that binds us all together.'

On that grand and visionary note the interview ends. Neat man in black has been pointedly waving his watch arm at Kim for the last fifteen minutes. I get the sense that he is used to Kim's expansive conversations. As he escorts me to the lift, I remark that Kim seems quite different from how he's portrayed in the papers.

'He knows what he's doing,' he replies cryptically, and then he's gone.

I leave the DCMS conscious of the impossibility of a straightforward argument, my picture of our nation's relationship with the entertainment it produces and consumes remaining muddled. Rather than hating entertainment, the minister of culture seemed passionate about it. And, having talked to him, the idea that entertainment can have all kind of good effects, but that bad effects are scaremongering, suddenly seemed one-sided. Although many record and games companies had defended their violent product with an 'it's only entertainment' argument, the fact that so many got behind the Disarm initiative (a week of anti-violence gigs across London) suggested an implicit acceptance of some of the other effects it can have.

At the same time I found Kim's equation of art with social betterment idealistic and simplistic. Or at least in the sense that he meant it. Speaking with Laurine and with Gemma, it was already clear that entertainment played a vital part in their lives. For Gemma, music offered an escape from an undeniably harsh life, while Laurine believed that the style of music that Kim had criticised for its macho posturing was – through its fuck this and fuck that lyrics – telling her something real and useful, offering her a guide to life. So much so that she forced her parents to sit down and put up with the cussing to reach the wisdom.

Under the influence

In September the mothers of Letisha and Charlene launch a campaign against gun violence, in association with Disarm, whose role is to generate funds for grassroots groups to divert young males from using guns. I get in touch with Bill Brown, the chairman of Disarm, and Beverley Thomas, Charlene's mother.

I wander around before the meeting at the South Aston Community Centre on the edge of Birmingham. Across the Expressway is the HP building, a brand and industry from another age. Next door is a primary school where kids in red sweatshirts run around. The sign over the front gate is written in five languages.

Opposite is Aldersea Drive. On the sign, someone has scrawled: 'Don't mess with this area.' There are a lot of imperatives on this small crowded redbrick estate but the majority aren't put up by the residents.

'Ball games prohibited. Keep off the grass.' Both above the same patch of dirt.

'Keep fireworks off our streets.'

'The street is being monitored.' And a CCTV logo. One of Britain's more successful brands.

The 'No Dumping' sign is a magnet for buggies, empty drums of cooking oil and a front door. There is trash everywhere, paint peeling off the doors, carcasses and entrails from cars strewn across driveways. But TV dishes grace nearly every house. I'm struck by the incongruity of the stuff going through these dishes – Sky Movies, endless MTV, celeb lives and home improvement programmes – and the dishes' environment. They are beacons that shine a glossy world into a shabby one. The gap between what we watch and how we live is one more of Britain's disconnections.

Inside, we sit alone in a large community hall. Bill is calm and friendly in a suit. He talks slowly and powerfully, and is joined by Doreen Bailey, a senior crown prosecutor and a high court advocate, who is spending a year doing community work.

Charlene's mum, Beverley, is quiet and young. She has sad eyes. She doesn't talk much. I find her looking at me a couple of times. I don't know how to look back. She wears a faded '22' T-shirt.

I ask her to tell me about the Safer Lives, Safer Communities initiative. She starts speaking, and then stumbles to a halt, looking over to Doreen who picks it up.

'It came about after the death of her daughter and also Letisha. The mothers wanted to redress the situation and they didn't quite know how but they came together with the Disarm Trust to start a campaign against gang violence.

'The campaign wants to educate young children about their responsibilities and teach them the dangers and the harsh realities of gun crime and also being in a gang because the media – the television especially and music – they tend to glamorise gang life. It's not glamorous when you speak to actual gang members; a lot of them are terrified, they can't walk down the road without looking behind their backs, they're always on edge. They don't lead particularly happy lives.'

As Doreen finishes, Beverley adds, 'I think that young people's brains need to be occupied.'

'Do you mean that people join gangs out of boredom?'

This time when she replies, she seems sure of what she is saying.

'They get bored or they're expelled or suspended from school, and end up walking the streets and end up in the wrong hands.'

'Things have moved on so quickly,' adds Bill. 'In comparison to other activities, school is not fun, it's not sexy, so you can't hold and sustain them in school. They get bored and they're out and when that happens there's no mechanisms in the communities to catch them before they actually drift into gangs.

'Once kids have been kicked out of school, I think there should be somewhere else to go rather than stay at home. Once they suspend or expel them, they're just left to do what they want to do.'

Beverley and Bill paint a picture of young people for whom school hasn't worked and who see little other option.

'Some of them are glad to be expelled or suspended.'

At this point we are joined by Mark Edwards, who Bill introduces as a disciple. 'Not biblical but modern-day disciple, new-age disciple.'

What this means is that he runs something called the Young Disciples, set up because Mark felt existing youth groups weren't connecting. His aim is to show young people that other options exist to gang life. Mark wears a leather jacket and heavy silver wrist chain. His hat is pulled tight over his head. He speaks passionately and quickly, with a firm stare and lots of pointing.

'I grew up in the inner city, witnessing a lot of serious crime myself, having seen one of my friends being killed, died in my arms. That challenged me and made me want to get involved to try and prevent it.'

Mark talks about some of the workshops he runs, aimed at getting people to explain how they're feeling. He describes a situation where a group is asked to ignore one of their members without letting them know what they're doing.

'So they'll all be in a circle having their discussions and this guy will be cold outside of it and after the workshop I'll ask how he felt. We get words like isolated, unconfident, low, drained in self-esteem because that's how young people feel: totally isolated, disengaged, they feel like no one cares for them, they feel unloved, neglected by the education authority, by the system, by their families even, that's how they feel. When you get deeper you see a lot of them are in a state of fear. They're carrying to protect themselves, and obviously they see it as "it's them or us". It's not just the war between themselves, they see it as "us against the system".'

This idea of a failing system recurs frequently throughout our conversation. Whether it's schools, the police, community groups or families, Mark and Bill, Beverley and Doreen create a picture of Britain where a significant number of kids are joining gangs because they have little else to do. Gangs, in their loosest sense, offer something that these kids aren't finding elsewhere.

As Doreen puts it, 'The gangs exist mainly as a family. A lot of these people need somebody to aspire to and there's always somebody older, there's always somebody that started the gang or was in the gang before you so it's somebody to look up to.

'There's also a sense of belonging, which nobody else has actually integrated them into. It's not like they're part of institutions or they're part of any club or anything. These guys are looked at as delinquents, as dysfunctional young people so nobody really wants to really integrate with them. They're left isolated, so being in a gang gives them a sense of protection, a sense of well-being and belonging with each other. A lot of them are coming from broken homes so they'll be looking on that structure as their adopted or secondary family.'

When they start talking about the spread of gun usage, it's in the context of having some influence and power, in a world from which they feel disassociated.

'I think it's part of their strength. They feel powerful with the gun,' says Beverley.

'Guns are even more accessible now, people can buy them, replicas can be converted, you can buy hand grenades, you can buy all sorts of weapons on the street fairly cheaply. Any youth can afford a gun and once you have a gun you feel this enormous sense of power that nothing, no one can stand in your way, and once you've used it that surge of power just increases.'

All this makes sense. But why – if society is not working for these kids, if gangs offer a family spirit that can't be found elsewhere – why the problem with entertainment?

'If we're talking about young people, they're very impressionable. It's so terrible, you've got a platform that could be so positive. The messages could be so positive and yet groups use this platform to sow seeds of discord. In a nutshell, these things do have an impact.'

'So, what do you think about artists who say they are not encouraging anything, but simply describing it?'

Bill is quick to dismiss this.

'They would say that, wouldn't they? They are describing how it is but it perpetuates the situation because people are listening to their words and subliminally they're acting on it.'

It's Mark, the youngest of the group, who is most critical of the entertainment that surrounds young Britain.

'Music is one element: but it's not just hip hop, you're talking about various genres of music, you're talking about radio, you're talking about TV, about films, about newspapers. It's coming from every single dimension. You look at the cartoons now, cartoons for young people. Child psychologists say that a young person's ethics and morals and behaviours are formed by the time they're seven years old. The cartoons presented to them are not educational cartoons about their lifestyles or about education, citizenship and being socially included. It's all aggression, hate, dysfunctional relationships. There are traumatising blood-bath scenes. Look at the Incredible Hulk. He functions through anger. When he's angry he's at his most powerful. It's like he's on self-destruct, and my nieces and nephews watch these programmes and I'm thinking to myself: this is what's polluting this generation.'

Mark is passionate and committed, but I find it hard to imagine what a cartoon about citizenship or social inclusion would look like, and who would watch it. And the Incredible Hulk has been looming greenly from our screens since Lou Ferrigno burst out of his clothes in the late seventies.

From cartoons the conversation moves on to gaming, and the video game Vice City is inevitably brought up. Both Mark and Bill attack Xbox and PlayStation, condemning an entire entertainment system, rather than some of the games made for them. I thank all four for their time, and they give me a friendly but solemn goodbye.

By the time I leave the community centre, I am struck by the passionate disgust that Bill and Mark hold for huge portions of our contemporary entertainment, entertainment that is enjoyed and valued by hundreds of thousands of younger people. Like Kim Howells, they recognise the pervasiveness of hip hop, gaming, pop videos, violent films, but they do not approve.

Mark's speech about the breadth of kids' isolation plays round and round in my head. This disengagement from society that he talked about definitely seemed to be an extreme example of something happening across Britain: the emergence of a particularly disconnected generation, which feels little empathy with or love from the country it inhabits.

I can't help wondering if the two things – the power of entertainment for a young audience, and a sense of disconnection from much of Britain – relate to each other. Has entertainment become so powerful simply because there is little else relevant to turn to?

Bleeding stump

'When I first used to go on the internet,' Stuart tells me, 'when I was thirteen, there was a website called Steak and Cheese which was just horrible shit, you know, nasty things like: this is a man who's been hit by a car while carrying a glass chandelier and now it's mashed in his head. And I used to spend ages looking at it because it was really funny and then got a bit bored. The internet desensitised me far more than any videos.'

I'm talking with Cordelia and Stuart, a thoughtful and well-balanced couple in their late teens. We're in their small front room in Reading.

'If you type in a word, like say you were looking for a song lyric and the lyric happens to be "bleeding stump" or something, you'll type that in and it will come up with something fucking disgusting like some real nasty fetid … '

'Gratuitously unnecessary,' adds Cordelia.

'But it'll be called "something or other bleeding stump" and you'll think: that's that song, and you click on it and there'll just be a picture of something.'

'Do you genuinely think that has desensitised you?'

'Yes, absolutely. It just happens so many times I'm not shocked by it any more. I'll get an e-mail and it'll say "Hello Stuart, good to see you last year, love Anna". You click on it and it's some picture of a naked woman trying to shove half a plastic shark up her arsehole or something.' He starts laughing.

'Does any of that bother you?'

'No, it's just stupid. I can't picture anyone actually taking it seriously, though, you know?'

'Or getting offended by it?'

'I can picture people getting offended by it, very much so. Older people, yes. Our generation had it from a young age, do you know what I mean? I remember the first time it happened: clear as day, me and my mate Robert we were looking on the internet and I was like, "I got an e-mail from some woman," and we both looked at this picture for about half an hour. It would be like: that doesn't fit up there, no, and then, you know, it happens so many times you get drunk, go on the internet: oh look, here's a video of some woman sticking a sledgehammer up herself, you know, let's watch that, and then eventually it doesn't amuse you any more, it doesn't provoke any reaction. I don't think that seeing stuff like that's made me a depraved pervert; I just think I'm not shocked by that sort of stuff.'

Charlotte, Majahid and Amanda are similarly dismissive. We're talking about the way that the press link music and computer games with violent behaviour. Majahid listens to rap, while R&B is Amanda's favourite music. Both watch a lot of music videos.

'That doesn't make you go out and do anything,' Amanda says with certainty. 'I don't care what anyone says, listening to that doesn't mean shit.'

'No, it doesn't influence nobody. If you look at something it doesn't mean you've got to copy it. It's like watching a video and you see someone ripping off his skin, you ain't going to rip your own skin off. It would be stupid to rip your own skin off.'

'If you go out and do something it's your own fault, no one else's.'

And Laurine is quick to put entertainment in the context of the real world, which is just as rude and powerful as anything glowing on a screen or belting out of the stereo. 'You go out on the street with your five-year-old girl and you hear someone say, "You cunt" – what is the first word that is going to come out of her mouth? "You cunt." My first word was dickhead, because of my brother. Everything with my brother was you dickhead, you dickhead; my first word was dickhead. It's not just because of the music, it's not just because of the TV. You've got to remember that the society of today is all about swearing, all about violence, about bad language, rape, everything, drugs, alcohol, shootings, gangs, everything. It's not just because of the TV, or because of the magazines or music. It's just the whole area.'

Frightening our children with horrible creatures

'For every piece of research that says watching violent films creates a particular form of behaviour, there is another piece that says it doesn't. It's very difficult to prove a correlation. Films and video are part of an overall picture. If you look at something like violence, people see more violence on the news, and that's real violence; when they go the cinema, what they are seeing, they know it's cinema ... '

This is Sue Clark speaking, the closest we have in the UK to a censor, someone who exists to monitor or control our consumption of entertainment. In Britain, the role of censor is carried out by the British Board of Film Classification, an independent body which gives age guidelines and recommends any cuts for films in the UK. In many other countries this is a government function, and I guess I'm expecting somebody stern, someone who will happily cut the best bits of film for the greater moral good of the country. Instead Sue cheerfully talks about scaring our kids, describing it as a longstanding, even healthy, tradition.

Compared to the media hysteria that seems to surround much of British entertainment, she offers a relaxed and pragmatic view.

'The number of films that come through that are pushing the boundaries are tiny and have a very small audience. The view that things are becoming incredibly liberal is nonsense. Out of the six hundred films that came through last year, you can count on less than the fingers of one hand the number of controversial films, and the fact that you can name them tells you that they're a very small proportion of what comes through here.'

Sue sets up a theme that recurs throughout 2003. That negative commentary tends to come from people outside the scene they are commentating on, and who have little understanding or awareness of it. A bit like criticising cricket because nobody scores any goals.

'We use the phrase "media literate". People who go the cinema regularly and enjoy the rules of the genre are much less likely to be upset or offended or prompted to complain than the people who inadvertently dip into something by mistake or go deliberately to be offended … Why did you go? This is not compulsory.'

Sue is keen to dismiss any simple equation between violent films and violent behaviour, and to place entertainment within the broader context of a violent society, and one that can recognise and respond to different categories of violence. She is also far less convinced than Kim Howells or Bill of the impressionability of young viewers.

'Media literacy starts kicking in at about ten, eleven, twelve. Eight-year-olds know there aren't dinosaurs out there so they're not going to bump into them on the way to school; they might have some bad dreams but kids have bad dreams about all sorts of things, and that's not a reason to prevent young children from seeing things that they will thoroughly enjoy. Violence has been part of our culture for generations. We've been frightening our children with violence and horrible creatures since time immemorial. This is part of our culture and you can't remove it. Film is just another way of portraying it. Half the time the parents are more concerned than the kids, who actually understand what they are watching. If you talk to children, they are far more disturbed by news broadcasts than they are by film, because they understand that this is just a film, but that isn't just a film on the news. I think people do become more tolerant of violence, but I think they become more tolerant because of what they see in real life rather than what they see in the cinema.'

This makes me think of Laurine's comments about the influence of the real world. Of course, 2003 serves up its fair share of visible, graphic – and real – violence; from the permanent threat of mobile terrorism, and a constant stream of suicide bombers, to the US decision to publish (in colour) pictures of the reconstructed corpses of Uday and Qusay Hussein. At home, we learn about the Camden Ripper, who tossed his victim's body parts into the nearest bin; papers go into explicit detail about the way that Ian Huntley disposed of Jessica and Holly's bodies; and a

Norfolk primary school complains about Prince Philip shooting pheasants within sight of the children.

'Everybody is influenced by what they see. We absorb things and are changed by them. But it doesn't mean they are changed for the worse. People can thoroughly enjoy violent films and not be at all violent. There is a school of research that says that watching violent films can be cathartic. If you think how many millions of people see a film, and because two people decide to copy it, it becomes a hugely influential film – what about all the people who did see it and didn't do what was in the film?'

In 1997, fourteen-year-old Michael Carneal shot three girls one morning after a school prayer meeting in Kentucky. In court in 2002, his defence argued that he had been influenced by games like Doom, Quake and Resident Evil.

The judges dismissed the possibility of a direct correlation: 'We find that it is simply too far a leap from shooting characters on a video screen (an activity undertaken by millions) to shooting people in a classroom (an activity undertaken by a handful, at most) for Carneal's actions to have been reasonably foreseeable to the manufacturers of the media that Carneal played and viewed.'

Warfare

At YES studios, a charity set up for young people either excluded from school or described as hard to reach, I chat with some student entrepreneurs. Set in a small converted house, YES offers music recording and video-editing facilities. I talk with Lionel, twenty, aka Silver Sharp; Romano, twenty-two, aka R9, aka Nezzy; Daniel, nineteen, aka Zom Beat.

In many ways, they embody everything that the minister of culture railed against. They are black. They wear box-fresh sneakers and gold. Baseball caps. One of them has a hoodie with a revolver on the back. They like hip hop and UK garage. They make music that represents life as they see it. They call themselves Warfare Records. They are massively confident that they are going to make it. Kim Howells MP might find that offputting, boastful. I find their optimism refreshing. Their remarks may be rougher than Sue Clark's, but the sentiment is surprisingly the same.

We sit in a scruffy room among old computers and handwritten posters on the wall. 'YES ethos: you have the solution.' I ask them about the music they make, and get a profound response from Romano.

'Music's a love, innit. Everyone's got love for music. It's a way of expressing your art. But what we do is like I'm writing a book for a blind man, you get me? I'm telling you how the streets are, what I get on with. Just that.'

After just a couple of minutes talking with these three, it's clear that any simplistic equation of lyrics with a call to violence is way off. They understand representation and the role of art as well as any critic.

'When people say that music influences violence, it doesn't,' Romano continues. 'It's just a way of expressing what goes on. It's like Picasso painting a picture. If he painted a picture of a man stabbing himself in the belly it's art.'

'Music's just art too,' mutters Lionel.

This echoes an interview I'd heard on Radio 5 with DJ Trevor Nelson, who had suggested that there are certain fictions we are more comfortable dealing with.

'If there is a serial killer on the loose, they don't ring Stephen King and start telling him off about what he puts in his movies or books, because we all enjoy them. We go to the cinema, we know it is not real, we go home. But as soon as this happens with this subject … they are knocking on every musician's door – from Eminem to whoever.'

Perhaps because novels and films have been around for longer, we are more familiar with them as artistic forms. Computer games or hip hop remain unintelligible to a much larger proportion of the British population. While we are quite happy to allow novels to be as violent as they please, hip hop is not credited with the same level of fictional distance, as if a rap track can't have a narrator in the same way that a novel can. To suggest that any lyricist who raps about guns is a killer seems as ridiculous as saying any novelist who writes about drugs is a junkie.

We get chatting about why particular types of music seem to get worse press than others. And the effect that music has on its listeners. Romano feels that criticism of hip hop and garage is the sign of a naive desire for fake stories.

'It's because the industry want manufactured. They wanna hear a certain kind of music which is not real. They want to hear about flowers. They want to hear about love.'

'Good times and that.'

'But in reality that's not what it's like.'

'People are just trying to make you understand what they're going through, what they've been through. If it happens to come out a bit negative then so be it. But that's their personal experiences, understand. You didn't live their lives, you can't tell them that, get me? Songs about guns: that's not going to influence me. If I'm a hearing a story about a next man's life, that's not going to influence me to go pick up a gat, and start shooting a man, you see what I'm saying?'

'Straight up.'

'So I don't believe in none of that really myself.'

'And what about the people who are criticising this type of music. Do you think they understand it?'

'They have no idea at all,' replies Daniel.

'It has to be, innit,' adds Romano. 'There's no other explanation.'

'They don't understand. Someone has lived their life the same as a rapper, they be like, "Yeah, I'm feeling it, I know where he's coming from." '

'Not saying it's only rappers that have bad lives. But they're the ones who express it. And get out there.'

Baseline Ladiez

I first talk with the Baseline Ladiez outside a gig for So Solid Crew, where they tell me that they make music with a positive message. On the night of the gig I'm struck by the gap between the media representation of the So Solid Crew, and the lifeless nature of the event. Despite the beefed-up security – 'No search no entry' – the metal detectors and the screens at the door ('Is that to stop people rushing in?' asks the dapper black BBC presenter. 'Nah. It's just hype,' replies the security), there is never any sense of danger at the gig. Embarrassed MCs try to get the half-empty room of under-eighteens going: 'I say So, you say … ' and just a handful of people shout 'Solid'. When Get Rich Crew come on they encourage the crowd to 'hold on to your best friend's hand' and it feels like one more pop concert. How quickly something stops being dangerous. And loses its appeal.

I return to Hackney to hear more about the Baseline Ladiez' positivity.

Walking to the pub I see flyposters for So Solid's second album, *2nd Verse*. Across the road a large poster put up by Trident – the Met police's initiative to tackle gun crime in black communities – warns: 'Don't let the gunmen prejudice our children's futures.' The message is covered with flyposters … for an Iraq demo, for some evangelical church, for a club night that advertises itself with an image of a girl with 'Fuck You' scrawled across her face.

We meet in a Wetherspoons pub. I order three Cokes, but then they're asked for ID, which none of them have. They're sixteen and affronted at not being allowed to order soft drinks. We go round the corner to a regular shabby English pub, and everything's fine.

The Baseline Ladiez are Toni, Lorelle and Ayesha. Although they tell me later on that they don't care about branded or expensive clothes, just stuff that looks good, Lorelle is wearing an Evisu jacket and Chanel earrings. Her friends tease her that they're fake; she tells me I better not put that in the book. Toni has black pants with Punk Queen across the butt in Gothic lettering. Ayesha has part Afro, part crazy plaits tight on her head.

Lorelle is currently studying travel and tourism, Ayesha media studies and English. Toni has a part-time job in a hairdresser but wants to get something else. She describes what they're up to.

'We're three girls, we're r'n'b, hip hop, gospel, garage. We've been together for around a year and a bit, and we just been recording, doing talent shows, getting involved with industry side of things.'

Like Warfare Records, they're unashamedly ambitious. They've played showcases in Poplar, and have appeared in *East End Life*.

'We're future talent,' states Ayesha. 'No way we ain't going to give up, there's so many things, so many people that tries to put us down, but cos we so strong-minded, no one's gonna put us down. They'd have to kill us.'

Everyone laughs. And Toni continues.

'We don't want to be famous. I don't like using the word famous cos famous just brings glitz and glamour and in people's faces with nothing to bring to them. I wanna be known … for my music and for the lyrics that we come with.'

'To make a change, not being pretty.'

When I ask them what kind of changes they feel are needed, they tell me about the level of violence that surrounds them.

'It's mainly around us, cos we see like people talk about "ahh I wanna be like this person", for no reason. It's stupid. We want to talk to people, try to get through to people, through music, and say: what is the point? Try and see sense.'

'If there was someone that we looked up to saying something we would definitely listen to it, and I would hope that some people would look up to us and think the same thing. It means a lot when someone you love or look up to is saying something important.'

Lorelle shares the disdain that Romano expressed for fake music. 'There a lot of people out there that just talk about nonsense. They just talk about love. It's nice to talk about that, but it's also nice to keep things, like, on the street. Things that are happening that aren't being talked about and it's nice that we can bring it up.'

'We don't want to escape the reality that is around us.'

'We want to talk about things that really happen in real life.'

'We like to promote no violence.'

'Yeah, cos people are up there and they're not talking about it, about the stuff that really matters or counts.'

'You know So Solid?' asks Ayesha. 'Like the government's always blaming them for black youths' behaviour, and it's not really them. If you listen to their lyrics, they're just talking about life. And then people, then governments want to blame them. But governments are not doing anything. They're just going round to other countries and just bombing them up, for no reason.'

Like the kids in Birmingham, there is no sense that you can blame external entertainment for individual behaviour. They take personal responsibility seriously.

'Most of the boys that we hang around with do understand about the no violence,' explains Ayesha, 'but the majority of them that we know are into fighting and guns.'

'You can talk about it but whether you act it out is different.'

'I think everyone knows what they're not meant to do,' adds Toni, 'and what they're meant to do. Even the boys I see that fight know it wasn't meant to happen, but once again it goes up to see who's the highest. A lot of the time it's up to the individual because there's a lot of things that go round us, like people beating up people for no reason, and getting into drugs and all that. And whether we get involved it's our choice but we decide not to. It really does depend on a certain person.'

'If they don't like it, they make it illegal'

A father is so worried about his two children falling into a life of crime that he has named and shamed them on the internet.

'British society is going to the dogs, all around us are foul-mouthed obnoxious children like my son. They are a small minority destroying all that is good for others.'

Evening Standard, January 2003

The government last week launched a crackdown aimed at tackling nuisance behaviour, including graffiti. As part of a pilot project, the Name That Tag campaign offers a 'bounty' of £500 to people who shop vandals for daubing graffiti on trains and buildings in Manchester. Chief Insp. Peter Holden, of British Transport Police, said: 'Graffiti is definitely not a victimless crime. It has massive financial implications for the train companies who are forced to take their trains out of service to be cleaned, which in turn has a terrible knock-on effect on customers.'

Stockport Express, November 2003

Mayday under control

They come with their pink hair and black flags, banging drums and waving placards. Some are wearing hoods pulled tight over their faces, and kerchiefs over their mouths, cowboy-style. A girl strides past, face painted white, in a dragoon's jacket, bright red with gold epaulettes and a fluorescent US marine's helmet. A small girl with pigtails waves an American flag where each of the stars has been replaced with a multinational's logo. A guy in a pink tutu gives the finger to a row of police. A kid with a pink Mohawk drives his BMX crazily through the crowds; a red banner reading 'Revolution' hangs from the handlebars. Weaving their way down London's Strand: a chaotic and messy parade of people, from proper ropy travellers to posh kids with their hair messed up, wearing hoods and masks but not on any wanted list. In true Mayday spirit I bunk off the first Thursday of my new job. It's an induction week and I figure I can always pick it up later.

In 2000 London's Mayday riots received global coverage. Crowds of media-styled 'anarchists' had run rampage through the City, attacking McDonald's and other symbols of corporate greed. Coupled with other anti-capitalist demonstrations around the world, for a few months there had been an energy around this kind of violent protest which had suggested that the disenchanted, the poor, the angry were making themselves heard. That their lawlessness would in turn affect the economic-political behaviour of the West.

Despite the scuffles that occur infrequently as the crowds of brightly coloured protestors surge towards the infinite rows of police, Mayday 2003 is never going to go off. Since the riots, which effectively signalled the end of free protest, each Mayday has been progressively more moody, more constrained as police use their numbers to squash and disperse any possible outburst.

This year the main agenda is the war. At 3pm Trafalgar Square is half full of anti-war protestors, pro-Palestine activists, trade union reps, and the socialist workers who turn up to any event that can be seen as anti-government. Their placards read: 'Resist. Revolt. F**k capitalism.' It strikes me as strange that a revolutionary body is less prepared to put 'fuck' out in public than a clothing brand. There's an assortment of other messages: 'Where do wars come from? A desire for what you don't have.

James 4:1.' 'If you are dumb enough to vote, then you are dumb enough to believe them' – written in chalk on the pavement. And the ubiquitous: 'Not in my name'.

I walk up the Strand to intercept the main march heading towards Trafalgar Square. McDonald's is being casually boarded up at about 3.30pm, only twenty minutes or so before the main gaggle of protestors are due to arrive. That's capitalism, making money right up to the last minute. And they've got their sums right, even feeding a few of the people who have turned up for Mayday. I see one kid stroll out, sporting a Rage Against The Machine T-shirt, sipping on a super-size McDonald's Coke.

The crowd marching down the Strand are outnumbered and corralled by lines of police and vans. There are a few skirmishes, but no threat to the police superiority. Like the endangered species some of the protesters are shouting about, these protestors have had their day. As the group circles through Piccadilly Circus, where shoppers look on, unthreatened and curious, it feels like one more tourist attraction, a quaint English pastime.

The sun comes out, and as people realise there are going to be no proper battles, no smashing of McDonald's, a more jovial mood descends. People skin up and the smell of skunk wafts over Trafalgar Square. For most protestors, Mayday has returned to being a carnival, just like it has been over the centuries, where for a few hours the normal rules are bent a little, but there is never any doubt about who is in charge. Contained, managed dissent.

Commuters tut at the inconvenience to their schedule, when their direct route to Charing Cross is blocked. Two ladies in their seventies stroll through after checking with police that it's safe. And a bunch of men in suits, calling themselves the Socialist Stockbrokers, do a short mime, making mad hand gestures, imitating buyers on a market floor, to the cheers of people sitting around.

A guy with bike-powered speakers starts playing techno, and the crustier protestors take their tops off, their faces scrunched up and their fists pointing in the air. A bit later the drums start up again.

At 7pm the police announce that they are continuing to detain the crowd because of a breach of the peace. And because they fear further breaches of the peace. Then the riot police arrive, with their helmets, shields and batons, and there is the surreal situation of being pushed from behind towards a row of unsmiling cops. You know they almost want it to go off, but you know that it can't, and that strangely you're safe.

By 8pm, a bunch of estate kids in Gap hooded tops and Reeboks hang out, staring at the hippies shuffling round another portable sound system. There are people dancing in the street outside Charing Cross to a song whose refrain is 'George Bush is an Islamic Fundamentalist'. Another song has mixed Ken Livingstone's anti-war speech over some slow dub beats. On one side they're hemmed in, on the other, they're just having a party. No one has won and the system remains, but for a few hours normal behaviour has been suspended.

Later, the protestors are told to disperse in ones and twos. They are funnelled through a long line of police, who make a big show of taking everyone's pictures. They have won through boredom and numbers. Against the colourful, playful diversity of the marchers, the partiers and the onlookers, they represent a solid unmovable world of black and fluoro jackets, of short haircuts, moustaches and similarity. Of displeasure and control. I know which side looks more fun.

Being young is criminal

Another favourite media story is about young people and crime. The refrain is similar to the ones about sex and drugs. More of them doing it younger and worse. The endless studies showing that 16 to 24-year-olds are responsible for a significant percentage of all crime.

Beyond the obvious crimes – the muggings, robbings, and so on – there seems to be a broader attraction towards a criminal state of mind by a large number of young people. The Mayday riots displayed just this: a colourful and vibrant mix of anti-authoritarian self-expression, positivity, personal politics, drugs and music. Taking pleasure in disobedience. And, while the Mayday protests weren't exactly endorsed by the police, they were permitted to continue, suggesting a tolerance towards a certain criminal mindset.

At the same time there is a growing tendency to come down harder on certain types of youthful behaviour – from graffiti to skateboarding. In November, a teenage graffiti artist by the name of Jack Jones is jailed for six months, a longer sentence than many convicted drunk drivers get. At the same time, a pilot project is initiated: the Name That Tag campaign with its £500 bounty for people who shop graffiti vandals. And later in the year, police start swooping on schools, taking photos of notebook doodles and matching them with graffiti styles.

Whether it's marching on Mayday and taunting police, or playing computer games which allow you to jack cars and kill hookers, this kind of behaviour has a distinct, powerful pull. Many aspects of young Britain seem to embrace and celebrate illegal or semi-legal activities, and in certain cases the force of them is dependent on their criminality.

The area that particularly interested me was where entertainment or art collided with criminality. Where entertainment was blamed for criminal behaviour, or where illegality was an inevitable side effect of entertainment. I was curious as to why so many things that young people get up to have a criminal tinge to them. Or why so many non-destructive elements of young Britain now feel criminalised.

I go to visit Martin Bright, home affairs editor at the *Observer*, because the paper had supported a Children Behind Bars campaign in conjunction with Nacro – committed to preventing children being locked up because of the damage it does them, and the belief that it sets them on a life of crime.

In the mirrored exterior walls of the *Observer* building, you can see a row of flyposters across the road. One set of them advertises So Solid Crew's Lisa Maffia's debut single 'All Over'. The title seems unfortunate and strangely prescient. Two nights previously, she was meant to launch her solo career at Turnmills, a couple of minutes down the road. She hadn't turned up, but several men and a gun had. They barged into the club, before emerging again. Shots were fired and a man killed as he drove away in his Audi TT, a car whose street popularity is due partly to its inclusion in UK garage videos and lyrics. As I walk up to the *Observer* building, I see two policemen standing guard outside Turnmills. Once again, UK urban music, and specifically the So Solid Crew, are being associated with guns and violence.

Martin is keen to do this interview and move on. He speaks impatiently, but as we get into the subject you can see that he fervently believes that teenagers, especially teenage boys, are being unfairly targeted by the government.

I start by asking him about the Anti-Social Behaviour Orders (ASBOs) about to be introduced as a measure to prevent public bad behaviour.

'What the new ASBO does is criminalise street-corner culture. It will make gatherings of two or more under-sixteens unlawful if a police officer decides they are a threat to other people on the street. There are also crackdowns on graffiti, on noise, on riding your bicycle on the pavement.

'A lot of the specific crimes existed previously; the difference is that now the police can demand that you pay forty quid on the spot, and failure to pay cranks up the offence and cranks up the punishment. You are criminalising a far lower level of crime, and that means you'll have an increase in the teenage prison problem. That's what really feeds into and creates serious crime. The vast majority of under-eighteens in prison could be let out and it would have no effect on the crime level.'

So while the legislators and much of the media blame hip hop and computer games for young crime, Martin identifies Britain's urge to lock up more young people as a key driver. His point is not that no crime exists or even that prisons can't sometimes be beneficial; but more broadly that the punishment is reaching far wider than necessary.

'It's a cliché to talk about an academy of crime, but the reoffending rate for kids who end up in prison is very, very high and that is the opposite of the intended purpose of these institutions.' He links this growing trend to criminalise non-conformist behaviour with a fear on the part of the people making the laws. In particular, he identifies one target for this fear.

'This government has been absolutely obsessed with teenage boys. There is a feeling on the part of Tony Blair and Jack Straw that if you could deal with a hard core of 100,000 or so young teenagers then most of your crime would be sorted out. This is part of an ideology of envy, of fear of young street culture's energy. It replaces harnessing that energy with punitive measures and I think that's a strain that has run through New Labour policy for a long time.'

'Why do you think Labour is so fearful of our street culture?'

'It's an attraction and repellent at the same time,' he replies. 'New Labour wanted to appear hip to ride the zeitgeist, wanted the label of Cool Britannia, but it wished to completely neuter any threat that came from that area. So while attempting to appear cool, and pushing the media image of Tony Blair as someone who plays the guitar and is at ease with rock stars, it was balanced with a contradictory message. That the source of fear comes from the very same people that might become Oasis but might just as easily end up being drug dealers. This fails to recognise that British pop culture comes from precisely that contradictory area and you can't legislate for it.'

This is a theme that surfaces repeatedly when I talk to people about the role of the illegal in British popular culture. Participation within an 'undesirable' street culture does not equate with criminality. And yet the two are often confused.

'The problem is that there's no genuine dialogue with the community and no genuine dialogue with young people on the street; they couch genuine problems in inappropriate language. If you talk to the black community or if you talk to the police, they will tell you there's an extreme problem to do with aspirational crime that surrounds hip hop and black American rap culture, and that So Solid Crew is a mixture of middle-class, lower middle-class and working-class kids, some of whom are hardened criminals and some of whom aren't. Kim Howells and Blunkett's characterisation of the culture is even more simplistic. There's no conception that the more they go on about it in parliament, the more kids will aspire to it.'

One of the accusations against the record labels had centred on them providing a voice for artists who represented gun culture as aspirational. Martin's comments suggest that the government itself is another influence on youth criminality. The more they go on about it, the more appeal and kudos it has.

'There's a complex network of ideas here, so that So Solid Crew may consciously say that they believe that guns are a bad thing, but at the same time they are representing the gun culture through their music and they attract violence to their concerts. Whereas the government might be talking about this in a very simplistic way, no one, including the people involved in this culture themselves, has any illusions that this is anything other than a very complex thing.'

Martin describes a situation where entertainment and the world it represents are intertwined, difficult to separate, and the line between criminal and entertainer is blurred. The government's response is to cast its net as wide as possible, so that any potentially illegal activity is covered. While this might appear logical from a crime-prevention standpoint, I wonder how young Britain is affected when so many desirable activities are labelled illegal.

Illegal appeal

In September 2003, 50 Cent sweeps the UK MOBO awards, winning best hip hop artist, best album and best single. The protégé of Eminem, his hip hop credentials include a spell of crack dealing and taking a handful of bullets. The UK success of 50 Cent shows how easily mainstream Britain embraces a message of violence, hedonism and prostitution. *Get Rich or Die Trying* was the 17th-bestselling album of 2003, ahead of Westlife's *Turnaround* or the Red Hot Chili Peppers *Greatest Hits*.

His single 'P.I.M.P', played repeatedly on stations like Radio 1 and channels like MTV Base, extols the virtues of being a pimp ... that is, getting bitches to pull in money so you can buy Benzes and 'gator shoes, and boasts about how little money he gives to the women who surround him.

The video features 50 Cent arriving at a mansion in a white Rolls, getting dressed in white by three bikinied women, and then attending his initiation into a pimp brotherhood consisting of other rappers, headed up by Snoop Dogg. In this context, the song is about him presenting his pimp credentials, showing the old school that he's ready to join them. By the end of the video, he's walking girls around on leashes, and rapping under a chandelier with Snoop.

Taken literally, it's misogynistic, materialistic and downright criminal. But the world of hip hop is not a literal one. It's all about excess and bling ... showing what you've got, because you didn't used to have it. And once you start taking pop videos literally, where do you end up? The entire genre is a fantasy one, and musicians have always taken on preposterous roles. Perhaps when Adam Ant came swinging in on his chandelier as a highwayman the gap between the artist and his video persona was clearer, but the dynamic these days is the same. Where the difference lies is in the flow between the two worlds. 50 Cent's record label publicises his criminal past as a way of displaying his authenticity. And shows like MTV's *Cribs*, which take the viewer on tours of musicians' sumptuous homes, reveal the similarities between the aesthetics of music videos and the realities of plush West Coast interiors. The videos present the artist's desired goals.

Beyond hip hop, it's easy to find more examples of crime worship. Computer game Midnight Club 2 describes itself as 'the future of illegal street racing'. You play as a member of the world's most notorious illegal street racing syndicate, driving round Los Angeles, Tokyo and Paris.

Illegality is part of many computer games, whether the subject is criminal or not. They are designed to be played better by people who cheat. Discovering how to hoodwink the system is part of the rules, endorsed by the makers themselves. Cheating is built into the gameplay.

Websites like Xtremecheats, Captain Code, Cheat Factory all offer a stream of cheats for most games. Cheat Haven's logo figures a halo over its name, suggesting that cheating can be divine. Others are more straight-forward: 'When you want some fun or are simply crap.' And of course, many of the cheats are submitted by players, so while you may be cheating the game you are helping others. These are brotherhoods of criminality, where techniques and tricks are swapped, conforming to the same dynamic that apparently exists in prisons, where experts swap tips for future crime. Cheats for Vice City include applying plane physics to a car, so it takes off at high speeds, making the car invisible, and changing the weather.

Less hi-tech but just as compelling is Ghettopoly – a 'stolen property fencing game' – a street version of Monopoly ... with properties like Westside Liquor, Tyron's Gun Shop, Lin Ling's Massage Parlour and the simple crack houses. There are Hustle and Ghetto Stash cards, with prizes like: 'You got yo whole neighbourhood addicted to crack. Collect $50 from each playa.' The logo is done graffiti-style and a black guy looms from the letter O, in white vest and bandanna, joint clenched between teeth, AK in one hand and bottle of malt in the other.

The website promises more games in the same vein: Hoodopoly, Hiphopopoly, Thugopoly and Redneckopoly. To accusations of racism and trivialising violent crime, drug addiction, prostitution, etc, etc, the creator, David Chang, suggests that we lighten up.

'It draws on stereotypes not as a means to degrade, but as a medium to bring together in laughter. If we can't laugh at ourselves ... we'll continue to live in blame and bitterness.'

In a flow worthy of Larry Flynt, Chang goes on to say that critics of Ghettopoly are critics of freedom.

'There was a time when expression counter to the ideals of the norm was repressed. Citizens were not free to publicly voice ideals that did not conform with the ideals of those in power. We, as a society, have progressed from intolerance to acceptance of individual differences and embrace the many ideas and views and opinions that our diverse society has to offer.'

Whether you go as far as David and see a celebration of pimping as a delightful expression of free speech, the pervasiveness of playful criminal imagery and language within modern entertainment is indisputable. The Criminal clothing brand says it most clearly, presenting a criminal state of mind as an essential youth attitude. From girls' vests with the legend 'I love criminals' to men's sweats sporting CCTV cameras, they make the aesthetics of illegality desirable and glamorous. Their website spiel goes: 'We're reclaiming the streets, covering our tracks and getting away with it.'

There is nothing new about the aspirational presentation of crime. Think Robin Hood, think Arthur Penn's *Bonnie and Clyde*, think half of Robert De Niro's back catalogue. Perhaps what upsets Britain particularly about music videos and computer games is that the distinction between artist, audience and the activities they describe is less clearly defined than it ever has been. But when 50 Cent sings 'P.I.M.P', he's not saying he's a pimp, he's just taking on the voice of a pimp. Is it any different to the narrator in *Crime and Punishment*? Does playing Midnight Club 2 make you more of a criminal than watching *The Italian Job*?

Neighbourhood watch

The appeal is evident; and the interesting question for me was not so much about the influence that it has (answer: it influences different people differently), but more about why the illegal has such appeal.

Ryan and Ursula, a young couple with a one-year-old child, tell me about the kids on the south London estate where Ursula used to live. Where the crime is not just stuff that is seen on TV screens or played over the radio, but a daily part of their lives.

'They haven't got people to be looking up to,' explains Ryan. 'They haven't got positive role models, they haven't got people to make them see the right from the wrong. It's like the person they'll respect will be one of them called Nicko, the one who can steal more than anyone, rob more people than anyone; all the kids respect him because he's the bad man. He's a little boy, you'd slap him in the back of the head and say go home … but because he's got twenty, thirty of the kids in the estates surrounding him, it's like certain people get intimidated about that. They haven't got any one else to look at. He's not a positive role model at all ... '

'The kids are aspiring to be criminals,' adds Ursula. 'The good thing to do, like, when you're at school is to shot it up and make money, so you sell weed when you're at school, so that's a good thing yeah, so you're making money, and you got the trainers, you got this, you got that, now you're somebody, everybody's looking at you, and you've got to keep on that ladder. Once you start with something and people are looking at you in a certain light, you have to carry on, and that's how lots of my friends got into dealing drugs, because once seen you're in that light, and people think, oh yeah, them trainers you got are wicked, that jacket, it's really nice, now you wanna dog, now you wanna Staff, you want a dog to walk down the street with; it's like a pressure, now blah blah's got a car, you ain't got a car, now you got a car, now you got a better car.'

From Ryan and Ursula I get a sense of the pervasiveness of low-level crime – robbing and selling dope – and the egalitarianism of desire. People want the same stuff – sneakers, TVs, cars; there are just different ways of getting them. As Ryan puts it, 'Even though they blatantly haven't got the money for it, it's like they'll go out and do dumb things. They'll go out and jack the other kids on the street ... it's like they're robbing from the poor. It's the dumbest thing you ever heard. It's like if you got no trainers, why you robbing off him? They all wanna be someone ... to prove who they are.

'For instance, there's two kids that live on our estate, they're like eighteen, nineteen; when you go in their house, they got a big widescreen, really nice car, Moschino, Versace, whatever you like, nice dogs, nice this, nice that, always got weed, always got drink, always blah blah blah. All the kids wanna be like them and all the kids are frightened of them and they get what they've got through drugs. You don't get nice things that quickly through work.'

There seems to be a sense, one that I also picked up from the conversations I had at the So Solid gig, that this criminal pervasiveness is a permanent condition of growing up in Britain. Few people talked about potential fixes.

'You can't stop what's happening and you can't control it. The only thing that you can do is look after the people who you love. There's kids I see who are twelve and I think if your mum knew that you was outside, if your mum knew that you was sitting down with those people … Some kids see that lifestyle and aspire to it and there's nothing you can do; it's always going to happen; no matter what anybody does, no matter what law's enforced.'

Ursula's cousin has appeared as we're talking, and she finishes off by saying, 'All you can do is give people information to make choices and some people make good choices, some don't; and there's nothing you can do to stop that. Everyone could go through school, could go to uni if they wanted to, if they made that choice, but everyone doesn't choose to.'

Ryan and Ursula's picture of youth criminality – jacking stuff to get more stuff – conforms to an old model of illegality and greed. What's more interesting is the amount of illegal activity – graffiti, pirate radio, free parties – that has personal satisfaction rather than material gain as its end.

Painting the streets

I visit Tom Dartnell, editor of *Graphotism*, Britain's leading graffiti mag, which presents and celebrates the international art of painting trains, walls and any other visible surfaces.

Graffiti is so ubiquitous that it becomes invisible. As with other forms of entertainment, it has realised that every surface is a potential screen. And on the train from Victoria to Hackbridge I look at the work that surrounds me. I note the etching on every train window, the pen on the seats. Every bridge is decorated, every electricity box covered. Even when any station seems miles away, graffiti flows to cover all available public surfaces. Graffiti, and its mutant cousins – stickers, stencils, etchings – are a public representation of the layers and volume of chat and communication going on in our culture. Message follows message. As pervasive as advertising. But more individual.

Like most other train stations in the UK, Hackbridge has been tagged and sprayed and chipped at and etched on. The station's roof is covered in Japanese characters. The tunnel boasts large white letters. The CC camera pole is scratched. Someone has written Fury right under the camera itself. And of course the graffiti has been graffitied. Tags sit within larger pieces.

Different colours cross and merge to create one mad scrawl. Whether it's defaced or enhanced depends who you speak to.

With its slick, art-directed graphics and hefty price tag, *Graphotism* balances the cool and the illegal. It started life as a black and white magazine, but now the print quality is astounding. Thick glossy pages of luscious colours. At £15, it's way above your average mag price. Bought by directors, ad agencies, stylists as well as a more street audience, it celebrates an illegal activity that causes millions in aesthetic damage each year … and inspires fashion shoots, book graphics and music videos. Brands from Sprite and Motorola to Land Rover happily use graffiti-style type in stores, on products, at festivals and expos.

Tom Dartnell shows me into the print office storage rooms. There are rows of spray cans in delicate shades. He shows me psycho pinks and a subtle range of greens, as well as the largest spray can in the world: Montana Triple X Large, holding a massive 750ml of paint.

We drink tea, and I begin by asking him who does graffiti. He asks me the same question right back. Teenage boys, I suggest.

'Right, I mean, that is essentially where it starts. But a lot of the people that are out there now are in their twenties, some in their thirties. It would surprise you, I mean, we know people who are married, who've got mortgages, and they're the ones out doing the trains. They're not necessarily doing the scratching and stuff like the etching but they're doing nice pieces on trains. I liken it to football hooliganism, you know. They do their job in the week, at the weekend it's their release.'

'And what's the difference between a teen and a guy in his thirties?'

'What you'll find is they've both got the same goal, which is putting their names up, but the older guy will not be too bothered about tagging or etching and just want to put up a nice piece, and I'd like to think that the young kid will eventually go down that route.'

For Tom, the drive behind graffiti is simple: it's about folklore and anecdote, about fucking the system and getting away with it.

'It's a sort of fame. Especially when you're younger, it's like getting fame among your peers, or other writers: that whole network. But then other people say they find it a way to unwind. You know it's fun to do. A lot of the older writers, when we speak to them, for a lot of them it's like an addiction. They can't go a few days or a few weeks without putting a tag somewhere. It all stems from the getting-your-name-up ethic. Your name's everywhere, people are gonna see it, and that's what it's always been about. If someone goes, "I know your work," then you'll be like, oh right, and it's a little ego boost.'

The magazine's existence and Tom's matter-of-fact way of talking about graffiti contrast sharply with police and media representations, which present it as destructive vandalism.

'Why do you think graffiti annoys people?'

'Okay, first of all, you know I'm not gonna sit here and say it's not vandalism. It is. If you're writing on someone else's property, it's not very nice. That's the main reason. Secondly, people who don't understand it think it looks ugly, and again I'll say that I think a lot of it looks ugly cos I can look at a tag and can know what's a good style. There'll be ten other tags around it that are rubbish but it's the whole thing, it's the learning process, like one day they're gonna be good.'

'And is graffiti's illegality part of the attraction?'

Tom nods enthusiastically. 'No doubt. The whole legal thing, it's rebellion, it's doing something that you've been told you're not allowed to do. And there is the thrill of the chase. If something happens, after that comes the whole folklore, "We got chased out of this train yard blah blah blah," and then stories go round the network of writers. You know there's some classics there.'

Tom shows me a piece of graffiti like I've never seen. It is bright, metallic and looks three-dimensional. It's painted on a canvas. It's by a guy called Diam from Germany.

'Everybody out there would want to be able to paint like that, you know what I mean? You do have the odd hardcore that'll say, "Oh no I just want to get my name up," but they'd love to paint like that.

'But you know if something like that,' he gestures towards the piece again, 'appeared on the side of the train, any train writer – and I'd like to think that a lot of the public – would go, "Wow, that is really good."'

Like every thing else, graffiti is about quality. At its best it makes somewhere more interesting and better to look at. It confronts and surprises people. It can make you smile and think. However, most of it is just practice: scrawls dreaming of being art. Like an inverse iceberg … you see about 90 per cent of it and it's shit. But the real stuff is the 10 per cent that's artistic, that you don't see unless you know where to go. It's hidden, under the surface, behind gallery doors, in train yards you'd never find on your own. Like all creativity, this artistic end has to grow from the streets, from the etching and the penning. It can't just come into being. It seems we want the sanitised endpoint without the process.

The fact that it is so hated says something about a country that prefers bleak, blank urban spaces to colourful swathes of communication. Graffiti is a very visible reminder of a group of people with something to say. Graffiti haters are perhaps the modern equivalent of those wise elders who believed children should be seen but not heard, because their point of view is not relevant or wanted. From the outside, graffiti, stickering, etching, etc might just be a mess: urban visual pollution, another product of a bored, thoughtless, destructive generation. For the perpetrators it's a different story. A rich one of finding a space and a surface where other people see nothing. It's about social communication, one-upmanship, local fame, audacity and reach. And so has much in common with many other youth activities, but with the extra buzz of being illegal, and therefore more exciting. The criminality of the act is one aspect of the work's quality.

We get talking about the way that an illegal, destructive and often messy public art form has been adopted by the music, fashion and advertising industries. Despite the fact that it must be those institutions who pay for a load of the issues sold, for Tom, once it comes off the streets, it loses some of its power.

'They'll use those on the edge of the scene who perhaps are more artistically inclined but as far as paying their dues in the core scene, they haven't really done it so it's not really an accurate representation. But then I feel a lot of people, you know, especially young people might be aware of that, they might be able to sort of smell the bad cheese ... '

Tom uses the phrase paying their dues a lot. Part of the talent and point of graffiti is that it's illegal and difficult. There are a myriad of ways of getting words and pictures on walls – stickers, stencilling, etching – but these are relatively quick. You do the art elsewhere, and your time at a site is minimal. There's less chance of getting caught. Tom isn't impressed. For him there is a purity about making a piece in a place where you're not meant to be, and taking your time.

'I'll be honest with you, I don't really like etching on windows and stuff like that, but I know it's part of the scene. The whole point of etching is: you start off with tags but they would get removed easily so you've gotta find a way, it's evolution as it were, to keep your tag there, so people then went on to using stuff like shoe dye in their pens. You know, like leather dye, and that's when you see a lot of the faded ones, where it's a faded purple. But then along came etching, you know, and then it's not so easy to erase. If you etch a window you've gotta replace the window, you can't get rid of it.'

'And does that mean that more traditional graffiti will disappear?'

'As far as the trains go, it's been going on here for over twenty years. If they haven't stopped it by now, they're never gonna stop it. Ten years ago, you could get sort of four or five hours in a train yard, you know, to do a piece. Now people are only getting half an hour, but they're still doing it. The trains are protected now: there's barbed-wire fences, there's video cameras, there's motion sensors, but the graffiti writers are still getting through.'

They managed to get through to Scarborough train yard in September. That's where the *Olton Hall*, a steam train whose normal route runs between Scarborough and York, is kept. It also starred in the *Harry Potter* films, which are filled with the nostalgic and good-hearted disobedience that much of Britain would wish on its contemporary youths. In September two carriages were covered in a futuristic cityscape and signed 'Slobs'. The picture of the train was all over the paper, as various pundits condemned the act of vandalism. The *Sun* gave it two pages with the heading 'Thuggle' and a huge colour spread of the 'defaced' train. As I read it, I think how the artist must be chuffed beyond belief. His piece, going in front of ten million readers. The *Sun* gave him the ultimate accolade.

On the lines

I get a rougher idea of the appeal and the illegality of graffiti from Chris and Ray in Gateshead. I'm there talking to a mate of theirs called Kiel about computer games, but they want to show me around their manor, so we go climbing over broken walls and above the railways.

Chris and Ray have been doing it for three years, and getting caught is an occupational, amusing hazard. Ray is currently doing community service for tagging, but doesn't seem too bothered by it. They start by showing me the approved graffiti sites. Untouched, positive messages: music, education, sport, a pristine version of youth. Then the other side, the places where you shouldn't be, the walls that aren't visible from the roads. They show me how to get onto the waste grounds and above the railway lines behind the Teams estate.

Out of sight, the walls are a confusion of colours. There are a couple of mattresses and piles of beer cans, the remnants of fires. Another disconnected space, apart from the rest of Gateshead. The local hero is Inch, whose tag covers every visible site. They tell me he's been seen in London and New York.

Chris, fourteen, and Ray, sixteen, talk about graffiti as a way of passing time, because as Kiel puts it, 'This summer's been crap, because there's nowt to do. Just been drinking. And smoking dope. That's our entertainment.'

'I got caught the other day,' Ray tells me. 'I got community service. I've got to spray graffiti off the walls. With like the jet gun. Power water. I only got six hours.'

But more important than the punishment is the fact that, through being caught, he's been put on a course that teaches him to do graffiti in approved areas, like the spaces they showed me, and this has given him his local fame.

'I got a photo. I got the newspaper in my house, on the front page of me doing the graffiti. You can do it in places where it's organised by the council.'

Kiel's unimpressed by the legitimacy of this. 'I reckon it looks shit.' And both Chris and Ray agree that, while organised graffiti is safer, it's just not the same.

'Non-organised you get a bit of a thrill out of it,' Ray tells me. 'And you have to be smarter.'

'He's changed his name about ten times,' Kiel says, pointing at Chris. 'And he's changed his name about twenty times. Game. Flame. Tame. Hundreds of names.'

'That's just tags. But if you do a big piece, then it looks good. There's loads round here. But they take time.'

'It's not so much time … you have to find a wall where nobody, like public, can see. Just say like you've got a main road, and you've got a wall and you've got a wall behind there, and then you go behind there and do it and probably not get caught.'

'So how did you get caught this time?'

'We were just doing it on the main road. I was doing it and he was just watching, waiting for us. And the police were waiting at the bottom of the road, and they had their dogs out, and I just looked at them and decided: I'm not getting bit by a dog, like.'

'I've been caught graffitting three times,' Chris adds. 'I've been put on the youth-offending team but I'm too young to get community service. You have to drop leaflets out and fix bikes.'

The three boys pose proudly as I take their photos in front of the painted wall. At the time they're excited about getting their names and pictures in a book. I speak to Kiel a few months later and he tells me he no longer likes the idea. 'I don't want too many people knowing my face,' he mutters ominously over the phone.

The reluctance to be pictured, and Chris and Ray's pseudonyms, go back to the origins of graffiti. In one street in Glasgow, I come across a pair of stickers on a door and a lamp post, both overprinted on Royal Mail delivery stickers.

Sticker one: 'Teenagers used to write their names on neighbourhood walls, but instead of writing their own names they chose nicknames, which in turn created a public identity for them. In 1971, a graffiti artist or "writer" called "Taki 183" from 183rd street in the Washington heights areas of Manhattan, went one step further … '

Sticker two: ' … and gave birth to the culture of today. Taki worked as a messenger travelling by subway to all five boroughs of the city. He wrote his name everywhere, including the insides and outsides of the trains and on every subway station in New York. His peers were impressed by his presence in … '

I don't find any more.

Of course, it's not just kids who are putting their names up on walls. Among the stickers and stencils that show you things for the first time – the ones that seem to have no purpose other than to make you smile – are the more familiar shapes: the leaping cat, the three stripes. Wherever creativity and communication exist, companies and brands will follow. And it appears from the stickers and illegal posters that record labels like BMG and Virgin, and brands like Boxfresh, Nike, Puma, Calvin Klein think that the law is as irrelevant for them as it is for the kids.

Except that the brands also have their advertising hoardings … they can afford to do it legally; unlike the graf artists and stickerists, for whom this is their only chance at a voice. And of course the legality of advertising hoardings again depends on who you believe has the authority to determine those laws.

There are two points here: one that record labels and other youth-targeted brands are advertising illegally on bridges, boarded-up shops, even on paid-for advertising sites. The other, more profound point is that their legal presence is just paid-for brandalism. One poster I see – a little more coherent than most – puts it like this.

> You might be forgiven for believing everything's just fine because the walls around you are nice and clean. Most of us never question the legality of advertising hoardings, although at least 10% of them are there without any permission. The average city dweller in the UK is subjected to over 3000 advertisements per day. Shouldn't some of them be selling ideas and not shampoo? The view belongs to everyone, even if the walls don't. If flyposting is vandalism, then advertising is just vandalism with a bigger budget.

GB fm

> '... yeah if you want this one for the reload it's 07956 398 269 you got to be quick ... turn up your music loud to this be proud of this ... r double e f to the a that's what it's about night and day ... who's locked on? North east south and west ... shout out to the subs crew ... just log on to all the w's unknowndotcom ... catch myself back here later ... hold tight the crews that rung up yesterday ... '

If graffiti is the illegal fuel for a substantial part of British visual culture, then pirate radio is the sonic equivalent. I talk to Outlaw and Wize, two DJs on Flex FM, one of London's longest-running pirate stations. They're in their early twenties, with baseball caps and shaved heads. They turn up in a white van ... Wize has just finished work and has time for a beer before going to set up the radio for the evening. Outlaw has a limp and has just come out of prison – a few weeks for something he didn't do. He's got a curfew, which means he can't go on air at the moment.

'With Flex we've been going so long now that the authorities aren't really bothered by it. They know us, they meet us on a regular basis, they still have to come and take our transmitter because it's their job. But when they do it, it's all very friendly, or not that moody anyway.'

They think it's a good run if they manage to avoid being busted for over a month. At about £300 a time to replace equipment, it soon gets costly. They are unconcerned about getting caught, and even less at the idea of getting punished. As Wize says, 'If they find you they can take you to court. If you're found guilty there's an unlimited fine. And a maximum of two years in prison. But the maximum fine that anyone's ever got is about £500. The average is about £200 if it goes to court.'

'Why is it illegal for you to transmit your own radio station?' I ask.

'The reason they object to it,' answers Outlaw, 'is because they can't police it properly and because we're not paying them licence or large amounts of money like the big stations.'

'At the end of the day it's a government-owned body. They just want to make money,' says Wize.

'It's just like the drugs thing. If they don't know how to deal with it, if they don't like it, they make it illegal. If there was a way of them making marijuana legal and tax it, cream a load of money off it, they'd do it straight away.'

Wize acknowledges that another reason is the lack of control over who says what. It seems that there are levels of conformity … that is, some stations can be more pirate than others. 'There's a lot of stations out there that don't abide. There's so many stations in London at the moment – up to about eighty at the weekend that will just do what they want; they'll be swearing Sunday afternoon. The DTI monitors pirates all the time. They record you for two months before they take you off. If you have got any indecent language they can use that against you.'

Talking with Outlaw and Wize, I'm struck by a sense of responsibility that is surprising given their lawless status. They have moved away from the garage scene because they didn't like its image. As Outlaw puts it: 'Since we've just taken Flex back on we've banned garage music totally from the station. Because we're not feeling it at all. It's not music, it's just noises. All these kids banging out their music on PlayStation 2. MCs are on there, they're talking about guns. It's not positive, it's not big, it's not clever. Half the little pussies, you shove a gun their face and they'll shit their pants. They're not talking about real stuff. It's not coming out of London.'

'It's a make-believe world.'

'Don't want to push a drug thing across,' Outlaw adds. 'Don't wanna push a gun thing across. If you come to our parties you have a good time, feel safe, not walk in, stand there, screw each other up and have a punch-up at the end, get guns in. Flex is not about that.'

Outlaw and Wize care passionately about their station. When I ask them why they do it, the response is immediate.

'It's a drug, it's like a drug,' says Outlaw.

'It's in your blood.'

Wize suggests that this kind of illegality stops him from being illegal elsewhere. 'I was doing worse things when I weren't doing radio. Soon as we started doing radio instead of stealing cars and doing drugs and things like that I was climbing up and down tower blocks sticking up aerials.'

'You channel your energy into something a bit more positive. Now we just can't give it up. We've been in some heavy situations; we've turned around and said we are never doing radio again, and look where we are now. We cannot give it up.'

And like any obsession it takes up a lot of time. Wize describes a typical day. 'Today I finish work, say three or four. I go to the radio, set the thing up, switch it on for bang on six, stay there for an hour or so and make sure everything's ready then go and see my girlfriend for a couple of hours, just try to fit her in, keep her happy and then I have to be back at twelve midnight to switch it off. Get home at one and got to get back up at six to go to work. Put it this way: girlfriends come and go but radio is always there.'

'That's why they call them radio widows.'

'At the moment mine's not very happy.'

Of course, being pirate isn't all about freewheeling and parties. There are downsides to acting outside the law. Wize describes some of the trouble they've seen. 'We've been shot at, stabbed, guns in the mouth.'

'Over radio.'

'Some people came on 103.6. We told them to turn it off. Basically two of our DJs was shot over it, one was shot through the leg, one shot through the wrist.'

'My car got shot at just over radio,' adds Outlaw. 'Two of my mates ended up in hospital.'

'My other MC got axed in the head. I held another friend's stomach in when I drove him to hospital. All madness but you try and stay away from it.'

Despite this, there's no end in sight. Wize wraps it up as he finishes the last of his pint. 'There's a law they are going to try and pass in October to make it illegal. Which is a load of rubbish but it ain't going to stop us. We want to keep pushing the boundaries. I have been doing this so fucking long it's all I know and it's always what I wanted to do.'

Each night they have to set up their transmitter, so after the lager, they take me to the top of a south London block of flats. On the way, they point out transmitters on buildings. Every other council block appears to have been used at some point in time. We take the lift to the top floor and then unbuckle the safety ladder to get onto the roof. There is an electrical tripwire on the door to the roof, so if someone comes to nick the aerial when they're on air, the circuit will break.

Pirate radio gives you a voice. You can say and do what you like. There's no contradiction between something that is illegal and something that is massively positive and productive. That ignores laws to spread a point of view and some great music. It is driven by passion and a willingness to create something worthwhile despite a level of personal and financial risk.

There are parallels between graffiti and pirate radio … both are forms of expression for people who have less access to acceptable channels, but a desire to be heard, and no patience to wait till they can do it legally. As Banksy – the graffiti artist who manages to sneak one of his pictures into the Tate Modern – says, when he describes advertising as pollution, it all depends who you decide has authority. A brand or a kid. The BBC, which forces people to pay money for something you might never listen to or watch; or Flex FM, which happens to play the music you love, does it for free, and will even shout out your crew's name if you put a text in. The choice is yours.

Make your own social

I meet Natalie at Mayday, running around with a girl with gold teeth. I go to her flat in Dalston a couple of weeks later. She talks with passion, enthusiasm and intelligence for an hour and a half, showing me photos, cuttings, articles, pamphlets … a very ordered documentation of protest and parties. Playing with her dreads, pulling at her lip ring, she tells me about squatting and dodging police, about the lack of faith she has in the British government, in British society, but it doesn't seem to matter, because with her friends, she has found everything she needs outside it.

As with most of the people I speak with, the government represents a distant, irrelevant force. She doesn't vote, and doesn't know many people who do. ('Why would we want to vote for them? It's like going into a shop and there's loads of stuff to buy but you don't want any of it.') So, in the absence of a democracy, you might as well go somewhere where you are represented, somewhere you do have a voice, where someone listens to you. For Natalie, those places are parties. She talks about rigs and parties and protests. Names like Reclaim the Streets. Manik. Panik. Random. Headfuk. They do free parties. Which is all about taking over a space and making it yours. With your laws. And your people.

'It was when I first moved into London and my flatmate took me to a rave. He kept going on about these parties, saying you have to come to these parties. And I didn't know what he was talking about because I'd never been to a rave before or anything like that, and so I just went along. It was in this theatre and I remember the guy on the door had a hardcore face, and he asked for donations and so I subbed him a few quid, and he pulled aside this black curtain and just got in there and there was just people running about, selling their shit, it was just people doing exactly what they wanted, just partying exactly how they wanted and my first thoughts were: I've found my people. I always knew there was this sort of group out there. And I never looked back.'

Like graffiti and pirate radio, breaking the law is part of the fun and the point of the party.

'Breaking into somewhere to set up a rig is a real buzz. You find somewhere maybe the night before, break the lock, or get through a window and then lock the door again from the inside. When you've got a nice place like a cinema, it's wicked, you just sit in the seats and watch the rig go up and dance a bit.'

'And there's no trouble when you're there. Leave us alone and there's no trouble. It's only when the police come and try to break it up or move you on that it can get nasty.'

From Natalie there is the strong belief that these apparently lawless groups of people are able to behave perfectly sensibly outside the law, as long as they are left alone. Because they are self-regulating and have their own codes of behaviour.

'It's safer to get drugs in there than in clubs. I'd buy drugs off anyone at a party. Because you know who you're buying off. Or someone knows them. And if they sold you shit then people would find out. It's not about the money or ripping people off. You can get most drugs: pills, ketamine, crack, heroin if you want but there's not much of a scene. It goes up and down. There was a crack scene for a bit and then some rude boys came in, and then more violence and some guns, and the parties were more moody. So they were less publicised, it became word of mouth, you'd get told by a mate, and so on.'

Parties conform to different rules, exist in different times and take place in different zones. Natalie talks with enthusiasm about their disconnection from normality.

'When you have a good party, you don't even think about anything bad that might have happened. You feel like you're one up on the world. They're all tucked up in bed or they're all doing such normal shit and you're breaking into a building on a massive high. Anyone's welcome, it's never more than about three quid. If it's a big party and there's a lot of rigs there it might be a fiver. If the pigs turn up it's just like, right, quick, everyone in, close the doors. They won't do anything. I haven't been to a party that's been busted for ages.'

Like pirate radio and graffiti, the party scene is driven by passion and the pull of a tight-knit social group. You versus the rest of the world.

'You got so many hundreds of people coming from everywhere, on their phones waiting for the address. It's a bit like cat and mouse. We're just having a laugh though. You feel like a kid again. But it's all safe, it's wicked. It's about community. I go to any party, here or in Europe, and I always know someone. Or bump into someone. Or sort something out.'

For Natalie, Mayday was one more party. 'For some people it is about violence. But lots of us are there for the party. I went to protest. I went to have a laugh. For a short time you're free.'

Accompanying her hedonism is a more active sense of injustice in the UK and an interest in doing something about it.

'The criminal justice bill really made things feel different: the British government seemed to ban everything that you liked. This Mayday was about the war: the arms, the oil. Every year it lightens your eyes up to something different. This year, I didn't realise the biggest arms distributor was in London.'

For all the focus on the party and pure hedonism, there's a nod to more serious theory. Natalie tells me about Temporary Autonomous Art Exhibitions that go on, which refer to Hakim Bey's work on Temporary Autonomous Zones (TAZs) and Pirate Utopias: spaces where, for a short time, normal rules are ignored and a more playful, less hierarchical set of behaviours can take place. As she puts it, 'We have to take spaces because we're not given them.'

The protests are perhaps when people like Natalie are most visible. They are the times when two ideologies rub up against each other. For most of the time, though, they try to keep as separate as possible. They have their own friends, their own clothes, names, their own social whirl, their own codes. Dodging police, blagging stuff, getting high. Creating a separate and independent world. Distinct and disdainful.

Not all the people I speak to about lawless spaces have such a positive image. Like Outlaw's tales of violence surrounding radio, I hear of squat parties gone bad. Cordelia, a polite and very middle-class girl who's planning to be a primary school teacher, but with a taste for pills and raving, tells me about a more scary experience.

'At first when I started going to raves I couldn't get over it, I was just like: it's free, I'm getting drugs. I can sit here wasted – you know, no one cares, this is fantastic. I loved it. And then you start to think: but no one cares when, like, DJ our flatmate was mugged, had all his clothes, everything taken off of him, left naked in the corner of a squat party and no one cares again, so it works both ways.'

UK does crime

Of course, illegal isn't just done by the kids. In fact, illegal is what most normal people get up to, maybe because we inhabit such a restrictive world. We just do it differently.

A study in September by Professor Susan Karstedt, from Keele University's Criminology Department, claims to have unearthed a middle-class crimewave: 60 per cent of the population engaged in illegal acts that cost around £14 billion a year; five times more than burglary. This time it's not graf, drugs or running pirate radio stations. Their crimes of choice are dodging VAT, not buying a TV licence, padding out an insurance claim – you get the idea. The report claims that the increase in this behaviour is to do with a general feeling that we are being ripped off by retailers and the government. The study identifies a sense of righteous indignation.

'People don't think they are doing anything wrong, and seem to have some sort of consumer rage that leads them to believe that they are just evening the score. Police seem to only concentrate on big corporate crimes or small petty crimes. We think this middle ground of crime could in fact be causing much more damage.'

So, Britain is a country where over half of the population are criminals. Does that say more about its terrible people, or the irrelevance of laws? The motivations behind a 17-year-old graffiti artist and a 37-year-old tax evader are the same: my worldview doesn't fit with the one that's being imposed on me, so I'm going to ignore it and make my own law. This partly explains the illegal appeal of so much entertainment. It offers scenarios where you can act outside the restrictive set of behaviours endorsed by the UK Government.

In modern Britain, the law is becoming less a question of right or wrong, legal or illegal, and more a series of transactions between an individual and the system/company/person they think is trying to hold them back or rip them off. A personally defined legal code rather than a state-imposed one.

The main difference is that the middle-class crimes seem driven more by personal greed, like the estate kids that Ursula and Ryan mentioned. In contrast, pirate radio, graffiti and parties are done with an appreciative audience in mind, play an important social role, and offer the perpetrator a chance to get creative and develop skills rather than just maintain a healthy bank balance.

Indeed, illegal for many people is how their careers start: photographers, film makers, designers, musicians … the people doing the kinds of job that tick the aspirational box. Perhaps illegal is an important career route because those kinds of job are less well supported by an old-fashioned education system.

Within these communities – the pirate radio station, the graf crews, the free party people – there is a powerful sense of self-sufficiency and pride.

What kind of effect does it have on kids to be told that the thing they are passionate about is illegal? Does it make them law-abiding, or does it move them even further away from the establishment that is making the laws?

The more I looked into it, the more I realised that illegality has become an essential part of youth entertainment ... and a vital fuel for British culture. Pirate is about making something that you want but doesn't exist. Ignoring restrictions and obstacles – whether they're laws or threats of violence – because you care so much about bringing this thing to life. Is it realistic to expect a country as varied as Britain to allow its behaviour, its creative expression to be contained by one set of laws? We might not like it all, but it inspires and feeds into areas that are acceptable and that wouldn't exist without it. From wall to record sleeve. From the top of a south London tower block to Radio 1.

As Wize puts it when he tells me how their commitment has influenced mainstream radio.

'Flex was gonna die, it was gonna die a death. I grew up on it so I was like, Flex can't finish, there's no way it can finish. We made it better, put up a website, brought live streaming to the world. We're the first innovators to actually do that. To live stream to the world: "Text message straight to our studio. Wherever you are in the world, you can give us a shout."'

'We beat Radio 1 and Kiss. Radio 1 started doing it about two months after we did. Now we've got regular listeners in America and Australia.'

'My mate's girlfriend has just gone back to Australia and she texts us when we're playing.'

'It's amazing to get e-mails from America.'

'It takes 10 seconds to come through. There's no real delay. It's wicked, it's like proper live.'

'Dance music would not have progressed so far without pirate stations.'

'Without pirate radio advertising, the club scene would die immediately. There's so much talent and energy that comes through it, if it didn't exist the British music scene would be much shittier.'

'We are loud, we are not scared'

Even if your teenager is still eating, and hasn't yet broken the law, the assumption is that for around six years, parents and offspring are locked into intense emotional conflict which can be broadly summarised as girls in screaming matches and boys retreating into a sulky silence.

Madeleine Bunting, *Guardian*, April 2002

The bill gives police new powers to exclude anyone under the age of 16 from an area after 9pm if they are unsupervised by an adult. On the authority of a senior officer, police will be able to disperse or send home groups of two or more unsupervised teenagers.

'The government seems very keen to talk about young people but much more reluctant to actually talk to them,' says Dillon, a member of the four-year-old UK Youth Parliament. 'This legislation is about young people and yet we were not consulted – surely this was something of paramount importance? Teenagers are being labelled so that when a pensioner reads about hooligans in the tabloids, and then sees a group hanging around, he will be ringing the police. I'm not going to defend the actions of those causing anti-social behaviour – but wearing a hooded top and a baseball cap does not exactly make someone a threat.'

BBCi News, October 2003

Keep moving

They come slowly at first. At 7.30pm there are only a couple of vehicles in the far car park of Thurrock service station. A cold November night, and later on there's going to be a full lunar eclipse. Ten or so people huddle round Oli's white Toyota, watching *Human Traffic* on the tiny screen next to the wheel. The car next to it belts out hip hop.

We're waiting for a cruise, but no one's quite sure if it's happening; and if it is, what time it's kicking off. A couple of people have seen fliers, but no one knows anyone who actually organises it. So, for the meantime, you just have to shiver and swap stories about previous cruises: the time that any car with alloys was banned from all garages; the *Max Power* photographer who published pictures from a previous cruise without disguising the number plates.

Then a chunky VW shows, with an Essexboyz numberplate. Bringing the news that it's all on for nine. Only another hour to wait. Slowly the cars turn up ... you can tell them apart from the other motorway traffic by the speed they take the corners on the approach road, by the UV lights glowing under the body and by the noise.

Within half an hour there are about 150 cars ... parked at mad angles, stereos blasting. People driving up to sixty or seventy in the entry lanes, pulling skids and doughnuts. A crowd stands round a car as huge flames roar out of the exhaust. Kids throw sparklers and fireworks. It's cold, and the uniform is Puffas and baseball caps. Hoodies and Reeboks.

Jonathan, a photographer from *Redline* magazine, one of the modified-car bibles, persuades a girl to take her top off. She is about five foot tall with massive breasts. Proper glamour proportions. She coyly covers her nipples while she leans towards his lens.

Suddenly someone whistles and people run to their cars. Within minutes a convoy of over a hundred cars is snaking out of Thurrock. It drives for half a mile to the Tesco car park. For this short journey, despite the absence of any modifications on my sober-coloured, unstickered car, I feel some of the power and pull of cruising. Everybody looks at you. No one can turn onto the roundabout because the cars are nose to tail. As we arrive at Tesco's, bemused shoppers look on.

I go and talk to Tesco's security, who have immediately called the police. They say it's private property and they wouldn't mind so much if idiots weren't burning up and down at seventy and doing wheel spins. There's a fair amount of showing off. Essexboyz, the group who have organised the cruise, persuade Jonathan to take a picture of the whole crew. The same girl gets her breasts out again, leans over the bonnet of a car and pulls her trousers down to reveal a tiny thong. The fireworks still going off as a hangover from November the fifth add to the carnival atmosphere.

I see a group of kids doing coke off a CD cover in the front of a car. A white van turns up and begins to unload some bigger speakers. There are hundreds of people in the car park. And then, of course, the police arrive.

They don't actually do anything ... but immediately the mood changes. There is less blatant bad driving. I speak to a couple of the cops. They seem relaxed, far less concerned than the Tesco security. As long as the rowdy element doesn't kick off they think it's fine. Safer to know where all the boy racers are, than split up across motorways. Also conscious that most of the kids don't want to damage their cars.

A girl called Leanne moans about how the police always ruin it and sure enough, half an hour after they first get here, the car park is thinning out as the more dedicated head off to Southend.

The whole thing lasts maybe two hours, and in that time offers a great model of contemporary youth sociability: frenetic, portable, temporary, fluid. Everything you need for a party is in the car: sounds, speed, people. There is no dependency on anyone else, no entry price, no dress code.

And it pisses people off. The Tesco security, the shoppers, see the irresponsible driving, the noise, the flirting and smoking and it looks dangerous, forbidden, antisocial.

But among the cruisers, there is little sense of it being illegal. Some people are surprised when I ask them if its illegality is part of the attraction. As far as they're concerned, they've just found a place for something to happen. Others know they shouldn't be there: they're not doing it to break the law but because it's fun. There is a strong sense that they should be left alone to behave how they want to.

Of course, they do know that what they're doing isn't approved by everybody. The Essexboyz website contains the following disclaimer:

```
The Essexboyz do not take responsibility for anything (so
what else is new!). The pregnancies were a rumour; and the
links to Saddamm Hussein are false. Also if you attend one
of our little social gatherings and get yourself nicked …
tough — you were obviously being silly and deserve
everything you get. We don't condone dangerous or illegal
driving, or anything that breaks the law … The fact that we
find it fun is mere coincidence.
```

'The fact that we find it fun … ' From Outlaw & Wize, Natalie, Ray and Chris to the cruisers in Thurrock, I started to notice a common thread that linked these disparate activities. Despite being illegal or, at best, antisocial, they were about pleasure and self-expression … and the perpetrators were often doing their best to keep these activities distant from mainstream Britain.

Graffiti, pirate radio, cruises, marches, squat parties are all about claiming space – whether it's brick walls, car parks, abandoned buildings or airwaves – that don't belong to you and using them better. Ignoring restrictions and doing it yourself. It seemed to me that much of the interesting – if controversial – activity in young Britain was taking place under these conditions.

On one of the cruisers' cars – where you'd normally find a GB sticker – I spot one of the most overused symbols of 2003: the skull and crossbones. From Busted to Murderdolls via *Jackass* (skull and crutches) and Top Shop to thousands of T-shirts, patches, sweat bands and badges.

The proliferation of the pirate symbol seemed to be no coincidence. Explicitly it's a thoughtless sign of rebellion, and it looks good; but it goes deeper than that. The pirate flag symbolised a ship's lack of allegiance to any country; the establishment of its own state; their own code of honour and set of rules. And the skull and crossbones remains a symbol of disconnection. It indicates a place, a state of being that is beyond the law of the land.

For the kids on the Thurrock cruise, and for cruisers like them across the UK, their cars are their pirate ships: colourful, mobile and beholden to nobody except speed cameras and grumpy store security. The cruisers are not interested in conflict or confrontation. Nor are they suggesting that the way they behave becomes normal or more acceptable. They are happy to carry on in the twilight places, the car parks, the service stations. To make something beautiful and pleasurable, even if it only lasts for a couple of hours.

Simultaneously a sign of impotence and power, the skull and cross-bones promises a place where things are better: a place of freedom, hedonism and irresponsibility. Places where you make up the rules. Piratopias. Disconnect/zones. I wanted to find more of them.

I done him in the car

According to a 2003 British crime survey, a third of respondents cited teenagers 'hanging around' as a big problem. And the introduction of ASBOs allows police to disperse groups of two or more people. These two facts suggest that Britain views teenage sociability as inherently problematic. There is also the implication that when teens get together they are wilfully antisocial, as if the main momentum behind their grouping is to intimidate or annoy people surrounding them. I was curious about the different forms that teen sociability took, and wanted to know what else lay behind the noise and apparent thoughtlessness.

Carina and Lucy, two girls I get speaking to at Thurrock, give me a sense of how completely cars form the centre of their social group. The following week they tell me they'll be at a McDonald's near Gravesend. It's a Tuesday night, but there are about ten or so modded cars huddled in the corner of the car park. Music floats out of a couple, and for the whole time we're talking, the two women constantly look beyond me, through the window and into the car park, to check who's turned up. One of their friends called Dan sits in to start with. They're all eighteen.

Carina and Lucy are tough and glam. Carina's wearing a Diesel jacket, and a red PVC top. Her earrings and necklaces are a mixture of safety pins and diamonds. When she smiles, something sparkles on one of her teeth. Lucy apologises for looking dowdy. She's come straight from work, but still manages to wear a skirt that 'let's you see my bum cheeks'. She lifts up her top to show me her doubly pierced belly button. A dolphin and a diamond. She tells me she's a model. Carina is training to be a hairdresser.

'This is the boy racer car park,' Carina tells me. 'It ain't at the moment, you have to wait until a bit later on; some nights it is packed in here, and sometimes it ain't, it depends on what groups of people come down here, and that is how we know everyone from coming down here, just from seeing them, talking to them, and if they say there is a cruise on, we all go to it.'

I ask them about the attraction of the cruises, the pull of hanging out in car parks, compared to pubs, clubs or TV.

'It is funner.'

'It is really the atmosphere.'

'I don't know if you have seen *Fast and Furious* before, but it is like that.'

'In a pub, you can't talk to people properly. Here, you all like the same thing. It is all about the cars. I think it's brilliant.'

They recount differing responses from the police and the security they come into contact with, but have little sense that what they're doing could be illegal, or even annoying.

'Sometimes if it is a nice gaffer, they are well all right,' explains Carina, 'and if loads of people have their PlayStations and DVDs and that in their cars, they look in the cars, don't they, and have a look at it and say it is nice and that, but if it is a nasty gaffer, they will try and pull you for things, like usually lights, but down here, they are well all right. Sometimes some people, we reckon it is that security guard, innit, that fat man, he probably calls them down here, not every night gaffers don't come down here, do they?'

'They come down here a little while ago because they were burning a car,' adds Dan, laughing. 'We got thrown out before for doing hand brakes. And we videoed it and everything. That was good.'

'Yes, wheel spinning and things like that … '

'And when it gets lively like that, do you get hassled?'

'Yes, the security guard comes out, he told us to go away, and he would set the dogs on us and we – the police said no we can stay in there.'

'The police don't care. The end of the day, what the police going to do, fucking arrest every single car, you know what I mean. Over what, being in a public car park?'

Of course, the cars and the noise and the showing off are not just about hanging out. Lucy and Carina talk of the charged atmosphere, made more powerful by the dark and the cold, illuminated by a mixture of street neon and car lights. A dynamic social scene, outside the influence of publicans or bouncers, a place where anything could happen.

'It gives you a buzz,' smiles Lucy.

'Atmosphere and everything,' adds Carina. 'I mean the boys grab the girls, and the girls go for the boys. It's like: nice cars, girls get attracted to them. I reckon … the uglier the boy, the nicer the car basically, innit. You get some proper like fat … '

'Are you trying to say something?' Dan chips in.

'No, not you … well, fat ugly bloke, but he has a well nice done-up car.'

'So is it partly about pulling?' I suggest.

Carina and Lucy look at each other knowingly and laugh.

'Yeah, they do it to get attention from other girls and that. And it is just a thing that in our age group, that's what matters most to people, their cars innit, I suppose. Like who has got the loudest tunes, whose is done up the best, who has the best wheels and stuff like that, innit.'

As with the pirate radio, with graffiti, and parties, doing up your car is about passion and putting in the hours. Carina and Lucy talk about their friends' obsessions with a mixture of disparagement and pride. They obviously love the scene and have told me that they prefer boys with nice cars; at the same time, they question the level of dedication.

'They get carried away with their cars so much, it's like that joke, "Why do boys wear baseball caps?" "To make their car go faster!" They just show off, don't they, and all the power goes to their head, if they have a nice car … '

The effort and money can be justified because they are creating an entire social scene. I have already seen how completely the cars provide for this group's entertainment needs: movement, music, films, games, privacy, contact, but Carina's story about her current boyfriend reveals the true flexibility of a souped-up hatchback. They don't just replace the pub, the club, the front room, the cinema, but also the bedroom.

Dan has gone outside to hang with his mates and Carina and Lucy get more explicit.

'Well, I am sort of seeing this boy, innit, down here, Ollie, and he is …' Carina begins.

'He thinks he is all nice with his car, but he is not, he is just a little boy.'

'About Ollie, this boy, I really liked him, yes, he comes down this car park, he might be down here tonight, and I went down Southend with him and everything, and other stuff happened … '

Carina trails off and starts laughing, so I ask her, 'What kind of other stuff?'

She looks across at Lucy, who's already laughing, and, eyes flashing, she tells me, 'I done him in his car.'

'You done him in his car? What kind of car did he have?'

'He has got a black Fiesta. V-tech.'

'And his name is Ollie!' adds Lucy.

At this point Carina also tells me his surname and address and tells me to stick that in the book as well. She then goes into more detail, although Lucy and she are laughing so much that it takes a bit of time.

'It was somewhere in Bexley Heath, and three times this happened. In my car an' all. It was in a car park, it was well funny. And his mates saw I was sitting in the car and they kept coming over to the windows.'

I ask if this was a one-off, and get a strange look from Carina. Of course not. Lucy comes in with her story.

'Me and my boyfriend had this thing that we had to christen every car that we have been in, and we borrowed his mum's car … his brother's car, his brother's girlfriend's car, and his own car. And we christened them and it was in Blue Water car park, and every time we got caught by a Blue Water security guard, through the window with a torch.'

So, while the cars might act as a replacement bedroom, there are drawbacks. Carina goes into the technical difficulties.

'I have only ever done it in my car and his car, and it was well hard, because I have got a small car. He was sitting down like that and I was on top of him like that, and my leg kept banging on the door, and it was well hurting … '

'Did ya?' asks Lucy.

'Yeah, it was well bad. And the only other time it was in the back of his car.'

'More room then?' I wonder.

'Yes, sort of – but he keeps saying he wants to do me in a bed now.'

'Have you had sex with him in a bed?'

'No.'

'Is that because you prefer it in cars?'

'Because I can't, I live with my mum and dad and that … '

The openness and obvious enjoyment about outdoor, slightly illicit sex reminds me of the glamour model-esque girl who had repeatedly got her tits out in Thurrock. I ask the girls if they noticed. At first, Carina thinks I'm referring to her, and she tells me that she also showed off her breasts. As I describe the girl I saw, she soon works out who I'm talking about.

'What, massive tits, she was really fat, wasn't she?'

'She was quite short and … '

'Fat! She was rough.'

'So does a lot of that kind of stuff go on there as well?'

'Yes. Because they want to attract the attention of the boys and say come on, look at my boobs.'

There is an exuberance in the way Carina and Lucy talk about their activities. It's clear that they see the car parks and service stations as their spaces, where they can act as they like, and where part of the attraction is behaving in ways that are less acceptable elsewhere.

'I pissed on that mini roundabout, and everyone was looking, it was well funny. But I don't care about stuff like that. And everyone saw, this car park was full of cars and that, and it was a Friday night, and we had just been out in Bexley Heath and I come back and I had a miniskirt on.'

'We are loud, we are not scared.'

When we leave McDonald's together, and walk towards our cars, they enjoy the calls that they get from the boys, and the fact that they're with some bloke no one recognises. They ask me to take their pictures again, so all the boys will see and wonder. In the last pic, Lucy stands behind Carina and grabs her breasts. I drive off and get a moody stare from one of the other cars. In my rear-view mirror I see a couple of boys stroll over to the girls' motor. A few months later, I'm talking with Carina again, and she tells me happily that later that night she met her current boyfriend.

Jesus is a cunt

I'm walking through the Download festival at Donnington Park, midsummer. A girl passes me sporting the T-shirt: 'I'm the girl your parents warned you about'. At first glance the whole festival looks full of the kinds of kids your parents warned you about. It looks bad. Like an ad for typical youth abandonment and antisocial behaviour.

Disturbed is playing on the main stage and encouraging the crowd to 'Put your goddamn devil horns in the fucking sky … Let me see your motherfucking fists in the air!'

Their lyrics are a litany of disaffection, of despair at an unkind world. With titles like 'Down with the Sickness', 'Numb' and 'Fear' they appeal to a sense of solitude, weakness and revulsion in modern society. 'Fear' sets up an image of misunderstood youth, a world of rejects and nobodies, while "Down with the Sickness" gets more personal, and presents a scenario of parental abuse and retaliation. Here 'the world is scary place' and the track ends by screaming fuck you to mommy, and calling her a 'stupid sadistic abusive fucking whore'. Many of the bands here – with names like Strung Out, Fabulous Disaster, Murder One, Funeral for a Friend – revel in their distance from society, take pleasure in their inability to fit in. It is an attitude reminiscent of Romantic poets, dour Russian novelists or downbeat French philosophers, who feel they are too sensitive for such a coarse world. Within the despair and anger is a sense of superiority. Download is mainly middle-class teens, whose anguished attitude towards growing up is facilitated by a relatively good education, and enough money and time to get upset about their situation.

I bump into three kids as they are running across a field. Their eyes are bright and they have manic grins. They are all carrying oversized yellow foam Kerrang! hands in the shape of devil horns, covered with signatures. They've just managed to blag their way backstage and have been hanging with Disturbed and Stone Sour. Holly is seventeen; she's wearing a cute rainbow wool hat, a pink and black tie hanging loosely over a black string-like top. And pink fingerless gloves. John is sixteen, with shaved hair, fluoro bangles, black armbands and a load of heavy jewelled rings. Chris, nineteen, has a picture of a raven on his T-shirt, done in soft-focus aerosol. It looks like the kind of image you'd find on a fat fantasy novel. They all sport made-up eyes, black nail polish and a smattering of piercings. When I take their photos they stick their tongues out and flash me their devil's horns.

They are bouncing off each other in excitement. So much for self-pity and anguish. Holly shouts at me: 'Disturbed fucking rule! I met them before and I cried and nearly died. And we went backstage with Stone Sour about fifteen minutes ago.'

'Fucking brilliant.'

'Fucking right.'

'Amazing.'

'Fucking quality.'

After that round of expletive superlatives, they go into a bit more detail about their passion. They all try to talk, but Holly's got the loudest voice and the most enthusiasm.

'Disturbed are … David Drayman is just so drop-dead gorgeous. He's idolised my whole life. I'd die without him. I licked his head. Licked his bald head.'

'We nicked some stuff from backstage,' adds John. 'I got two drumsticks from Gordon from Raging Speedhorn cos he owed them me from a gig ago.'

Chris goes deeper. 'He describes my whole life. That's the way it is. Most of the music's about getting bullied and how much shit they've gone through their whole life, and with my past experience, getting bullied and getting crap off other people, this music just mellows me out, it makes sense.'

I talk to John a bit more. Despite the wild, just-bust-out-of-a-gothic-psychiatric-ward look, he reveals the sensitivity and uncertainty that have brought so many of these teens here today. He loves his nu metal and death metal, bands like Arch Enemy, Slipknot and Shadows Fall. His dad was in a punk band called A.W.O.L. and his mum was a punk so he's not surprised he likes the music he does. That, and the fact that they connect with how he's feeling, and often act as a kind of therapy.

'I like this sort of music because when I'm in a bad mood it helps me cheer up. It is my escape from everyday life. Without it I would be a wreck. My life is a complete fuck mainly because of myself so a lot of Eminem's music pretty much describes my life. Music is bloody important. It is my life. I can't sleep without it. I have it on first thing in the morning and last thing at night. My life is evolved around my music.'

I guess he means his life revolves around music, but I like the sense that he evolves in response to the music he listens to.

He talks about the extremes of emotions he goes through: 'My life personally is like a rollercoaster. I would be on a major high one minute then the next I would be majorly depressed.'

I leave Holly, Chris and John recounting their backstage adventures, and stroll further through the festival. The fashion is a visual correlative to the audience's moods. There are boiler suits and black everywhere. Chains, tattoos, spiky hair, black eye make-up and boys with black scuffed nails. Five pointed stars. Skulls. The aesthetic is 100 per cent antisocial. All about flipping the bird to supposed norms. But the look and the language is tougher than the people actually are. All the dreads, piercings, gloomy make-up, spikes, psychiatric ward jackets and devil horns don't hide the fact that this is an energetic, almost polite festival. No moodiness. No fights. They might look like Satan's offspring, but they behave like well-brought-up children.

The T-shirts reveal a further anger and tendency to exaggerate: they are an overdose of slogans and shock. But in these numbers it just passes for normal conversation, a conversation that goes: curl up and die, addict, mainline, fuck you, leftover crack, never surrender, protected by satan, masturbation is not a crime, fuck posers, jesus is a cunt.

For sheer overload, Takumi, seventeen, from Derby wins hands down. On the front: 'What a great fucking T-shirt'. On the back, as many permutations of fuck as you can squeeze on there: fuck your father fuck your ass fuck for fun fuckbrain fuck yourself FUCK IT.

I ask Takumi and his girlfriend, Vicky, if the moodiness and visible anger that fills the place is reflected in people's attitudes.

'It's nothing like that at all. I mean, a lot of people have got their own thing but that's why you come here … you don't have to worry about it. Most people are just friendly people.'

'And what about all the hands in the air and the devil stuff?' I ask.

'It just gets you up there … it gets you going,' Vicky answers. 'We're not exactly Bible bashers. But we're not devil worshippers.'

They might not be dangerous, but they certainly are passionate. Kids know the lyrics. Everyone I speak to lists their favourite bands and songs, and tells me it's about the music. Fourteen-year-old Liam shows me Dan from Disturbed's plectrum that he caught between his fingers when it was thrown into the crowd: 'I was trembling for ages after I caught it.'

Around all this black and anger, the ads that are shown in the breaks between bands on the stage TVs seem out of place, from another, lighter world. Even more unreal and distant than normal. Lynx, CKY4 may be aimed at this age group, but surely not in this mood, in these surroundings.

I'm being sizest but I can't help noticing the number of overweight people. I wonder if big people like rock, or if rock makes you eat more. Or maybe it's just about drinking more beer and doing fewer drugs. There is the smell of dope everywhere, the familiar huddles of spliff buddies, but little of the wide-eyed abandonment of other festivals I visit.

Despite the verbal and visual onslaught of expletives, I see lots of families, here for a day out. Kids of twelve with massive T-shirts, tiny legs and grubby sneakers walking a few paces behind their dad. At some distance from the stage, there are loads of mournful couples holding tight to each other. Swaying rather than dancing. In fact, there's no dancing at all. Just hand raising, head shaking, jumping and moshing. I walk over couples snogging on the grass, and groups of lagered-up boys on the way to the Scuzz tent, which is younger and punkier than the main stage.

Outside, there is a long line of kids waiting to get bands to sign something. The list reads like a manifesto of discontent and pain: Disturbed, Spineshank, Mudvayne, The Darkness, Bouncing Soles, Stone Sour. Inside the tent a couple of hundred people at the front of the stage are leaping around, throwing bottles at bands, falling to the ground and getting back up again. There is the inevitable tumble of bodies as people hurl themselves at each other in furious time to the music. Kids emerge from the crush: sweaty, hair plastered over their face, covered in red welts from a careless elbow.

Download reveals an inverse relation, a disconnection between appearance and attitude. The more antisocial the clothing, the more polite, nervous, bullied the kids. Compared to the Essexboyz – with their neat sportswear and glam girls – this lot are much more visually offensive. But I know who I'd back in a fight.

This is all about the split between sign and meaning. People who only read the signs will always get it wrong. This gap is further reflected in the simulated fighting that goes on in the mosh pits.

Carl gives me the lowdown on moshing, the name for the frenetic activity beneath the stage. He is wearing a wide-brimmed black leather hat. His right hand is a mesh of silver jewellery, covering most of his fingers, so it seems like he has intricate metallic digits, jointed and decorated with teeth, horns and stars, each one coming to a point. He describes his style as 'black metal, Cradle of Filth, that kind of stuff'.

'One thing you'll find in the middle of a mosh pit, if you're knocked to the ground, you'll find about seven people gripping your arms and pulling you back on your feet. You might get knocked down again, but you'll always find somebody. It is a very tight-knit group, especially when you're listening to a very punk band, you get a lot of skinheads going in there. They can get really rough, letting a lot of aggression out. I think it's a vent for aggression rather than going out into the middle of the street and causing a punch-up. It is a simple, easy relief that allows it to be expressed in an environment where you're not going to be prejudiced for doing it. Everybody who comes here and has a good mosh generally enjoys it. A very healthy release for most people.'

The Gnome Girls agree. Rose, Andrea and Katie have heavy black eyeliner, black striped tights and scowls. Andrea and Katie have T-shirts proclaiming themselves to be the Gnome Girls, because that's Less Than Jake's name for them since they presented the band with a gnome. Katie is wearing skin-tight tartan trousers with the message 'Anti-Youth' scrawled across them. I ask them if they're as aggressive as they (are trying to) look.

'To be honest with you,' Andrea replies, 'you get the aggression out in the music, and you find festivals like this and gigs and clubs and the people in them are really cool.'

'You don't get no trouble,' Katie adds. 'We're all a family, like a community.'

Andrea backs up what Carl has said about the mosh pits: 'You know you get the mosh pits. If someone you don't know falls over, you pick them back up. There's rules.'

Like about half the festival-goers, Rose is wearing a Marilyn Manson T-shirt, his white face staring balefully out at the world. I ask why they like him.

Andrea replies: 'I really like his music, his image, what he stands for.'

When I ask what he stands for, the answers come immediately.

'Freedom of expression.'

'Be yourself'

'Just doing what you want to do.'

'To anyone.'

'Don't take shit from anyone.'

The goths and the townies would never get on. I can't imagine Carl tearing up Tesco's car park in his black hat, and the idea of Carina tottering around the fields here in her Louis Vuitton shoes and handbag combo seems impossible. But the urge to be with others who share your somewhat antisocial passion is the same, as is the affinity they feel to the people around them.

No-go cities

If modified cars are the pirate ships of youth sociability, then the Download festival makes me think of a gated community. Traditionally excluding people on the grounds of being too poor or too young, Download works on different criteria. Don't bother coming if you're too old or too polite.

This hijacking of space doesn't just occur in car parks and distant fields. Choose any city centre Friday or Saturday night across Britain and there is the similar sense of exclusion for those not taking part.

A survey by Mori in the autumn claims to show that city centres have become no-go areas for most people at weekends. Whereas in the 18 to 34 age group, 45 per cent go at least once a week, most people over 35 – particularly in their fifties – stay away. This is, of course, picked up by papers, who manage to get a quote from business leaders in Aberystwyth describing it as a 'drinking Mecca', while Bournemouth's Chief Superintendent compares the town to Faliraki and warns that 'mindless idiots' are ruling the centre at night.

Over the year, I visit a number of town and city centres, from Bournemouth to the Bigg Market in Newcastle, and find one of the more repetitive aspects of youth entertainment. The location might change but the action remains the same: the streets of cavernous pub chains – Youngs, Yates, Wetherspoons, etc – and the more individual, pricey bars with names like Revolutions, Liquid, Cage, Kiss, etc, etc.

The style gets smarter the further north you get, but it's all coming from a similar place: imitation bling – girls in blouses, strappy tops, heels, short skirts. Boys in open-collared shirts, two buttons rakishly undone to reveal the heavy chain, jeans/slacks and loafers. It's the geezers, the townies, the charvas.

There's little of the inventiveness or visual wildness of clubs and festivals – although I do see girls in nurse's outfits and boys in seventies gear – but a similar spirit: abandonment and the sense of being in control, of owning this zone. Groups of guys eye packs of girls. Each bar offers its own journey to intoxication. Happy hours. Doubles and triples. Cocktails in foot-long glasses.

The British High Street is a rudimentary piratopia; in this case the entrance criteria are about intoxication. If you're not pissed then you don't want to be there. It is lawless – I see people buying pills, a guy getting a hand job in an alley, fights, tantrums and comatose kids – and purely hedonistic.

But the presence of moody bouncers, CCTV and the regular police drive-bys prevent this lot from truly gaining pirate status. It's only halfway there. And perhaps sensing that these kids aren't completely lost, in the Bigg Market at least, I watch a group of Evangelical Christians talking to people at their most vulnerable. I see them approach a girl sitting alone, drunk and sobbing uncontrollably. Talking to two guys who are squaring up to each other. And, inevitably, they approach me. I must look like a victim. I've spent the last hour wandering alone up and down the same stretch of pavement. Getting into short conversations with people. Quite often being knocked back, or laughed at, especially by groups of pissed girls. The woman who tries to talk to me is small and earnest. I think she's surprised when she realises I'm not drunk. I ask her what she makes of such a joyous and happy scene. She replies that so many unfortunate, unhappy people in one place upsets her.

'Isn't this what weekends are for?' I ask her, gesturing at the screaming, vomiting, scrapping, snogging melee that is Newcastle on a Friday night. She looks at me bemused and hands me a crappy leaflet.

I'm not the only one to resist the lure of Christ.

'Jesus dies on a cross for you,' she beams at some passing girls.

'He died for nowt,' one yells back.

As I walk off, a boy of about sixteen asks another of the God Squad if he's selling any ecstasy tonight.

Jesus was a skater

Any weekends or evenings, you can see them. Skating on concrete expanses, blatantly ignoring the No Skating signs. The constant clunking of trux on pavements, as skaters go through their continual, gradual improvements.

I find some skaters in London at Waterloo. Just like at Download, their T-shirts protest their toughness and nonconformity. A thirteen-year-old wears one stating that he's a dealer. Another encourages you to 'Enjoy death'.

As with Download, they are thoughtless obscenities. There is no force or nastiness to back it up. There are kids smoking dope and a boy hands round a quarter-bottle of vodka, but this is all about the hanging out. The illegality is just a side effect. Like clubbing, skating creates a close-knit culture and spawns a whole range of creative social activity. And like pirate radio, graffiti and driving too fast round Tesco's car park, at the centre there is an obvious passion attached to being into something.

I get talking to Nick, seventeen, from Surbiton. He's got a pierced lip and a red pierced hole in his ear. His Guttermouth T-shirt indicates a certain disdain for social niceties. Their discography includes titles like 'Cram It Up Your Ass', 'I'm Destroying the World' and 'Looking Out for Number #1'.

There's a No Skateboarding sign about ten metres from us when I ask him if it's legal to skate here.

'Dunno, I think it is. There's an underground office under here and you're not allowed to skate here on weekdays but I think you are on weekends and holidays.'

'Would it bother you if it was illegal?'

'Yeah, it would piss me off because it's a perfect place to skate and if they made it illegal that would make me angry.'

Jon is fifteen from Newbury. He has been skating for three years and knows why he likes it.

'It's fun. You meet a lot of people, travel places, learn stuff that you wouldn't learn in school.'

I point out the No Skateboarding sign to him and ask if that causes any problems.

'Not really, but it depends, the police don't really mind but sometimes they go properly nuts or be really gay.'

Where he comes from, the police are tougher.

'We get fines in our town, like a fifty-quid fine, but we never get caught, we always do a runner. We're not doing any harm. It's not as if were ripping up signs. If it's not destructive I don't see the problem with it. Lots of other groups do a lot more damage than us. It's not as if we're going round graffiting stuff on walls, putting windows through and stuff. It's not doing any harm.'

But skating here is better than using an approved skatepark.

'Places like this, you have to travel to find them. Some parks are all right, but not that good for everything. You can't olly anything. But people hate it, and if you skateboard you're classed as a troublemaker.'

Like Outlaw and Wize, Jon grades his own antisocial activities as less destructive, more personally fulfilling than others. Skateboarding fills up time that might be spent on other activities.

'You keep out of trouble, you meet lots of people. I see other people that have quit skating, and they've turned into doing drugs and stuff, so it keeps you out of trouble.'

Skating is an activity that can support and encourage a whole range of other activities. The constants: fashion, music, film, design, hedonism, breaking the law, risk, boys and girls.

Skating, cruising and waving your mutherfuckin devil horns in the air. All activities that say fuck you to the places they take over. But within these broader shows of social disrespect lie tight-knit circles of friends and partners, almost feudal in their organisation and independence, answering the twin needs of young sociability: it puts you in touch with loads of people, and it teaches you skills that might go on to be useful elsewhere.

'You go everywhere,' Jon tells me. 'If you're in other countries you'll always meet people. Skating can get you into different jobs, like film editing and photos and stuff. A creative way. Find a job you want to do. You can do so much with it; you can film a skateboarder and then go and film other stuff. I just bought a £500 computer because I want to get into it. Use Adobe Premiere and iMovie. We just been filming over there.'

'How long will you carry on doing it?'

'Hopefully until I have no legs or something. I'm pretty committed to it.'

Join the Biggest Party on Earth™, make friends, get laid, get addicted

Face Party's claim to be the biggest party on earth is backed up by serious numbers. It's an online community that lets users upload words and images about themselves. And then cruise other people's profiles in search of someone to chat to. The site gives a true sense of the infinite hunger for contact that exists within young people today. On top of the basics, it has a whole host of other add-ons – or Cool Tools™ – to make your cruising more efficient or more pleasurable. Undercover Agent lets you track who's visited your profile or who's added you as a buddy. You can edit your photos to make yourself look sexier or weirder, and AVS (Adult Verification System) lets over-eighteens post and view others' X-rated photos, while the 'No More Gimps' control lets you block access to undesirable visitors. All this with the endpoint of making it easier to get in touch with people you think you might like and keep away from people you don't.

But while Face Party provides the space, it's the users who breathe life into it and provide the energy and the flavour. The site is like an online car park or field. A blank space waiting for people to fill it. There is little centre, or sense of control, or organisation; the event is created by people turning up and participating. It is peer to peer rather than top down. Everyone brings something different to it. Although, unlike the physical spaces, Face Party is always there. There is always someone to speak to.

And scrolling through the thousands of users, it's possible to get an idea of the multitude of social that Britain contains. Because everyone is on show and competing with the rest of the site, you get a sense of exuberance and self-promotion ... pages and pages of big smiles and exclamation marks.

I go to interview Dave Bamforth on the night that Face Party throws a surprise party for its millionth member. Sam Bradley, aka princess sam83, thinks she's coming to London for a bit of shopping. But on the sixth floor of the Kensington Roof Gardens, something a little more special is waiting.

One table is laid with eight places in the middle of the floor. Nineties' music stars Goldie, Shaun Ryder and Bez are chatting on sofas. In the garden two flamingos stand motionless in the roof river. Dave is in a dinner suit and red and black corset, with one spike of hair sticking up Tintin-style from his shaved head. In a fairground box, George and Zippy from *Rainbow* are shouting inanely to each other. Saddam Hussein (or at least one of his looky-likeys) is lounging against a pillar. Glamour model Jordan turns up, tiny except for her breasts and an evil teddy handbag swinging on her thigh.

The party seems an appropriate symbol for the strange connections that can be made online, not bound by location or reason. It's the most random bunch of celebrities I have ever seen in one place. This is Sam's prize, dinner with a bunch of people she's never met, and who are linked only by the fact that at some point in the last ten years (or thirty years I guess for Zippy and co.) they have been famous in Britain.

Face Party's website described the collection as 'our celebrity friends', but Bez and Shaun's PR agent tells me that they only got the phone call at the last minute, and the offer was too good to refuse. I assume she means the payment, not the dinner party. I talk to Bez and Goldie; neither of them seem that clear as to what is going on. I catch Goldie reading the Face Party literature with a slightly bemused expression.

As we're waiting for Sam, Bez starts telling me about the book he once wrote, and the difficulties of dyslexia. How his kids have got it too, but at least they recognise it as a condition these days. I think about making a joke about whether he's got dyslexia confused with dyspraxia, and if that explains his dancing style, but as I'm working out which bit is the punch line, I get distracted by Grim Rita (the online agony aunt) comparing her cleavage with Jordan's. Two unreal worlds collide here somewhat uncomfortably: celebrity and the virtual. Neither of them seem as beautiful, interesting or as much fun when they're real.

Sam arrives and seems simultaneously over- and underwhelmed. She poses on a bridge in the garden with all the celebs and then with her boyfriend in front of the flamingos. As she kneels somewhat uncomfortably, you can't help wondering if at the back of her mind she wishes the disconnected sign had popped up just as she was sending her profile.

I finally get to talk to Dave when Sam and her surprise guests are sitting down to dinner. We go out into the garden. Dave has a lot of energy. His eyes are bright, his words often tumble over themselves, and throughout the interview I can see a pill on his tongue. I take a look at the packet he's popping them out of. Nicorette. His assistant tells me later he's been on them for months, maybe a year. But he used to smoke sixty cigarettes a day. So at least that's an improvement.

Dave has always dealt in unreality. He started off doing raves in the late eighties, he has dabbled in porn – that's where he got his web smarts – and now, of course, he presides over an online community of people who mainly have never met each other in the flesh.

I ask him how much traffic the site sees. His reply is superlative.

'We do 424 million page impressions a month. If you put every magazine in Tesco's and add up the circulation we beat all of them combined. It costs millions to run. We use a thirty megs a second. Most websites don't use that a month.'

Dave describes the organic nature of the site, and by doing so, indicates one of its key strengths. The fact that despite its size, it still feels unknown, private.

'We are the twenty-seventh most visited site in the world and still no one's heard of us. We are the second most visited community in the UK. It's a real underground thing. You either know about it or you don't. It's weird to be so massive but still underground. We've never advertised. It's all word of mouth.'

'What's the secret to your success?' I ask.

At first he doesn't want to share it with me. After much deliberation and another half Nicorette, he goes for it.

'We are basically a kind of dating agency but nowhere on our site does it say date and every other dating site is like date online or super-date. No one's gonna use that. What kid's gonna want to use a date agency? But we're a dating agency. But because we call ourselves a party and we organise parties, it's socially acceptable to use it. It's not just dating. But we've had loads of marriages on it: fifteen marriages! Our user group is sixteen- to nineteen-year-olds mainly so to get marriages is really weird. Grim Rita gets letters every day saying I'm in love with someone I met online and she's like, for fuck's sake, you've never met him.'

For certain users, it seems that Face Party becomes a key element of their social lives.

'Kids especially are addicted. There are certain members who you see on there the whole time. They wake up, turn on, turn it off, go to bed and literally some people use it eighteen hours a day every day. Finding out who's been rating you, who's been looking at your page is the favourite tool. To find out who's got a crush on you. People will look at your profile but they won't write to you. But you can find out someone who's looked at your profile.'

While Face Party's success has been driven by the fluidity and range of access that an online world can provide, Dave is keen to bring this energy into the real world.

'I want to concentrate more on doing parties. The vibe is more important than the medium. Face Party's like just the brand. We want to do a stage for up-and-coming members who are DJs at our next party.'

Dave's ache to bring the excitement and velocity of Face Party back into the real world is evidenced not just by his desire to throw parties, but also by a conviction that behaviour online can seep back into this world and change it. In November the site encourages members to put their collective presence behind something more worthwhile.

> We've got over a million members, all with different skills
> and talents. It's about time we put those talents to use!
> We want your suggestions for a ridiculously BIG FEAT for us
> all to achieve next year. Perhaps we could build a school in
> Africa, or stage the world's biggest custard-pie fight — it
> could be anything you want, but it's got to involve
> absolutely thousands of members … and it's got to be BIG!
> So how does it work? Well, send in your ideas and we'll put
> them to public vote. Let's say, for example, the winning
> project is to build a school in Africa. Face Party will
> manage the whole project and, with the help of our members,
> source all of the materials we need for free. When it comes
> to building the school, we'll need loads of different skills,
> ranging from plumbers to painters. If one of our members is a
> plumber, we'll fly them over to Africa for a few days and so
> on — whatever it takes to get the job done. Everyone can be
> involved — whatever your skills, we'll always be able to find
> a task for those who want to help out.
>
> If every person does something tiny, with over a million
> members we can achieve something amazing. Everyone can be
> involved — so long as they're prepared to give their time
> for free.

I find such an ambition simultaneously audacious, charming and naive. The idea of flying some plumber over to Africa for a few days 'to get the job done' (a blocked cistern in Accra?, sewage problems in a Nigerian slum?) makes me smile; nevertheless Face Party is testament to the collective desire of young Britain to link up with multiple people and hang out.

With Face Party the number of friendships that people desire and even maintain reaches into the thousands; it points to a time of permanent connectivity, when you can be in touch with like-minded people, where depth is not the only value to be sought from friendship. It's also about frequency and novelty, the velocity and possibility of new conversations. It suggests a simplicity of contact, where the barriers of potential embarrassment and rejection are smoothed out by volume and distance. Like the apparently violent mosh pit at Download, or the Thurrock cruise, it is exclusive and tribal; in a place of apparent distance and disconnection is a set of rules for new ways of connecting.

Friends online

By mid-November Face Party boasts 1,771,188 members. I decide to talk to a few of the nearly 8000 members online. Face Party is like a menu of potential buddies and lovers. You type in your preferences – age, location, sexuality, whether they're online, whether they have adult pictures – and are presented with a stream of people.

When I first join, I feel slightly unnerved at the idea of posting my picture up for anyone to see, laugh at, comment on. I realise how outdated this resistance is. Not putting up my picture would immediately put me in the class of misfit, make me a Face Party gimp with something to hide. Most of the images have faces staring provocatively, seductively out of the screen, tempting you to click them, not to move past. They are on show.

And it's some show. I click randomly on a girl's face and get a sense of the volume of attention that someone with a confident smile can receive. Her home page states that she has had 16,969 visitors since 21 August. That's two hundred people a day, checking her out.

I move through the site, looking for people who are online and whose photo and brief profile seems to work best, indicating difference and liveliness. I ask them if they mind answering a few questions. Most of them are happy to help.

Couthmeat is from Cumbria but hopes to move to Manchester. From her photo she looks like a goth. She's sixteen and one of the pictures on her site features a pale guy with his top off and arms waifishly across his chest. According to the description, this is her husband, Steven, although when I go back to her page a couple of months later it's been replaced by a picture of someone else – 'my sexy bf' – playing guitar. The fact that 'Kurts death treated like suicide! rargh!' makes her sad. She's into loads of different music. 'Linkin park, Nirvana, Placebo, Murderdolls, Muse, Metallica (old stuff), Puddle of Mudd, THE DARKNESS!, Foo Fighters, Papa roach, Slayer, Pantera, Iron maiden, You get the point!' rotten.com is her favourite website and she says she doesn't read.

How long have you been using Face Party?

a year

How often do you use it?

every day

How many different people have you been in touch with on it?

about 100

How do you choose who you want to talk to?

i send them a message & if they reply we talk. i look for music styles and things before talking to people, whats the point in talking to some one on the internet that has nothing in common with you ?!?

Tell me a bit about how you write your descriptions.

i just update my pics as i get them taken, if i get a new pic i stick it on. and i update my profile nearly every time im online, because my life changes as the days go on

Do you think the friends you make online are different from the friends you make in real life?

nope i feel like friends online are just as cool as real friends

Do you behave differently?

yes, because i normally use words like 'coz, kool, wot, ehh, u'

Do you think you can reach the same level of depth online as you do offline?

yeah i do think you can reach the same depth online as offline, you can get really deep into conversation

Do you get in touch with people just by what they've put on their home page?

if i think its cool i will say that i think its cool, so yes i do

How did you decide what to write about yourself? Was your aim to encourage others to get in touch with you?

no not really, i said who i am, n i dont want any one to try and change me, if ppl dont like me for who i am they dont message me! simple!

Have you ever met someone in real life after talking to them on Face Party first?

yes a guy who is now one of my best friends! he lived down the road! weird! :)

stubley45 is seventeen. What makes him happy is 'bein immature n havin loads of fun n laughin'. His bad habits are 'bitin me nails, swearin'. His body type is 'average, smooth'. His perfect partner is 'Tara Reid or Cameron Diaz'. His favourite food is 'those greasy cheeseburgers from vans at fairs'.

How often do you use it?

Everyday

What's good about it?

meeting new people and expressing yourself

How many different people have you been in touch with on it?

god knows … over 500 probably

Do you talk to the same people all the time, or do you meet new people?

some people ive talked to for months but alot of new ones each week

How do you choose who you want to talk to?

Their personality, intrests and looks

Do a lot of people get in touch with you?

About 10 a week

Do you think the friends you make online are different from the friends you make in real life?

Yes, because of how often we talk, how little we know of each other and their backgrounds are unknown

Do you behave differently?

yes. Talk as if I'm trying to pull the individual, almost like I would if i was out in a club, whereas people i see everyday I have a more basic conversation

Stubley indicates a heightened sense of contact, where every conversation is loaded with the possibility of something richer than swapping text. And with pictures and profiles like lauren121, you can see why.

lauren121 is seventeen. She stares provocatively from the corner of her eyes out from the screen. One hand running through her hair. (I go back a month later to ask her a couple of extra questions, and the image has changed to her perched on a bed wearing a nurse's outfit.) She describes herself as 'Tha Original Little Miss Naughty™' and lists her bad habits as 'Flirting :: Logging Into Face Party :: Texting'. Her favourite food is 'jaffa cakes' and she likes 'Hard House and RnB'.

How often do you use Face Party?

    Whenever Im bored

How many different people have you been in touch with on it?

    OMG! Thousands! I have had like 80,000 visitors so far! LOL
    [laughs out loud]

How do you choose who you want to talk to?

    If they seem friendly and not borin or freaky

Do you think the friends you make online are different from the friends you make in real life?

    errm yeah coz u dont reali knwo them

Do you behave differently online?

    Not reali, im jus myself

It's not just Face Party where chat happens. I get talking with people on a variety of sites. On teentalk, both Sexy Strawberry and girl_vixen suggest that there is considerable difference between online and offline relationships.

    The friends I make online have nothing to do with real life
    friends most of the time. I've made a couple of very special
    friends on the net, but since I've talked to hundreds of
    people on the internet I can't say it's the same to make
    friends on the net and offline. The difference is that you
    don't see the people, you talk to them but you don't see the
    way they act, the way they talk and the way they treat other
    people. I think that all the things I say on the net could
    be said to anyone offline. I like to say what I think.

People are definitely less honest online, I don't trust
humans …

Sexy Strawberry

the friendships are always different online, my own personal
friends i can tell everything to but i feel restricted to
what i let people online know because of nasty stories you
hear on the news etc. people are less honest online, online
you can become anyone!

girl_vixen19

Online contact is not a replacement for human contact, but a different way of doing it. It provides an alternative set of codes for contact – for example, Stubley's parameters of approachability: 'their personality, intrests and looks' – and sets up a level of interrelationship that would be impossible to duplicate offline. Cool Tools creates the perfect conditions for communication – where you can approach as many people as you like and the possibility of rejection is tempered by the endlessness of contact. In one sense, it is a testing ground for friendship, where you get the opportunity to move through vast numbers of people, some more sticky than others. Sometimes sticky enough for meetings to stretch beyond the computer screen.

Face Party is about numbers and novelty. It stems from Dave's desire to create a bigger, more permanent rave, one where you present yourself as you choose, and where there is always a whirl of new faces. It's about being able to get a tangible fix on your popularity, and so offers a model for a more frenetic, multiple and efficient type of sociability: pointing towards an era of large-scale, perpetually shifting contact that sits alongside more regular friendships. There are obvious parallels here with our broader consumer culture, where experimentation and choice are built in to every brand's offering and where you would never contemplate buying without trying. Even the language is similar … the home page invites you to browse members, like they are a type of interesting product. Friendship on the same level as buying a CD or a book: you look through thousands to get the one that fits you best. And, of course, you can manage your own identity (or identities) to keep them lively and appealing.

Spending an increasing amount of time in online friendships will unquestionably affect the way that we do any friendship. New criteria are introduced. Sometimes friendship can be no more than a practical movement through people. Discarding those who don't fit requirements. Learning which parts of our own personality work hardest.

Online sites might encourage us to value frequency over depth, but perhaps they can also teach users how to be better friends. On Face Party, personalities are dissected by their owners to form a checklist for compatibility. Personal characteristics are detailed like items on a shopping list. It is a compact way of presenting yourself – teaching people to itemise their good and bad points, to present themselves efficiently to a hyper-active audience. It provides fragments of people to surf through, to chat to, or move on from.

Mobile life

The net offers the possibility of permanent and multiple random contact, but for keeping in touch with your mates, you can't beat a mobile. Portability is one of the key themes of modern life. The ability to take anything with you wherever you go. Always connected to your friends, to entertainment, to news and information. At the appropriately named Mobile Life Event you can explore the visions of a mobile future.

The event is split into zones, where different brands show off their wares and services. They indicate a time of connection creativity when these tiny devices help you realise your full potential as a communicative and connected individual. 3 promises to extend your senses: 'see and feel'. Siemens offers a stream of messages, as if it cannot choose between the multiple wonderful benefits it provides. Its statements seem more appropriate to a therapist than a mobile phone manufacturer: 'Be individual. Personalise. Be inspired. Free your creativity. Express yourself. Fight the boredom. Your senses long for satisfaction.' Kodak, the old guard: 'Share moments. Share life™.' virginmobilelouder.com promises new music, gigs, festivals, events, news and more.

Whatever brand you look at, the message is the same: boundless optimism, the fear of spare or dead time, of boredom, of loneliness. Instead: a creative, social heaven that phones open up for you. The core

messages transcend individual brands. The designs may be different –
Nokia's mixture of future-facing text and graffiti, T-Mobile's pencil-drawn
ads attempting to hide the Teutonic mass of this multinational phone
company; 3's contrived future aesthetic: space-age white capsules and
spheroid seats with gadgets hanging over them – but it's all about
connectivity and enhancement. About maximising time and pleasure.
Time is different here: it's distorted, layered, managed. The web page for
mobilelifeevent talks about the 25th hour ('you get out of life what you
plug in'), the imaginary extra time that proficient mobile use can bring
you. Of course, mobiles don't really give you time; they sell it to you. In
chunks. In bundles of seconds. This new level of sociability costs. You're
paying for your permanent accompaniment. Games, music, news. Pennies
for seconds. Pennies for friends.

The brands are certainly making more noise than the visitors – a
mixture of wideboy teens, families and tech heads. The most popular stall
throughout is the Legends Shoot Out, where punters try to score goals past
David James. I see a line of people waiting to get their Kodak photo taken
with Phil Tufnell of *I'm a Celebrity* … fame. The *FHM* tent fills up steadily
throughout the day, as teenage boys are snapped next to models. Probably
the best use of a phone camera they'll ever have. Getting phones, pictures
and pleasure hardwired into them.

What you have here is a concerted attempt at social engineering.
Accelerating the way that people interact. The way they do friends.
Everybody knows that some time in the future we will carry around
devices that show films, identify colleagues, find your nearest chip shop
and check your e-mails. It's definitely going to happen. Unfortunately
for the companies saddled with their massive 3G debts, people aren't
taking up all this tech quickly enough.

I visit Mobile Life in the week following Orange's ambitious relaunch,
featuring a young kid as educator. Posters announce the world of
knowledge that their phones can reveal … if only you know how to use
them. The main thought centres on how you're only using 20 per cent of
your phone, and this implicit reference to your brain is spot on. For many
people, phones have become a sort of external brain, storing numbers,
names, pictures. Memories. Emotions. They make sense of the world
around them. Phones are a great illustration of how totally and swiftly
technology can become part of us. An essential element for modern

communication, opening up a different level of fluid social contact.

Of course, phone training is not really for the younger mobile users. I talk to one of the trainers, who's on a seven-week tour round the UK's malls and exhibitions. Spreading mobile knowledge and phone wisdom. It's mainly the older people who approach her, she tells me. Very few teenagers. 'They're more clued up.' The Orange ads may feel fresh, but they're still working to an old model. However fresh, funny and unpedantic you make the instruction seem ('Give a man a fish and he'll eat for a day. Teach his phone to find the nearest chippy and he'll never go hungry again'), it's still instruction. And learning works differently now. No one tells these kids how to use their phone. They'll work it out themselves. Quicker and more appropriately than any lesson.

The enthusiasm of the phone companies is not matched by the visitors to the event. Hardly anyone I speak to has bought their tickets. They have been won, sent through the post, had invitations texted to their phones. The phone companies clearly see this as an additional way of using their marketing spend.

I talk with Alicia (3310), Catherine (6100) and Pia (8310). They're all fifteen and have had phones for about three years. They know the model numbers of each other's phones. Catherine's is the best, with a colour screen and photo attachment. They get a new phone or upgrade at least annually and their parents cover the bills: 'They've got credit cards.'

'How important are phones to you?'

Pia replies with a sentiment that everyone I speak to repeats: 'Can't live without them.'

'I only know about one or two people that don't have phones,' adds Catherine, who happily admits to using her phone in school during lessons. 'It's so much easier to text someone than call them … especially when you're in lessons. I get 500 free a month, so I probably send about fifty or a hundred a week.'

'I have 300 free a month, and I don't go over.'

'I just don't really count … just whatever I need. Send another one … '

The appeal of phones is simple: 'It's communication between friends.'

When I ask them about their address books, it's clear that numbers count here too.

Alicia starts the betting. 'Mine's full. I've got a hundred. If I could have more than a hundred, then I'd go over.'

'I've got about 115.'

'About 150.'

Although they admit there are some repeats, they also talk about how they constantly have to delete and replace names. Keeping their record of friendships permanently up to date. Friends are judged by frequency of contact and each girl seems to be in a continual process of editing friendships. As with the visitor logs on Face Party, mobile address books offer a tangible way of working out who you like most.

While they have seen many of the displays, they remain underwhelmed by the enthusiastic brand visions. Mobiles represent one of the fastest-changing categories in tech history, having had more effect on our social behaviour than any other individual item, and yet the continual upgrading and launching of new services is met with little passion. As Catherine puts it: 'They've done the main bits, and now it's just like, let's do this, let's do that.'

'There's like video mobiles,' explains Alicia. 'You can make videos and stuff but they are just too big. I'll wait till they're smaller and cheaper.'

Pia points to a key rule of connectivity – that a network grows in value depending on the number of people who have access to it. 'Now it's pointless having one cos none of your friends have one. It's not worth it until enough people have one.'

'And there was a leaflet thing that I filled in and it said if there was one thing you could add to a mobile what would it be, so I think they're still trying to look for things to add.'

'Would you ever ask someone else for help using a phone?' I ask – rather naively, if the funny expressions they exchange are anything to go by.

All at once they reply: 'No, no, I don't think I would.'

'I think it's just part of learning,' explains Catherine. 'You don't really learn how to write, you just pick up a pencil and know. You just pick up a mobile and learn yourself. By buying a mobile, you choose to learn how to do it. It's all part of it.'

'So if you say, I need that service, then you need to learn how to do it.'

Outside Legends Shoot Out I get talking to Ryan, fifteen, and Paul, sixteen. They're in football tops and baseball caps and are hanging around because one of the models talked to them earlier on. They think the best bit about the event is definitely the women. As Paul tells me: 'There's some very nice women here as well. Yeah. Very nice women. Down at the 3 mobile stand there's three Charlie's Angels lookalikes and they all look really nice.'

But they've got another reason for being here. A bit of a scam worked out. Paul shows me an 8310 that he picked up for £15 yesterday.

And then Ryan chips in. 'I got loads yesterday, but I sold them. Had a little deal.'

'That's the point.'

'Basically we come here, buy the phones for fifteen pounds each and then sell them on for fifty pounds.'

Yesterday Ryan sold five and Paul sold four. Ryan takes me through his day's work.

'Sold one for sixty, one for fifty, one for thirty and sell another one today for forty-five. To me mates, to my little brother.'

Business aside though, they're phone evangelists. Paul's had one since he was twelve.

'I rely on it. Can't live without it. It's like if you go out with your mates and get lost or something, it's easier to have one in your pocket. I go through ten pounds a week credit, easily. We're both with Virgin, so it's only 3p to text to each other.'

Like Alicia and co., they're aware of the new developments, but don't see them as relevant yet. 'The trouble is at the moment, the 8310, they're two hundred and fifty quid in the shop, but the camera phones at the moment are too much for kids to buy. So you have to wait for it.'

Remembering Pia and Alicia's reaction, I feel a bit stupid asking if he'd look for help using a phone, but he goes easy on me.

'The way I see it is, if you're an older person, me personally I think that they need more help with using their phone. With me, I can pick up a phone and learn how to use it in seconds. I can know what to do and everything. I don't really need any help in controlling it.'

'And what do you think about some of the messages that the phone companies are putting up? Like that one over there … "Be inspired"?'

'I don't think you need to be inspired to use a phone,' Paul snorts. 'I think it's just like in everyday life. Most people have got one. I think it gets younger. My cousin's got one and he's only like seven.'

Many of the people I talk to equate phone ownership with their social life. As Becky, sixteen, tells me: no phone, no life. 'I wouldn't not have one.

I use it for hours every day. For talking and texting. But mainly for texting. And I get free landline after 7pm.'

All of the people I speak to mention the importance of having a good phone. One that looks all right, isn't too heavy, can do the ringtones, hold the images that make it personal. But few of the teenagers have the latest model. It becomes clear why the telecoms companies have had to put on such an ambitious consumer event. People aren't upgrading fast enough.

There is great attachment to their phones, but little excitement. The inspiring straplines and latest models don't really seem to get this lot going. Phones just are. They're part of their life, and they expect them to keep on getting better, smaller, smarter. But it's not that important to have the latest model. What counts is a more democratic connection. There's no point having a video phone if none of your mates have got one. Because the phone is not a piece of self-congratulatory style technology. It's a tool. Every phone that I look at is battered and scuffed from overuse. All are personalised … with ringtones, stickers, figures and screensavers. Their phones ring and beep the whole time … as unobtrusive but essential as the sound of your breathing.

This sense of absorption into the body's functions is echoed by one of the phone trainers who jokes: 'My memory's gone, because I used to know all of my numbers off by heart. If I lose my phone, I've lost everything. I don't even know my boyfriend's number.'

'The bigger the mirror, the bigger the line'

It's quite worrying that we might end up in the next 10 or 20 years ... with our psychiatric hospitals filled with people who have problems with cannabis. Recreational use of cannabis is something that any government and any community should think very seriously about.

Professor Ghodse, a former INCB president and in charge of studies into addictive behaviour at the University of London's St George's Hospital, *BBCi News*, February 2003

Dope porn

Like most centrefolds this one seems too good to be true. Larger than life, bursting with health; glossy and forbidden. You would never see anything this perfect in the real world. Good lighting, maybe some retouching makes the image almost fake, certainly unobtainable.

This is the centrefold for *Weed World*, a magazine dedicated to the various pleasures of marijuana. It gives tips on growing weed, it interviews professional smokers, tells hilarious stories of stoners and smuggling, and this month's centrefold is 'the freshest Indian Minali'. Solid, shiny lumps of brown hash, sticky on the outside, crumbly within, reach out to the reader. On the consecutive page, a proud hand holds 'the best from Belize', a pile of light green grass. On the next: a chronic bud, a potent form of skunk, as praised by Dr Dre in the album of the same name, and by other West Coast rappers since the mid-nineties. The plump leaves are coated with crystals.

Dope porn for weed dreams.

The magazine's contents page carries some small print, incongruous among the distinctive pointed leaves that surround it. If you bother to read it, if you can make your smoke-addled eyes focus for long enough, you realise it's a disclaimer.

'Weed World in NO WAY accepts responsibility for the use of products advertised within the magazine ... All information within this magazine is for educational purposes and is not intended to condone or promote or incite the use of illegal or controlled substances ... All products advertised within this magazine are for novelty value only, they are not intended for illegal use.'

And so on. The magazine is clearly aware of the law. Apart from this solemn reminder that the world does not share its passion for hemp, *Weed World* is about celebration. The contents page promises news of the Paris Hemp Festival, an article on parliamentary injustice (presumably a regular column), and various specials: Judge Dready, Cannabis Journeys, Sonia Skunk, Medical News ... something for everyone who loves pot.

As you would expect, the articles are a mix of earnest support for legalising marijuana, buying and growing guides, and the anecdotes of space cowboys. But to the novice reader, the big difference from your regular mag is the ads. No Gucci models, no sleek sports cars or wide-screen TVs. Just page after page of smoking and cultivating paraphernalia.

Mr Beam, Grotech, Hydro Light, Kentish Green ... all touting their hydroponic lighting kits, which will enable any kid with a few seeds and a bit of space to get growing. And the choice of seeds ranges from the usual suspects: Durban Poison, Northern Light, Purple Top, White Widow, to the more extravagant stars: Early Girl, Afghani Hindu Kush, Hawaiian Maui Wowie Skunk.

And then there's the smoking equipment. If a few Rizlas and a roach are a bit basic for your toking needs, then this is the place: grinders, bongs, pipes, silver palm leaves, electric bongs, vaporisers, pollinators. All with the aim of providing you with the smoothest, most satisfying smoke. There are a lot of people here making money from selling equipment for consuming an illegal product.

In a nod to its controlled status, there are a few ads for kit to make drug use invisible: Quick Fizz – effervescent detoxification, ZipnFlip – fake urine sample bags, and Get Clean shampoo.

Of course, marijuana might be illegal, but in Britain at least it seems that fewer and fewer people take any notice of this. It's certainly not going to stop you if you like a smoke. And lots of people do.

Up in smoke

Government research suggests that fifteen million people in Britain have tried cannabis, and puts the regular users at a few million. The UK's cannabis economy is valued at £5bn. That's about same size as the global sales of companies like Cadbury Schweppes or Interbrew, responsible for another of the UK's top narcotics in the form of Stella or Boddington's. Cannabis is not a niche drug. This is part of Britain in the 21st century.

Of course, the kids aren't the only people not taking the law very seriously. In January 2004, the drug was downgraded from a Class B drug to a Class C drug, which means that although the government isn't exactly endorsing it, you're unlikely to get a caution if you're caught with a small bit of personal. This freewheeling acceptance goes further than dope: it's also reflected in the sprouting up of psychedelic mushroom stalls over the summer of 2003. From Psyche Deli on Portobello Road to Joint in Portsmouth, it's now easy (and legal) to buy fresh magic mushrooms – although the stall holders are prevented from giving you any advice about how best to prepare and consume them.

Ex-chief superintendent Antony Wills, who retired from Scotland Yard in May, has compared smoking cannabis to getting drunk. 'I would have no problems with decriminalising drugs full stop. Policing cannabis is a waste of time. I don't feel the effects of cannabis are any worse than overconsumption of alcohol.'

The pervasiveness of drugs in the UK means that there is little controversy surrounding their consumption among the people who take them. Everywhere I go – from clubs to marches to modified-car meets – kids smoke dope, drop pills, sniff coke and chase ket. For them, it is no big deal; an alternative or, more frequently, a companion to alcohol. Despite the illegality of ecstasy and cocaine, availability rarely is an issue; and for most users, the illegal status is little more than an inconvenience.

But teenage drugs use, like teenage drinking, is presented as problematic. The £3m 'Talk to Frank' government campaign that launches in May is a big step on from the authoritarian 'Just Say No' efforts of the eighties, but nevertheless focuses on the health and criminal risks of taking drugs. Clearly, there are both, but these remain distant for most users. Like pirate radio and graffiti, most drugs remain illegal, and so provide one more example of how the British government criminalises huge sections of the population because of something that is done on a regular basis for amusement and pleasure. Just from the numbers it seems likely that hundreds of thousands of people use drugs regularly without getting busted or going mad. I asked myself what this drug use felt like, and if it always had to turn out bad.

Free the weed

The annual Legalise Cannabis festival in Brockwell Park, Brixton, is a sign of the normalisation and widespread acceptance of the drug. On a sunny Saturday in April, I go to check it out. At first glance it looks like any other festival. Groups of teenagers sit on the grass. Children run around their with parents and dogs. A band plays on a large stage. Trance pulses out of a tent. The smells of hot dogs, jerk chicken and popcorn waft out of a multitude of stalls.

It's only as I walk round the stalls that the festival's true purpose becomes clear. They are like the pages of *Weed World* brought to life. Like a swimsuit fan at a motor show, you get to see the centrefold in 3-D. Only here you can buy it as well. The stalls don't sell dope, but they are overloaded with the culture and products that surround it.

There are signs for herbal highs, smart products, natural ecstasy and other products for a legal buzz. Sky High promises pipes, skins, bongs and, strangely enough, hats. More smoking slang, or just to keep your head together? Next door, Head Heaven offers a range of bright knitwear as well as the obligatory kit. Coloured plastic bongs, curved china pipes, small metal tubes, foils, gauzes, enormous rolling papers, rolling mats. Bandannas decorated with cannabis leaves at two quid, wacky backy stash bags going for £2.50. Rollwiviit smoker's trays. And even a smattering of politics. A placard with the message: 'Which Bush kills? George or ganja?' lies discarded on the grass.

Of course, the real sales, the ones that count, are going on all across the festival. Outside the music tents, dealers who normally hang in Brixton are openly selling small bags of grass. And it's not just the locals taking advantage of the widespread disregard for the law. A student from Bournemouth tells me he has bagged up his entire homegrown supply and is hoping to earn a few hundred pounds.

The festival's purpose is evident in the huddled groups scattered all over the ground. Circles of mates lick Rizla, empty out cigarettes, crumble hash, scatter weed, tear off roaches and light up. Everywhere.

I ask two policemen their thoughts about what's going on. Don't they feel an urge to get a few arrests in? Hit their weekly targets in one afternoon? They don't want to get into the legalities of what is happening, or why they are letting thousands of people break the law. They are just there to make sure there is no trouble.

I get chatting with Deedi, Louisa, Emma and Sonic as I'm looking through another stall's paraphernalia. They're all locals and are enjoying the day, the fact that a bunch of people can come together and hang out. They're eighteen, wearing oversized torn-up jeans and battered DC sneakers. Deedi is blowing bubbles and wearing a Sesame Street hoodie. Sonic has a Mohawk and a knackered rucksack with a 'fuck you' patch.

I ask what they're doing here and Sonic tells me. 'I'm blazing. That's what I'm doing here, I'm blazing.'

While they agree the festival's a great thing, they don't believe that cannabis should be legalised.

With a fat joint in his fingers, Sonic gestures at me and states, 'I reckon it should stay illegal.'

'I reckon the only reason it would be legalised is so the government can tax it,' states Emma thoughtfully.

'I think it's a good thing that this is allowed but not legalising it completely. I just don't want it to become mainstream, man. It's cool how it is.'

'It doesn't have to be legalised completely. I think it would be worse for dealing and stuff.'

'And that would bring advertising into it and stuff and that would ruin it,' concludes Louisa.

This interest in dope retaining its illicit status surprises me. I had assumed that everyone would be for greater freedom. But a range of attitudes emerge as I speak with different groups. While some resent the fact that the government has any influence over how they choose to play with their minds, others support legalising marijuana but not class As, while some have no problem with things as they are. Presumably partly because the law is so irrelevant to their ability to score and enjoy drugs. And also because doing something illegal – however widespread it is – offers an appearance of disconnection from mainstream, safe Britain.

Sonic has been smoking dope since he was twelve, the others since they were about fifteen. For all of them, it's a normal part of their lives. A lot of their friends also smoke. Some of them don't. It's not a big deal. But none of them like the idea that someone else should be telling them what to take and what not to take, whether it's the government, teachers or friends. For them, it's just a normal part of their lives: nothing complicated about it at all.

'Quite a few people have told me that you gotta stop doing drugs, man, all this crap, but I don't care,' Sonic explains cavalierly.

Louisa joins in, mimicking a serious adult: 'It's bad. Don't do drugs.'

'It's my choice whether I want to fuck myself up.'

'It's all about choice, I guess, until you push it too far.'

'If the only person you're hurting is yourself …'

I find a group of kids who are more vocal in their support for legalisation. Their style is strictly urban in Reeboks, tracksuit tops; baseball caps for the boys, scraped-back hair for the girls – although Jamie is wearing a green floppy hat with Heineken patches all over it. They're sixteen, seventeen and have been smoking dope for two to three years. Jamie a bit longer.

When I ask what they're doing, they're in no doubt.

Jamie says, 'Supporting the cause,' and the rest of them chime in: 'Yeah, yeah, yeah.'

'There's people from all over the country, ain't there?'

'Yeah, loving it, loving it. Showing support, innit? For the cause.'

'And do you think that dope should be illegal?'

'Nah, not really, not really at all. It should be decided by the whole population. That's the other thing, see. If they decriminalised it, it would knock out all of the dealers and shit like that. You wouldn't have to deal with any of that any more. I know so many people as well who want to grow their own. When it's decriminalised I reckon home-growing is the way it's gonna go.'

'What about other drugs? Do you think they should be legal?'

A chorus of nos from everybody, and the definitive answer from the expert in the group, Jamie.

'They should stay class A.'

'What do you get up to when you're not here?' I ask them.

'Smoke more dope,' laughs Amy.

'Smoke pot in someone else's front room.'

But of course that's not it: they work, go to college, a mixture of the two. I ask them if they think it stops them functioning.

'No, not at all.'

'Of course not.'

'And are all your mates as laid-back about smoking dope as you are?'

'A few people have a problem with it,' replies Jamie.

'I was like that to begin with,' says Amy, and Olivia agrees with her.

'What changed you?'

'I went out with him,' Amy laughs, pointing at Adam. 'I like used to screw at him when we were younger and when we first started going out but I got used to it and started doing it. Loved it.'

'Yeah, it's great,' chips in Olivia.

'We had a party one night. Adam rolled a humongous spliff.'

'A big pure skunk spliff.'

'We got fucked after a couple of tokes.'

'And liked it after that' – Olivia is still laughing – 'and saw the way.'

Jamie comes back with some more philosophising. 'That's the thing if you think about it – it's like once you tried it you realise there's nothing that bad about it. It's not like it influences you. It's a realisation, innit?'

'You don't think of it as a drug,' adds Adam. 'I don't smoke cigarettes. I just have dope instead.'

As I walk off they're packing a clear glass bong. I ask if they always bring it out with them.

'No, this stays at home. It's too valuable. And it's not exactly subtle, is it? For special occasions only.'

Judging from the light brown stains on the inside of the glass tube, special occasions come round frequently at Jamie's house.

As well as the townies and the rude boys, and the scruffy, middle-class kids, there are the ones who really do look like the dope fiends. The kinds of kids who don't have to be at a cannabis festival for people to stare at them and wonder. There is a woman on stilts, dressed as an enormous cannabis leaf; there is the guy in a two-piece Moschino-style denim outfit, but rather than some Italian logo it is emblazoned with small green leaves. I ask to take his photo but he says: 'No. If I let everybody who asked, I'd never get round to smoking nothing.'

Sophie, Ash and Matilde are sitting with a big group of friends. Ash is wearing a grubby fluoro roadworker's jacket and a shirt with some flowery pattern on it. It's possibly a pyjama top. He says he's a space cowboy. Matilde, in her own words, has silly hair. It's shaved at one side and sweeps over the top to run down her back. Sophie looks stunning. She has green and orange hair with a cutesy pink ribbon holding it in an innocent-looking long bob. She is wearing a knitted chunky white, pink, orange, green, red, purple sweater. And a flowing set of skirts – part ra-ra, part tu-tu, all trashy. She's twenty, from south London and a rubbish fairy. Matilde is twenty-three, from Mozambique and Liverpool and currently living in London. Ash lives everywhere.

I ask them if they support legalising cannabis.

'Depends who's growing it really, and what they're putting in it,' Ash tells me.

'I reckon it's all about decriminalising it and not legalising it,' adds Matilde. 'All our mates would be out of fuckin pocket if you legalise cannabis. And the money would be going to the government. They'd be reaping in the taxes and all that. So it's about decriminalising it.'

Both Ash and Matilde have a slightly cynical view about why this festival is allowed to take place. They're happy that it's going on, but see it as a pressure valve, that keeps potentially troublesome elements quiet. Behave for 364 days and get one day to smoke dope in public.

'It's a communist weekend, innit? Just like yin yang. You have one lot doing up their ties and us lot doing up the reefer. What would you rather be doing now: smoking reefer or looking at your bank balance?'

'Here it's just like a nice weekend. This weekend is special. It's not like this every weekend in London. I don't know if it's connected to Mayday but it's a special weekend so I reckon it's like: lump it all in at the same time. And keep it here to avoid it spreading out and becoming troublesome. Get them to have their fun at the beginning of the summer, you know, everyone's happy and that's about how it works really.'

'In a way though this is where we've been good boys and girls. This is the weekend we get to smoke dope and the old bill just watch from a distance. But it's important that it happens. That it doesn't just stay hidden. People are thinking more now. It's not just about getting high, say when you're with your mates and you go to someone's house.' Ash gestures around the park. 'We're in a big shared house at the moment, having a big smoke.'

Ash's comment about it not staying hidden makes me think about other zones of disconnection, and how momentum and size can make them more visible, so they cannot help but rub up against the broader world. In this sense the cannabis festival acts as a social experiment, checking how much disruption or disorder a park full of potheads can cause. For a day, Brockwell Park offers a accelerated vision of the future, where laws are less national, more fluid, and spaces exist for different styles of living, for more permanent disconnections.

When I go, Sophie writes in my book: 'Recycle, make mess, find underground happiness', and invites me to come and visit her shop.

With everyone I speak to the fact that cannabis and other drugs are illegal is at worst an inconvenience, but mainly an irrelevance. Nobody talks about the dangers of getting busted. And nobody seems to have any trouble getting hold of stuff, whether it's weed, pills, ketamine, speed or coke. It's freely, easily, permanently available.

Some people think it should be legalised, others don't. It's not a simple yes/no thing. Some of the smokers like the fact that it's illegal, still deemed outside acceptability. Others prefer their mates to be making money from it rather than the government or multinationals. But most don't really care that it's illegal because it has no effect. The law doesn't stop anybody smoking as much of it as they like. And days like this just confirm the arbitrariness of its illegality.

As one kid says to me, jabbing in the air with his spliff: 'The fact that this can go on shows that nobody really cares about it. That it's just a stupid law, that they don't know how to change. You can't imagine a legalise robbery day, can you, where it's okay to go round thieving stuff, and the police don't do shit? Or a legalise murder day, can you?' His friends agree and they laugh as they take the joke further; legalise violence, legalise bomb-making ('that'd be fun ... to watch'), legalise graffiti. They think maybe you could have a legalise speeding day as long as you kept the children inside.

'They might want to do something about the clothes, though,' he says, pointing to a white kid with a few sparse dreads and a red, green and gold T-shirt with a large cannabis leaf on the front. 'That kind of outfit, now that should be illegal.'

Psychoactive vaults

As I chat with Ash at the cannabis festival, he starts talking about some of the free parties he goes to, and about the experiences he's had on different drugs. I lose track when he starts telling me about the stones having messages on them. It reminds me of essays by the psychonauts – Huxley, Leary, McKenna, Jensen – who wrote about their drug-taking in spiritual-medical terms, keen to get beyond the simplistic high and to bring back more coherent reports from the multiple plains of wasted. In those days it was only the scientists and the legends who could get published, but nowadays any budding chemical author can share his experiences with like-minded users.

Erowid.org is one of the most comprehensive sites devoted to recreational drugs. The numbers give an idea of interest – 'Nearly 25,000 people visit the site each day, making more than 2.8 million unique visitors in the past year' – and point to the compulsive chronicling of this illegal activity: 'Over 16,000 documents related to psychoactives including images, research summaries & abstracts, media articles, experience reports, information on chemistry, dosage, effects, law, health, traditional & spiritual use, and drug testing.'

Erowid is a useful source in a mediascape where horror stories outweigh the good times. Its home page explains why it exists.

'Although the risks and problems are widely discussed, it's also clear that psychoactive plants and chemicals have played a positive role in many people's lives. Erowid is founded on the belief that a healthy relationship with psychoactives is one grounded in balance, where use is part of an active, intellectual, physical, and spiritual life.'

The site originates in the States, which might explain the somewhat worthy vision, as well as the order with which contributors describe their experiences, giving precise dosages and often using the correct chemical names for drugs. Nevertheless, in these accounts it is possible to get a better idea of the kind of effects that go on when people take drugs.

In the personal experiences section, the accounts have titles like 'Impossible to understand reality', 'Opening the soul's eyes' and 'Unimaginably intense'. As well as the more unfortunate: 'Why I'm never touching LSD again' and 'Maybe I'm an addict'. They give the time and amount of dosage, as well as method of ingestion and form of drug.

FreedomFreak on ecstasy: 'The music was surrounding me in trance-like comfort. The sound spoke to every nerve in my body. I could enjoy the "Here and Now" – any time a thought of something unpleasant from the world would arise, I could look at it without stress, then gently push it out of my mind. It didn't matter that I had a project and exams. This state was pure, free, uninhibited.'

Anonymous on acid: 'Everything shifted into cartoon form and looked very fucked up, everything became 2-D and flat. The part of me that was floating above the car changed form so its now 2-D face grew a zig-zag mustache and one of its eyes became a spinning spiral while the other became a flickering eye of horus, which shot occult symbols out.'

Tathra on ketamine: 'I can see in more than just three dimensions, it's hard to describe … everything had much more depth and was way more refined. Simply by looking at my arm, I could see all the valleys and mountains that are my flesh with extreme clarity. I feel completely at peace, as if this is the only reality that exists.'

What is valued here is the radical shift of perceptions, a slanted view on the world. As a destination it is different from alcohol. It's not about numbing your senses, but expanding them, letting your eyes, ears, brain work differently. Erowid introduces the notion of drugcraft, the slightly contradictory idea of being smart with drugs that normally mess with your head. These are people who take their drug consumption very seriously, who have thought about why they play around with their consciousness, and aim for altered states.

'The art of drugcraft is to get more euphoric with less drug. Psychedelic drugs safely produce relaxed attention … but also something more … one such example: kinesthetic perception whereby our heightened visual, auditory, tactile, olfactory, and gustatory senses merge so that we can taste sound, listen to color, touch an aroma and SEE … as we have never seen before … before experiencing EUPHORIA!'

This mantra feels like a throwback to the sixties when drug-taking was seen as a way of achieving a higher consciousness, rather than just a different – albeit more pleasurable – one. In all my research I didn't come across many people who talked about drugs like this. And the ones who did were often the most drug-guilty, and felt that they had to offer a reason more complicated than 'it just feels good'. The British, it seems, like their drugs a bit more messy.

Getting messy

It's a sign, both of recreational drugs' illegality and the fact that they can have crazier effects on the brain than alcohol does, that such a literature of justification and description exists. Alcohol is much simpler: drink, get drunk, feel good now, feel bad later. It's only among the serious wine buffs that the same meticulous approach and veneration for mind-altering substances occurs. But even with recreational drugs, the psychoanalysts are in the minority.

For most people, it's not about getting deep. It's about getting high. And having a laugh. Compare the analysis-heavy pages of erowid.org and other Terence McKenna-influenced sites with the pages of *Mixmag* and *Muzik* magazines, a far more common representation of why kids do drugs. Within these pages there is none of the weighty righteousness of drug bores. And none of the drug guilt either. No descriptions of length of effect or precise dosage.

Instead you've got a graph in *Mixmag* under the heading 'Do drugs make you go bald?' which plots famous hedonists (from 'dabbled' to 'one long party') against follicle count ('bald as a coot' to 'werewolf'). In *Muzik* magazine, there's a page feature: '20 reasons why ... eggs are better than Es' which gives such tips as: 'Visiting an ecstasy dealer is often a scary and hazardous activity, whereas visiting a dealer of eggs usually involves lots of fun chasing about a farmyard yelling, "Here, chicky chick chicken!"', or 'We've never felt the need to eat one more egg, just to even out the comedown from the last three eggs a little bit.'

There are anecdotes celebrating drug-taking – 'The first time I wore my rubber batman suit it was amazing, I got to meet so many people. The first guy I met said, "Batman, do you want some free pills?" Holy Ketamine!' – and tips on how to do it better. In *Muzik*, Cypress Hill's DJ Muggs shows readers how to make a Philly blunt, and *Mixmag* features Smoker's Corner, where they give you conversation topics to discuss when you're stoned: 'Sesame Street is adding a muppet that is HIV positive. Spark up and discuss.' A Ministry of Sound ad is promoting its Sunday Papers sessions, 'Saturday night till Sunday morning', and just in case you didn't get the pun, the woman in the photo is waving a pack of blue king-size skins.

Reading these magazines, it's clear that the people who know best, who consume the most and are embedded in an intoxicated culture, don't take drugs very seriously. Or rather, they take them seriously every weekend, but the whole thing's a bit of a joke.

So *Mixmag* invites readers to contact its Mongo hotline, either calling or texting, and prints the best messages.

'I'm not sure why i'm lying on my bathroom floor at four in the morning but i presume my journey here was both magical and expensive.'

'U should c these trippy lines there well freaky'

And in reference to the tranquilliser ketamine: 'I'd just like to say, if it's good enough for horses, it's good enough for me.'

And if that's not enough, at the bottom of the page, Mongo in a Mess asks readers to show the goods. 'Got a pic of you muntered you feel you need to share with the world? Text it to us from a picture messaging phone.' Online, *Mixmag* directs you to the Gurner's Gallery, where hundreds of photos of huge pupils, wobbly mouths and pale skin are arranged.

The Mongo in a Mess is sponsored by Vodafone. Radio 1 teams up with *Mixmag* to support the 'Weekender Bender – Calling all hardcore clubbers. *Mixmag* want to know who you are!' Kiss 100 plays out the Mongo hotline from 4am on Saturday mornings. And of course *Mixmag* is published by EMAP, which also brings out *New Woman*, *Heat* and *Trout & Salmon*. Despite some of the activities that these brands associate themselves with, they know their consumers and how to connect with them.

The section at the back of *Mixmag* is called 'Chill – stuff to read when you can't read no mo'. I ask Nick Stevenson, *Mixmag* editor, why so many people send in stuff where they look or sound out of it.

'*Mixmag* readers are very loyal to the mag and like being part of it. People ring up because they like to see their own ramblings in print and I guess there is a feeling that everyone around the UK at 3am on a Sunday morning is talking gibberish and coming out with enlightened bollocks, so why not all share it? That's why there is a Mongo hotline show on Kiss 100 at the same time.'

I wonder if their carefree treatment of the subject has attracted any criticism.

'One woman rang me to say that her son is in prison for dealing drugs and believed that it was our handling of drugs in such a matter-of-fact way that led to him becoming an ecstasy dealer. To anyone with any real intelligence this is rubbish. By talking about drugs in the same tone as our readers, when we give advice and useful knowledge we are a more trusted source, with important safety, legal and health advice. Much better than a lot of the government and other press saying "Hey, kids: drugs are bad."'

Nick confirms my sense that for most young drug users getting wasted is something to celebrate and show off about.

'I wonder if sometimes people ring up and pretend to be fucked just so they can get their ramblings in the mag. Some of the stuff is very inspired, well-thought-out and shows the real clarity of thinking that is achievable through narcotic use. Saying that, most of it's just drugged-up bollocks.'

When I ask Nick about Vodafone's sponsorship of the Mongo in a Mess section, and whether they know that they are supporting a column that is about people being out of their heads, he suggests I take it up with Vodafone. I put a call into their UK marketing department, leaving my mission and questions on an answerphone. But they never get back to me.

We love Homelands

This easy acceptance of intoxication is burned into British culture. It's not just in the back pages of *Mixmag* that FTSE 100 brands court young consumers by aligning themselves with drug-fuelled hedonism. We live in a country where the possession and dealing of class A drugs remains punishable by hefty sentences, but hundreds of thousands of people shift and consume millions of pounds worth of stimulants every weekend. And throughout the summer there are vast zones across the country where this is encouraged. Where Britain PLC, via booze and media brands, happily leaves the TV and the bars and rubs shoulders with kids at festivals.

Homelands, May 2003, and the brands are more subdued than a few years ago when main sponsor Ericsson stamped its giant logo all over the place. But you can't miss the neat logos and flash tents. Bacardi, Strongbow, Mars. The most visible and audible brand there is Radio 1, shouting out its youth credentials. The line-up's pretty good, if traditional – Audio Bullies, Timo Maas – but the whole affair seems a bit too pleased with itself. The logo towers above the decks and every ten minutes or so, wherever you are at the festival, you can hear the MC above the rest of the festival racket: 'Radio 1 – doing Homelands.' 'Yeah, yeah, we know' someone mutters as he gets in the huge line for the toilets.

Compared to the liberal family day out that was the cannabis festival, Homelands is full on. It looks like a small village has been transplanted into Matterley Bowl, near Winchester. Tents, stalls and fairground rides fill this picturesque site.

But as you approach the entrance, you can see that there is something else going on. Large yellow and black signs line the entranceway: 'Police Notice: Drugs Amnesty bins. Last chance to deposit your illegally held drugs. Warning. Police drug sniffer dogs working ahead on entry points. Offenders will be detained.' Climaxing in the bin itself, yellow with a small slit and a large chain holding the top down. The anti-drugs bark seems worse than its bite: there's no sign of any sniffer dogs as I walk through the gates.

In the whole time there I only see one likely drug arrest: four scared-looking teens being led out in plastic cuffs by a bunch of 'undercover' cops, whose skin-tight stonewash jeans and bulk surely give them away to all but the most insensitive dealer.

There are about 50,000 people, and the majority are here to get high and have fun. Festivals aren't perhaps the best place for in-depth interviews – there's always something more interesting to be doing – but there is concurrence in motives and viewpoints among the people I do talk to.

And there are all sorts here: from gangly fifteen-year-olds taking their first pills and chewing their lips, to forty-year-old men, with beaten faces and calf tattoos. Cybers, townies, even a few punks and goths. United by a desire to muck around in the middle of the countryside. It's more carnival than festival: people jumping over sleeping bodies, play fights, screaming. The Bacardi tent has a branded truck parked outside which is overflowing with people the whole night. By the morning, the windscreen's busted and the bonnet dented. I don't see it being driven away.

Some of the people I speak to are full-time caners; especially when the summer comes round, they flit from one festival to another. But many are studying or working. The bank holiday just gives the workers another day to get over it; the half-term gives the school kids a whole week. Nobody I talk to has any qualms about discussing their drug consumption, although one eighteen-year-old girl does write in my notebook, when she gives me her home phone number: 'Don't mention the pills on this no.'

The stalls and clothes say it all. I recognise a few from the cannabis festival. Then there are the more rave-specific. The 'class A citizen' stall: 'cheeky threads for the chemical generation'. T-shirts with a big Mitsubishi logo and the words: 'Authorised dealer' underneath. Or the more extropian 'Chemically Advanced'. As well as the admission that sometimes taking drugs can stop you working: 'This unit is temporarily out of order'. And for those who are in any doubt as to why, three favourite brands of ecstasy are there, all of them logos pinched from somewhere else: Mitsubishi, Motorola and Superman. Speed, communication and superhuman powers. Sounds about right. Perhaps the best, only available for women and under the offensive section, is the one that says: 'Cracksmokingpornfreak'. I don't see anyone wearing that at the festival, though I do smell a couple of kids smoking crack later on, sucking on an empty beer can that's peppered with small holes.

But of course there are loads of other T-shirts around, all about attitude and consumption: 'Fucked up.' 'I'm just a social drinker. But I do drugs like a professional.' 'Dosse posse' underneath an Adidas logo that has become a cannabis leaf. The girl with the simple 'Nice tits', who obligingly pushes her chest out as far as it will go when I ask to take her photo. It's the same kind of attitude found in the back pages of *Mixmag* and *Muzik*: drug-taking as pure entertainment. Overdoing it as something to laugh at and celebrate. Showing off to fellow consumers.

William, seventeen, has come down with two friends. They're sitting watching one of the rides, and smoking hash. He's wearing a bright yellow rain cape and glasses. He's very polite and eager to talk. He looks like someone from an Arthur Ransome book: gingery hair, pale, skinny but wholesome and enthusiastic. It's 7pm when I talk to him. He likes festivals because of the people and the vibe.

'I love the atmosphere. Everyone's so happy. Everyone's loving it. No one comes here for rucks; that's great. DJs are great. They make you feel a lot better. We just love it. Everyone's happy. We are the love generation. And we shall stay the love generation. People are here to have a good time, have a laugh, no one cares what they look like. It's just the atmosphere. Do what you want, you know what I mean. It's just great.'

'Have you taken any drugs yet?' I ask.

'Well, I've took five pills tonight. I'm pretty fucked on class As. I can honestly tell you I have no sense of the time.'

'Will you take any more?' I wonder, given that there's another eleven hours of festival to go.

'Oh yes, oh yes,' he replies. 'Mitzies. Mitzies are great. They're the best really. Mitzie triangles. Fat ones.'

Rebecca and Jane are sitting nearby and ask what I've been talking to William about. I explain, and they're keen to add their own opinions. They're both nurses and they see no contradiction between their weekend of illicit pharmaceuticals and their day job of dealing with legal ones. Although they know which is more fun. Rebecca and Jane, both twenty-three, are from Australia but now living in Peterborough (or Peter-boring as they have nicknamed it): 'There's nothing fun there at all. There's a cathedral and that's it, and we haven't even been to that.'

This is their first British festival, but they've been to a few in Australia, and it's a familiar sight.

'Everyone dresses up a bit more here.' They dress safe: jeans, hooded tops and fleeces.

'But Australia's much more relaxed.'

I look around at the groups of people lying around on the grass, the smell of cannabis drifting across the field, and wonder how much more relaxed it can get.

'What's good about festivals like this?' I ask.

They both laugh before Jane says, 'You want us to be real honest, right? Just coming to dance and … ' – both in unison now and laughing – 'take loads of drugs.'

'What do you like taking?'

'Anything you put in front of me. Pills and coke.'

They plan staying till six and assure me that they've 'got enough stuff to get us through'.

As it gets dark I spot two girls in pink fluffy fairy outfits sitting on the grass. With Cordelia and Sam is Stuart wearing a 'High again' T-shirt. It's his nineteenth birthday and somehow this means he hasn't had to dress up. Usually he does too. All three of them are in a very good mood. It's Cordelia and Sam's first festival, and Sam has recently dropped her first E. I ask them about their clothes.

'Well, I'm like this in my head, I think,' Cordelia grins.

'Pink and fluffy is us both.'

'Fluffy from the land of buzz, that's what we are.'

They're as enthusiastic as William about the event when I ask them why they're here.

'The atmosphere, the being out in the open with loads of people who are all having a fantastic time. Everyone working for the same thing. Fantastic music. Loadsa shops. And everyone, just chatting to everyone. It's just brilliant.'

I ask if they've taken any drugs. After laughing – 'Can't you tell?' – they go on to elaborate.

'We're trolleyed out of our skulls. On blinding pills.'

'It's my first time. It's amazing. I love it.'

'They're green Toyotas. We picked them up from London specially. Because they're so good.'

'And they are blinding.'

Stuart comes in with the technical details. 'The guy we get them off makes them, and they're pretty much like 50/50 MDMA and gelatine, so if you do half a one it's like double-dropping Mitzies. It's mad. They're real good.'

Clearly having a great time, Cordelia slips in a couple of thoughts about how ecstasy could become a political force. 'The guy from the Streets says they could settle wars with this if only you could imagine the world's leaders on pills. So right, though. Cos everyone here is so, you know, mellow. It's fantastic.'

'Amazing,' Sam says for the second or third time, so I ask her if she thinks she might do it again.

'Oh yeah. I love it.'

'She was on the straight and narrow until she met me.'

'It's amazing. I love it.'

I ask her why she decided to take pills tonight.

'Just seeing everyone else doing it, and seeing her come up' – pointing to Cordelia – 'and then wanting it.'

A few hours later I speak to two tiny girls huddled in a blanket, just their pale, wide-eyed faces poking out. They say they're eighteen, although they look about fifteen. Their names are Bouncy and Phenella. They talk in posh, slurred accents and tell me that they've been to lots of illegal raves. They think there's a good vibe but remain unconvinced by the drum and bass tent. They think it's a bit much.

I ask why they've come to an organised festival.

'Always a good ex … ex … what's the word? … ' Bouncy drifts off and looks at her friend.

'Reason?'

'Yeah, I guess you could say reason for getting really fucked and having a good time.'

As the night goes on, it becomes more difficult to have productive conversations with people. They're keen enough to help, but too wasted to be much use. Legs tapping, eyes wandering and losing focus (one teenager I was speaking to just drifted to a stop, closed his eyes and toppled backwards). Sometimes there is a momentous pause as I ask a simple question, and I feel like I'm about to witness something deep. But it doesn't come. Sentences become shorter. Tangents get more random. More questions. Fewer answers.

Homelands is not really about talking through stuff or analysing why people are there. There's little of the philosophy that you find on Erowid and similar sites. But it's unquestionably about changing states. It's about being in the moment. Being in a tent with thousands of other people, listening to the bass, watching the lasers, hearing one song mixed into another. Watching the Oblivion ride that turns into a giant light show at night. Feeling your arms tingle and your vision get messy. It's about playing with the chemicals in your head so that music takes you somewhere else, so you want to jump and scream and smile at whoever is next to you. It's about pure, immediate pleasure.

Of course there are the casualties. The ones who haven't quite got the equation perfect. The pupils threatening to consume the irises. The uncontrollable chewing. The figures hunched over, dry heaving. I see one boy lying semi-conscious on his back, one hand stuffed down his trousers, moving rhythmically as his mates sit round and laugh. A few girls in tears. Drunk arguments. But for most people Homelands delivers what it promises: a load of music and freedom to behave as you like.

The English weather is not kind to twenty-four-hour hedonism. By 4am it's pretty cold, the grass is damp, and there's nowhere to sit. The carnival now resembles a battleground: there is trash everywhere; wide-eyed kids stumble around in the dark, looking for friends. The glamour and energy of the evening is dying. Figures curl under blankets, looking like the corpses of a rave. While others seem oblivious to the cold, wandering around in T-shirts and tiny skirts, pale faces, dark eyes and blotchy skin. Inside the tents, the music continues and crowds are still dancing, but for those who don't want to dance the options are limited.

As the sun comes up, a steady stream of people walk out of the Bowl to their cars. Stereos play and a few hardcore party people shuffle around. Everyone is still skinning up. Others drink tea, checking their pupils in the mirror, to see if they look straight enough to drive. There are police at the exit gate, but they don't seem to be stopping anyone, despite the fact that a good proportion is driving while semi-high.

Pink and fluffy from the land of buzz

Cordelia tells me that she has lots of opinions, and that it would be good to talk more. By the time I finally get to catch up with her, she has just moved to Reading with Stuart to start her teacher-training course. Their street does not look like the land of buzz. It's a dark row of terraced houses. Their flat is sparse and neat and suggests nothing of the visual creativity that their Homelands costumes revealed. Only her hennaed hand and pink fluoro bracelet hint at a wilder lifestyle.

I go to talk to a pink fairy and find myself in conversation with someone who wants to teach autistic children. Cordelia is well spoken and lively and she keeps reminding Stuart that he needs to get a job. At the weekends she takes pills and gets wasted. She has spent the summer living in a squat with a ketamine dealer and tells me stories of finding huddled bodies, vacant stares and piles of vomit whenever she'd get up. Later on she reveals that what she really likes is cocaine. It's her favourite drug. Special-needs teacher and weekend drug-taker are not contradictory. They are both Cordelia.

She mentions that she messed up her sixth-form college but goes on to talk sensitively and passionately about her chosen career. She describes herself as motivated.

'I've always wanted to do teaching; I've always known I'm meant to be in special education. I want to be a head teacher some day. It does make a difference. I've felt myself almost being stuck up at a lot of raves and squat parties because I've just been like "I really enjoy all this but I like it for the weekends". I like to have a job and a life and a car and I want to teach.'

This balance between hedonism and the desire for the good suburban life is further echoed in Cordelia's thoughts about politics. In contrast to many of the kids I spoke to who saw no value in voting, she is strident in her defence of it.

'I think everyone should vote. It bugs me when people say, "We've got nothing good to vote for so I'm not going to vote." It's a human right, I think, to choose who controls you. And also these people will be the first people to sit there and say, "Ugh! I hate this, I hate that, fucking government, fucking don't do this, fucking don't do that." Well, if you voted for the opposition then you can criticise but if you don't vote at all, you know …'

While Cordelia sits across the table from me, talking almost non-stop, playing with her ivory necklace, making sweeping hand gestures, Stuart is laconic and cool on the sofa. Every now and then he speaks, something thoughtful, and often funny. Half the time, Cordelia waves him quiet or just carries on talking anyway. She does indeed have a lot to say. For the next hour Cordelia talks to me about the importance of voting, how she learnt about sex (from *Just 17* magazine), her decision to stop being a pikey and become a hippy, and her Marilyn Monroe outfit that she uses for handing out fliers. The conversation lurches between subjects somewhat chaotically, but this seems to be her life, a constellation of apparent contradictions that nevertheless fit very well together. Throughout the summer she worked to save money for college, living in an environment of ket-inspired squalor, without being too bothered.

'We lived in a flat in a place called Liss and it was a guy who we knew who'd moved out and said, "Oh my God, don't move in there," and we were like, no, no, there's a massive room, the rent is so low, it's a really big room and the guy next door's like a DJ – you know, I thought this was a good thing. You know, "We'll go to all the raves, he's got a big rig and, you know, teach me to mix and all this stuff. Brilliant!" Of course, three in the morning, a great big rig against the walls going "boom boom boom" and I'd got work in the morning. Every night, people all over the place snorting ketamine, you wake up and there's people sick in the sink, there's people all over the floor, your flatmate's snorted eight grams and tried to kill himself again.'

At this point, I'm feeling concerned, and nod thoughtfully as she speaks. She just bursts out laughing, and the anecdotes continue.

'There were so many people coming in the house that you didn't know or trust because the guy we were living with was actually dealing, and he pretty much supplied the whole county with ketamine, and it was coming in and being cooked on my best frying pans.' She starts laughing again as the incongruity of having best frying pans in a semi-squat strikes her.

'They took the mirror down from the bathroom – when I first moved in I was pretty cheerful about it all – and I was like, where's the mirror gone?, and they were like: "We thought we'd take it down because we heard this song that said the bigger the mirror, the bigger the line." So I thought, oh that's funny, so I did some art and wrote: "The bigger the mirror, the bigger the line", and I thought that was all fine but then of course sure enough, they're actually doing lines as big as the mirror and it was just pathetic. They might have been fun in their heads but they weren't fun to look at.'

Cordelia's final disparaging comments about the ket users in her house are telling because they reveal the subtle judgements that substance users make about one another. Nearly all of the users that I speak with believe that they have sussed the best relationship with stimulants, and are often critical of others. So non-ket users will criticise ket users for being messy; ket users see pillheads as tame, and missing out on something. Most drugs users regard alcohol as blunt and inferior, although few of them are teetotal. Like fashion and race, drug use offers another axis of disconnection and attraction. So, while Cordelia will knock her ex-flatmates' excessiveness, she happily admits to her own wasted times. She relives Homelands and describes Sam's first pill.

'At Homelands I got fucked and I came up and it was just fantastic and Sam was like, "I'll just have a tiny bit," and I was like, yes, sure; a tiny bit of these pills will still knock your head off. We were in a shop called Heaven and we were just looking at all the clothes and I'm just like, yes, this is lovely, you know I love you, you're my best friend blah blah blah, and suddenly she was just like …' – Cordelia makes a sighing sound, indicating extreme pleasure – 'you know, she was just like, "Oh my God, I just feel so good, I just can't explain it" and it was as good seeing her come up on that as it was me coming up my first time because she is one of my really best friends and I love her to pieces and I did – even though it seems really bad but I did really want her to experience it because I always – certainly when I'm doing it, I'm having a fantastic time and I want her to share in it, and I think that's the way pills work.'

But surprisingly – given the hippy beads, the stories of raves in fields and the faint smell of joss stick in the air – her true passion lies elsewhere.

'My drug of choice,' she says, laughing again. 'I just can't even think about it else I start going all … is cocaine. I love it. Someone will mention that they're going to get me some cocaine and everything else goes out the window. All I can think about is, like, when are they coming round? Shall I phone them, shall I nag, you know, when are they coming … ? Yes, yes. Cocaine is – and this may offend every man that does it – but cocaine is a girl's drug.' She's laughing again, at this appropriation of a drug for one sex. 'I love cocaine because you can go out clubbing and there's nothing better than cutting up a line on the toilet seat. Sounds really stupid but you go in the loos and all the cubicles will be going … ' – she makes a sniffing sound – 'and you're in there and you're going with the girls and, you know, it's really good. In fact, dreadful as it is, I cut off a line for my little sister on a toilet lid once in a pub in Petersfield.'

We get talking about balance and I wonder how her weekends of excess and abandonment fit in with her plans to be a teacher, and whether there is any contradiction between the two types of lifestyle. She replies that contradictions are only there if you believe they should be. And that people make assumptions that taking part in one activity precludes you from another.

'I once got into an argument with a guy. We were talking and he said, "What do you want to do?" and I said, "I want to be a teacher." And he said, "Isn't that those who can't, teach?" and I said, "No, those who can't, share their best mate's bedroom and snort cocaine all day."'

As Cordelia finishes her anecdote – which I think is meant to show that people can manage multiple interests – Stuart returns to the room from taking a phone call, and their suburban dream life gets one step closer.

'I've just been asked back for that thing on Friday.'

'Well done!' Cordelia exclaims, laughing. 'Stuart has not got a job. We've had real trouble and he's just actually been asked for a second interview.'

Going back to our conversation she tells me that she can balance partying and studying easily, and that she considers her weekends of drug use 'moderate'. And I guess, compared to the flat where she spent the summer, they are. The one allowance she makes is to try not to get busted, by letting Stuart carry the gear.

'At Homelands the drugs we took in, Stuart – it was his birthday but because I'm going into teaching – he put them in between his bum cheeks in lots of plastic because they had sniffer dogs and someone we knew got done for possession.'

From sniffer dogs on to the law, and, unsurprisingly, drug legislation is presented as an irrelevance.

'We always go on the legalisation march – does anyone pay the remotest bit of attention to that law? No, I don't think so, apart from the fact that you know if you do it in a public place you'll get arrested.'

I mention that their portrayal of their drug use, which they talk about in a light-hearted tone as a normal and amusing if sometimes chaotic pastime, hardly fits with the way that teenage drug use is written about in the press.

'What do you think about the way that papers present drug use?'

'There was one story saying: "Cannabis addict commits suicide".' Stuart joins in. 'Right, guy's an art student and he's like manically depressed, parents have split up and at some point he smoked pot, went to counselling and gave up, they said he gave up for six months, right? He was going to counselling, everything was fine, failed his exams, commits suicide. Headline is "Cannabis addict commits suicide".'

'Rather than art student ... '

'Why do you think those kinds of stories exist?'

'Because old people – middle-aged people – are happy in this. It's a market, it's a targeted market to our parents; it's almost like it's scaremongering I think but they need to read it. They think: "Oh my God, my child. I need to read this because it may tell me how to look for signs in my child who may be dying because they ... " They worry, don't they, and I think it's cruel ... because it's making them worry about stuff that isn't really, you know, viable to worry about.'

'It is cruel because there is misinformation; or not misinformation as such. It's just very ...

' ... economical with the truth.'

' ... biased information. I don't think that it's possible to get a newspaper that's not biased but with those particular issues they're so biased it's frustrating when you read it. It's like there's another one I read, "Girl on pills crashes car and kills mates", and it's a girl who took some ecstasy and then a week later crashed her car.' This makes both of them break into laughter again. 'And it's just one of those things. I mean, parents will worry about things and they'll want to find it out and the media kind of, they – what's the word – they rip it up. They make it sound so bad and the parents are like, "Ah, I'm informed about it."'

'Yes, yes, they now think they're with the kids and they can make a judgement.'

Getting it straight

It's easy to find users who will tell you why drugs are so good. And the volume of anti-drug literature and opinion is everywhere. From government reports to a leaflet published by the Church of Scientology called 'The Truth about Joints!', which puts them as the first step on to inevitable heroin addiction. 'Tomorrow's drug addicts are today's joint smokers … a joint is terribly destructive and the consequences of smoking it are catastrophic, particularly for adolescents and children.' The leaflet goes on to blame hashish for the collapse of Arabic society in the fifteenth century.

I wanted a more impartial view as well. To get an idea of the extreme effects that drug use can have on young people, I visit Paddy Screecher, a team leader at the Hungerford Drug Project in Chinatown, London. The service was set up in 1970 and provides support for street homeless people with drug problems. As Paddy explains, 'This is where drugs began in Soho. The first recorded death – the first coke death – was an actress. Cocaine and opium first hit the scene in Chinatown through the docks. The result of that was the first drugs legislation, which was the DORA act, the Defence of the Realm Act. They were worried that foreigners would be making our soldiers take drugs. And they would not be able to defend Britain properly.'

Hungerford uses a mix of creative and complementary health sessions to help 'the most demotivated, chaotic street homeless'. They are designed 'to fight pleasure with pleasure' and they work with the full range of usage: alcohol, heroin, crack, Valium, Rohypnol, cannabis ('Everyone is smoking cannabis on and off as a sort of gentle friend to sit with alcohol') and in many cases a combination of all of these: 'The poly drug users, people who are using heroin and crack and have a Valium habit and drink alcohol as well. The true troubled people at the very bottom of our society.'

Paddy tells me about heroin users with no injectable veins; about people who have turned to the street after physical and sexual abuse at home; about crack users who can't raise enough money through begging each day, and have to turn to robbery and mugging.

'It's very hard to live on the street for long without using a drug. Crack wants you on the street. Everything you can sell eventually you will, including any place you're living in. The street and drugs do go together very well. It is very rare that we meet anyone who lives on the street for a substantial time and doesn't use alcohol or drugs.'

Despite his ongoing contact with the rough, sad, bleak end of drug-taking, Paddy does not believe that drugs inherently lead to bad effects. Even with the extreme cases it's possible to 'see how clearly their drugs were like any other decision you make: a creative attempt to solve a difficulty'.

I arrive expecting cautionary tales and suddenly I'm being told that drugs can have a therapeutic effect, insofar as they allow you to experience a new range of emotions or sensations. To get to a stage in your life that would have been unimaginable without that drug experience.

'I had a bloke who grew up on a Glasgow estate who was at war with his family. People were shot, people were cut in the face. He had crossed scars across his face from a punishment cutting. He discovered heroin when he was sixteen. It was the first time he had ever experienced peace in his life, the first time he had ever had a night's sleep in his life. And only after two or three years of that was he able to learn the experience of peace so he could then go and look for it authentically. And he would know how to recognise it when he found it.'

Indeed, Paddy presents drug use as a way of addressing absences or problems within your life.

'If people's lives are short of magic or meaning, hallucinogens can solve that. They may solve it in such a way that they can drop out the hallucinogens. If people have never experienced confidence or courage then crack or coke can absolutely help them do that. If sex has been a minefield, a terrifying nauseous dangerous place, then heroin can provide salvation. There are so many people who use drugs as a way of pressing a pause button so that, in time, they can get to go somewhere else. And then they can drop the drug.'

Perhaps you shouldn't need to use the drugs in the first place, but in a country which sees over ten million annual prescriptions for SSRIs (drugs like Prozac and Seroxat), the idea of mood or behavioural adjustment via chemicals is embedded. And of course they're acting in the same area. Both Prozac and ecstasy affect the flow of serotonin in the brain. They make you feel happier. Illegal drugs are just a clumsy – and often unpredictable – form of self-medication. But whether they are used to escape problems or to attain rapture, there is the same drive at work: they get you to a different place. They make you feel different.

To see drug use as problem solving or problem causing is to focus on the minority. Paddy knows he sees the worst cases, and perhaps because of this, he realises how distant most drug use is from his experiences.

'It's got to be said that 95 per cent of the people who use drugs in this country do so absolutely unproblematically throughout their lives. The choice to go skiing kills more people each year than the choice to take ecstasy but nobody is legislating against skiing. There is an unspoken moral which as far as I can work it is: it is wrong to change your mental state by taking a substance unless it is given to you by a doctor.'

'Do think the idea of unproblematic drug use is growing among younger people?'

'This is a generation who have taken the full range of pharmaceutical options that are available to them. They have put them into the bit of their head that prior to 1965 was for alcohol. Someone using coke at a party is exactly as normal as someone using alcohol, is exactly as normal as someone smoking dope at the party. Attitudes change, and a younger generation will soon have more power and the law might be closer to expressing their views.'

Paddy makes an analogy between the drugs debate and the euthanasia debate, mentioning a British couple who recently went to Switzerland to commit suicide. Once again, the expansion of personal choice is brought up.

'It's my life, I can do what the fuck I want with it, and you can say that's an expression of existential 21st-century despair or you could say that it's an exciting discovery of a right.'

Getting it straight 2

I go to see Harry Shapiro, director of communications for Drugscope. Waiting near the reception desk I pick up a book – *Waiting for the Man: Music's Relation with Drugs* by Harry Shapiro. I flick through anecdotes about Warhol's factory and amphetamines, about black bombers and ludes, about the early nineties and ecstasy, and wonder which drug typifies our time. And then realise that we've moved on. Drugs are no longer important enough to define a time or influence art. Even as recently as the early nineties, as dance music became mainstream, drugs were the subject and the point of music. You wrote lyrics about drugs for people on drugs. You wrote music that only worked properly when people were high. This still goes on, of course, but it's so embedded in the way we do entertainment that the drugs themselves have become invisible. Drug use is so widespread, so normalised, that drugs are just one possible option, a part of the furniture, or, as Noel Gallagher said: no different to a cup of tea.

Drugscope is a UK charity with two main functions: to provide a public information service on the use of drugs, and to provide help and guidance to professionals who work in the drugs field. It is an enormous resource – the online database is free to use, and contains 90,000 documents on all aspects of drug use.

Harry starts by reeling off the obvious risks associated with drug-taking – from blood-borne diseases to failed relationships to imprisonment.

'Given all the risks,' I ask, 'why do so many people use drugs?'

'It's the same reason why people smoke, why people drink, why people eat chocolate, and gamble. It's to do with escapism, it's to do with risk taking, particularly for young people. It's to do with enjoying the effects. It's a pleasure thing. People don't take drugs because they're horrible. People might not necessarily enjoy all the experiences but the basic motivation for getting off your face is that for the vast majority of people it's a pleasurable experience that does them no lasting damage. So that's a hard one for a lot of people to get their head round. It's not just the mad, sad or bad that get involved in drugs.'

Harry's answer fits easily with the casual approach to drug use that I have found among younger users.

'For the majority of people who have ever tried an illegal drug, even on a reasonably regular basis, they're unlikely to come to any great harm. Some will, but it's the same as cigarettes and alcohol.'

Perhaps one of the biggest factors in young people's drug use is that their experience is very different from the way that drugs are portrayed in the media. Drugs become news because of problems – addiction, crime, mental and physical ailments. But most users do not relate to these shock stories.

Like Paddy, Harry is conscious of the positive effects that drug use can have, and of drugs' potential to get you to places you otherwise might not reach.

'I've talked to people whose experiences of ecstasy have been pretty horrendous and they are really sorry they ever got into it, and other people who were wallflowers, very introverted sort of people, and they have taken ecstasy and it's transformed them, in the sense that they now have social skills that they didn't before. They don't take ecstasy any more but they've actually come out of their shell. They are different people in a positive way.'

Most importantly, Harry presents drug use as the normal human condition. He feels that the war on drugs cannot ever be won, and suggests that our refusal to embrace drug use is an abnormal blip in human history.

'All of the evidence going back, anthropological, archaeological, going back five thousand years, tends to suggest that we as a species are on the constant lookout for ways of altering states of consciousness. However modest that might be, from a bar of chocolate or a mug of coffee to crack and all the stuff in between. If you accept that it's part of our genetic make-up, you might as well try to have a war on envy. It doesn't appear there are any mechanisms, however draconian, that will actually stop the natural desire to change the way you feel.'

'I saw your book in reception. What kind of effect has drug-taking had on popular culture?'

His answer suggests that today's entertainment and fashion culture was kicked off by drugs. For Harry drugs have part created the way the world is now.

'Without cannabis and LSD you wouldn't have had this social phenomenon called the sixties. Up till 1964, from the postwar period, everything was grey. That generation wanted peace, quiet, tranquillity; they'd just come through the Second World War; there was the threat of the Russians blowing them to kingdom come, and then you've got a group of people – artists, musicians, photographers, whatever – suddenly got their hands on this stuff, and transmuted what they saw under the influence of these drugs into popular culture. They brought it all in, and all of a sudden people are walking around in bright yellow and reds and flowers and all the rest of it. I can't possibly see how such an explosion could have happened without a catalyst like that.'

Stealth highs

The UK government might be unwilling to face up to the complete penetration of drugs into contemporary Britain, but other large organisations are not so slow to spot our willingness to improve our physical and mental states through chemicals.

Edwin Moses is a director of eight life science companies around Europe, including Oxford Asymmetry International, Evotec and Inpharmatica. He suggests that not all recreational drugs are produced by criminals, and points towards a time when drugs and recreation are more intertwined. He quotes Viagra as an example of pharmaceutical companies accidentally discovering a drug with vast recreational potential. As well as the people with erectile dysfunction, it's used by many simply to enhance their performance.

'Pharma companies are aware of what they call non-label usage. They are aware that very often drugs are used in much larger quantities than for the application they were developed. So they'll register a drug for a certain application because it's easy to get it registered, and they know full well that people are buying it in bagloads for something else.'

Edwin has little doubt that the use of chemicals for recreational purposes will continue to grow, because of users' desire and because of pure market forces. And that pharma companies will continue to encourage stealth recreational usage.

'The market for that is huge. How many people have got any one disease? Not a lot. How many people would like to have their taste improved? Well, every single one of us.'

I take this thought a bit further, carried away by the idea of a stream of legitimate, safe chemicals. How many people would like to be happier, smarter, less tired, etc? Every one of us, of course.

'The market is the world. How many people can use Viagra? Well, half the population can. So you've suddenly got the entire population as your market for recreational drugs, rather than a subset.

'Viagra is the biggest-selling drug in the world because of its recreational use. You don't have to be particularly smart to realise that this is interesting. I think the sense of smell and taste are ones you could look at. Visually you could imagine a drug that might improve 3-D vision to tie in with PlayStation. Or something to improve your reaction speeds.

'The main problem with recreational drugs is that currently they're used in a non-regulated fashion. They're made in the back streets with bits of everything in, or used in an uncontrolled fashion. If you regulated that, both in the manufacturing and then sub-typed them to the person who was taking them, and find out where it was safe to take ecstasy, then you get rid of all the safety problems.'

And then it's a question of morality and law. And whether, as a society, we are able to accept a broader range of chemical playmates. Of course, as Edwin points out, there are other influences too.

'Nobody thinks twice about having a couple of pints and that's mood-altering. There is no difference in my mind at all between marijuana and cigarettes. The line is entirely historic and taxation-related. Some of the legal drugs are much more harmful. Governments will think in terms of taxation. The lost revenues of cigarette taxes. A way to make up that revenue would be to get the population hooked on another drug that was safe. That will not be beyond the politicians. If you legalised and controlled drugs you'd clear away a lot of the problems. A lot of the dangers that exist now are caused by the lack of regulation.'

From my chats with users, and from reading a bundle of drug-related publications, I am convinced of the large number of people who use drugs as a means of expanding the range of available sensations, of growing their opportunities for pleasure.

'Do you think drug use can lead to a fuller life?'

'It is possible to have a different life. Some people won't take any stimulants at all. Other people think stimulants are exactly what they need to do. It's about personal choice. But I think the opportunities for that personal choice will be increased considerably.'

Drugs are normal. Are you?

According to most media and the government, drugs are a problem. They ruin lives. They kill people. A war exists that can be won. Despite widespread and generally unproblematic consumption, the media focuses almost entirely on a small number of freak accidents. Two of the more visible stories in 2003 are about a five-year-old ecstasy victim and a woman who pulls all her teeth out while on GHB to stop a luminous pink and green fly from choking her.

But for millions of young Britons it seems drug use is completely normal. British youth loves drugs. They love taking them, talking about taking them, snapping photos of each other when they have taken them. Wearing clothes that boast about their ability to take more of them. I had been aware of drugs' omnipresence at the start of this book, but following my festival visits and conversations, I get a much better sense of how easily they fit in with most elements of young Britain.

Among the users and the drug workers, the bong sellers and Mongo hotline editors – even among the big pharmaceutical companies – there is a practical acceptance and positive attitude towards recreational drug use that has outpaced any governmental or public action or any mainstream media utterance.

At the core of young Britain's love affair with drugs is the fierce belief stated by nearly all of the kids I talked with – and echoed by Edwin, Harry and Paddy – that nobody else should judge what you do to yourself. That what you do to your head is your business. And for these people that business is about pleasure. Getting high is a legitimate activity.

But official Britain is a place where certain drugs become harder or softer depending on the prevailing political climate. Where you can be prosecuted for being a dealer if you sort out a few mates. Where ecstasy is a killer, and smoking dope is one small step away from banging up smack. Where you're allowed to feel well, but not better than well.

This government-endorsed reality is so far from anybody's experience that it is irrelevant: opponents and users might as well be considering a different topic. There might be a slight shift towards making a couple of drugs slightly less illegal, but absolutely no attempt to represent or understand the perceptions of millions of satisfied users. Users who see illegality as an obstacle to scoring but not much of one. Who see no problem with using drugs to alter their moods or develop their personality. Who use drugs weekly, daily, without problems. Who use drugs to get high. To get somewhere else. Wasted is a popular place.

On one hand, they are wasted. But from their point of view they are using drugs because it makes sense. Drugs make music sound better, lights look weirder, conversation go faster, funnier, loopier. They make you see, hear, feel things differently. They are about experience. Immersion. The goal of drugs is hardly different from the goal of great literature or surround-sound widescreen TV. It's one more PlayStation game. It's about changing your perceptions. Only the means of getting there is different.

As Deedi puts it: 'It's just: people like getting high. I like looking at the world in a different way is all.'

Drugs are one more option among multiple entertainment choices. Experiences are enhanced. Added to. Stimulus is used in a different way. And so, on the other hand, nothing is wasted at all.

'Have you had a threesome?'

Children as young as five should be given sex education lessons, experts have recommended. But Robert Whelan, of the campaign group Family and Youth Concern, said: 'We are opposed to sex education in primary schools. It is far too young. It is a form of child abuse. You are robbing children of their innocence and giving them information they are not ready for. You're taking away their childhood.'

BBCi News, July 2003

... the growth of porn has accelerated to a point where definitive statistics are virtually impossible to compile. Many of the numbers stretch way beyond what most of us can comprehend. Nevertheless, to give you some idea, here are some random examples. Some 200 million people are online worldwide, and studies place pornography at between 20 and 30 per cent of all internet traffic.

If they are halfway close to the truth, our relationship with porn begins to seep into the banal. Pornography is treated more like fast food than sex; a casual everyday snack.

Observer, March 2003

Sex in public

The image shows a close-up of a woman's thigh. Moisture drips down it. You can see the bulge of her pubic hair behind the semi-transparent panties. A hand rests provocatively on flesh. But this isn't porno; it's the poster for MJ Cole's album *Cut to the Chase*. And it's fliered all over cities across the UK. On bridges, and walls, telephone circuit boxes and spare ad hoardings. There for any kid or respectable couple to see.

The streets have gone sexual. What used to be kept on the top shelf and protected from under-eighteens now swarms everywhere. It's not just MJ Cole who's at it. The murky and unregulated world of flyposters continually puts out.

French Connection is perhaps partly responsible. The genius abbreviation of the brand name to FCUK in 2000, and subsequent heavyweight ad campaign, meant that, to anyone who wasn't anagram incompetent, the English language's second rudest cuss was suddenly unavoidable.

Since then the Androids' poster has asked the public: 'Who would you do it with?', in bold type above the images of Kylie, Christina, Madonna and Pink lookalikes. An ad for the movie *Rules of Attraction* shows teddy bears in all kinds of positions – from missionary to bare back to doing it teddy style. And of course the brands have got in there too.

In May, Mates condoms runs a campaign, ostensibly promoting their website – ishaggedhere.com – but really just an excuse to stick up a bunch of posters with euphemisms for fucking. So you're greeted by the Mates logo glistening like a fresh shot of sperm and 'reverse cowgirl' or 'parking the pink bus' snaking along a wall for 20 metres. In the run-up to Christmas, Ann Summers goes public with an ad for its best-selling vibrator, the Rampant Rabbit. A giant poster welcomes drivers on the Cromwell Road with the message: 'A rabbit is for life, not just for Christmas.' Other messages flyposted around town include: 'Santa's little yelper' and 'Oh come all ye faithful'. The ad doesn't feature the vibrator – a cute bunny is the only image – but the fact that millions of London women are being encouraged to buy something to help them wank better shows how far sex has leaked into public space.

Britain is a highly sexualised society. From music videos featuring nearly naked young girls to celebrity confessions (in November, Britney Spears – that one time no-sex-before-marriage puritan – gives an interview where she boasts about how often she masturbates and how it makes her a better lover), to documentaries (*Club Reps*, *Ibiza Uncovered*, *Teenage Kicks*, etc, etc), to the growing explicitness of mainstream cinema (Meg Ryan's *In the Cut* begins with an incredibly realistic and lengthy blowjob scene), sex is everywhere. Watch any of the music channels, and it's non-stop. Jiggling booty, grabbed crotches, bare midriffs form a backdrop of flesh and suggestiveness. And the sex tips that used to be the domain of *Cosmo* have drifted younger and to the other sex, with magazines from *Men's Health* to *Sugar* flaunting their latest advice on the cover. Even the theatre gets a look-in. In April *La Fura Dels Baus* comes to the UK. *XXX* runs in the Riverside Studios for a couple of weeks, and features endless nudity and some fairly authentic sex scenes where you can't quite tell if they're using a prosthetic penis or not.

While the pervasiveness of sex crosses the whole of Britain, once again, it's the younger participants who bear the brunt of criticism. Sex may be public, everyone may be at it, but for teens it tends to be presented in problematic terms. The story about sex and teens is one of inappropriately early sex education, an explosion of STDs and a casual approach to fucking that makes the sexual revolution of the sixties sound like a Victorian piano rehearsal.

If drugs are one topic guaranteed to fluster the tabloids, sex is another. As with most stories about teens, what makes the headlines, what influences the documentaries, is the extreme, the consciously wild and irresponsible. In July, I'm drinking tea, reading the papers, and the cover of the *Sun* is all about Shevaun Pennington, the twelve-year-old girl who spends four days in Europe with an American marine after meeting him in a chatroom and apparently convincing him that she was nineteen. The story has everything that plays on Britain's fear of sex: an underage girl, contact via the sexually drenched internet, a runaway.

Such attitudes towards teen sex and the internet are further supported by companies like Symantec, whose ad for their internet security product shows a young girl at a computer. Her mother reads the newspaper in the background, oblivious to whatever her daughter is surfing. On the front of the newspaper, in huge letters, the warning: 'Stalkers could use the internet to contact your children.'

On the same day that Shevaun takes the *Sun*'s front page, the paper's centre pages continue their week's series of visiting Britain's sexiest cities and talking to the teens and twentysomethings about their rampant sex lives. With titles like 'Surf's up, pants down', and 'We love to get our Southend away', the series finds a host of kids who are happy to flash their undies and confess to wild outdoor sex.

From celebrating the lusty appetites of young Britain, the paper lurches into full panic mode. One headline reads: 'The sex plague: Britain is in the grip of a terrifying increase in sexual diseases. Cases of AIDS and other potential killers are soaring out of control.'

Southend, Shevaun, Symantec, Soham. These are the stories Britain tells itself, our cautionary tales. The two main archetypes: unashamed disease-ridden hedonism; and older men preying on young girls. Extremes of excess and innocence with little in between. But these are the edges of young sexuality and hyper hormones. Are they really the inevitable endpoint of a sexually explicit Britain? To get a fuller picture I talked to fetish models, sex clinics and campaigners for virginal marriages. I also spent an afternoon surfing porn online. Doing it during daytime seemed less shabby.

Oversexed

The eroticisation of our streets has become so acceptable, so invisible, because we have got used to sex elsewhere. And nothing is more responsible for exploding the volume of sex that kids see, hear and talk about than the internet.

Sex, or more correctly porn, has been described as the engine of the internet. Porn sites have led the way in innumerable innovations: from online payments, to Adult Verification, from pioneering the use of live cams to growing loyal audiences. You came here first.

The ways of measuring the amount of sex available to any surfer are multiple and probably unreliable, but whichever you choose they point to a lot of clicking. Whether it's favourite search terms, the stat that a quarter of all internet traffic is sex related, the quote that '10 per cent of e-mails are pornographic'. This stuff gets around.

The net is not as free or unregulated as it once was. Many more sites require some form of Adult Verification – which in turn requires a credit card – before you can see much, but for anyone who can be bothered to spend a few minutes looking around for free pix, the rewards are bountiful and various. The net has made sexual imagery accessible, a commodity. And it shows the extremes of sexual possibility, the endless permutations and iterations that are possible when people get naked and have a camera pointed at them. As with other areas of contemporary entertainment, there is no end to what is on offer. There is always more.

As well as the usual – the twosomes, the threesomes, the lezzers, the giant cocks, the oversized and the tiny breasts, the teens, the Asians – there are the more specialist. 'MILF: Mothers I'd like to fuck.' 'Chix with dix.' 'Spunk Farm – for women who love animals.' And so on. Conjoineddreams.net presents a series of doctored photos: naked women in various stages of duplicity. The creator confesses to an interest in identical twins. Since there aren't that many conjoined porn stars, he's had to make his own. Most of them have two heads, but from then on it's fluid. Two, three and four breasts, separate torsos but shared legs, a pair of identical torsos that meet at the waist. And all of them smiling coyly, brazenly, sluttily at the camera.

It goes on: `X-rated slut cams, free porn in your e-mail, real-life housewives hungry for hot cum, UK Housewife XXX fuckfest, watch juicy teen pussies get broken in and pounded with hard cocks! Free Sluts. Adult Dreams. Nasty Black Sex. Pure Teen Porn. Obey Me Slave. Planet Lesbian. Sorority Review. Fantasy Latina. Tiny Petite Babes. Nice Butts. Anal Valley. Hot Asian Cherry. Get Hung. Anal Debutants. First Lesbian Kiss. Awesome Orgy. Transsexual Uniform Voyeur XXXXXXXXXXXXXXXXXXXXX`. An entire alphabet of porn.

A blur of panties pulled aside, pouting lips, blowjobs and sperm-soaked smiles. Page after page of different women and men. You can never outrun porn. And the webmasters understand this weariness. Not for porn the passivity of other websites, where the user decides when he will leave one site and go elsewhere. In porn world, you click on an image and several windows open. Even as you close them, others appear, urging you to seek out one more cumshot, one more housewife, one more titwank.

In a world where sex is about pleasure far more than babies, the real fecundity, the procreation is here. Where pix give birth to more pix, windows open on to more windows in an endless generative cycle.

It's not just the dark corners of the web that show you sex. If you visit the Mates site, you find a brand-endorsed celebration of outdoor sex. At the home page, the two g's swim across the screen like sperm to make the word shagged, and you are invited – of course – to come in. Once there, it's public stories about public sex, showing how happy people are to discuss what used to be considered a private activity.

```
i beat u
your attempts don't even compare to mine!! 1) under a willow
tree 2)back of a bus 3) front of a bus 4) my parents bed
5) my best mates kitchen unit 6) in a cab 7) my college
common room 8) restaurant wash room 9) against a lamp post
10) in a museum (we got caught!!) 11) the balcony of a
theatre (the play was boring) 12) a car parked on a high
street 13) in a hospital 14) my work stockroom
15) chessinton 16) a white sand beach 17) a fun fair 18) his
auntie's swimming pool 19) the fire escape stairs … and last
but not least … 20) the infamous aeroplane toilet!!! i know,
i know, i'm a hussy!!!! but, can anyone beat that?!?!?!
                            this story has been uploaded by danlyn2413
```

This willingness to tell all is evident in many places. On Face Party, Shelley16, a nineteen-year-old student from the West Midlands, smiles up at the camera in pants and a bra. Her profile tells us that sex makes her happy, not getting sex makes her sad, and her bad habits include not wearing any knickers.

And at the back of *Max Power* magazine – one of the modified-car kids' bibles – as well as in the babes section of the website, girls are quizzed about their sexual preferences. These aren't models … just the girls who turn up at some of the cruises. But they seem happy to answer anything. So Emma, sixteen, from Ipswich smiles up at the camera.

Favourite sexual position: *Legs behind ya head*
Consider a threesome: *Already done it*
Spit or swallow? *Swallow*

Such a casual and lightweight approach to sex does not always lead to irresponsibility, though. Carina and Lucy, the two girls who tell me quite happily about their sex with boyfriends in parked cars, display a mixture of playful eroticism and personal morality that is more complex and sensitive than the papers would suggest. After both telling me about doing their boyfriends in car parks across Essex with obvious glee and no shame, Lucy's tone changes.

'I have only slept with one person. I can blatantly put my hands up and say I have only slept with one person in my life. And I have been with him for three years.'

'But *we* do things … '

'I mean we do stuff together, to wind boys up and that.'

'We kiss each other. Grope each other.'

'Snog each other, always do it.'

'We always get off with each other, we say we are bisexual and stuff like that.'

To prove this, they make a point of touching each other's breasts while looking at me and laughing. They might as well be holding each other's hands.

This casualness towards sexual contact is further typified by Carina's story about watching her friend have sex on the front of a car.

'My mate done someone on the front of his car, and she was completely naked, she was all drunk one night … out the front of my mate's house, on the front bonnet.'

'Of the jeep.'

Both Carina and Lucy are in hysterics by this point. When they stop laughing, Carina continues, lurching from voyeurism to disapproval in one sentence.

'And there was a blue flashy torchlight and I kept shining it on her, it was well funny. But things like that are just, do you know what I mean, sex is well bad these days, everyone goes with everyone. All these youngsters that everyone goes with everyone.'

'Having babies and that.'

'I am saying that my groups of mates, like my sister's groups of mates, they have all slept with each other and they think it is normal. My sister said to me all her boy mates, they have slept with all the girls. They just think it is normal. They go yes, I have done him, done her, and things like that.'

'You don't agree?'

'I am not like that, no. I haven't.'

Wait a minute

To get a flavour of the damage that our sexualised society is causing I go to visit Robert Whelan, director of Family Education Trust, working title Family and Youth Concern. I find their website when looking for British organisations who recommend sexual abstinence before marriage. I knew of several in the US but wasn't sure if that brand of restraint had found its way over here, and if it had, how it was being received by our oversexed teenagers.

Abstinence is not a popular word these days. People don't like being told what not to do; or more importantly not to do something yet, because it will be better later. Abstinence fits uneasily in a world of instant credit, instant food and condom machines in every club and bar toilet.

And I wasn't sure what I expected; surely not the furious preaching of American stadium-fillers, whose zealous and sweaty pulpit-bashing just convinced you that they had a fifteen-year-old waiting in their tasteless limo out back. I knew that the FYC was a secular organisation; but an American woman had answered the phone when I'd called to set up the meeting …

The FYC is a couple of minutes from Waterloo station. To get there you walk over raised sidewalks, two storeys up, that would have looked great in the architects' drawings (avoid the traffic, view the City like a bird) but invariably end up full of graffiti and piss. Three hairy tramps puff on roll-ups and count change in the spring sun. Kids spit down the stairwell to street level. There are burn marks along one wall, giving a textured backdrop to the flurry of tags. I imagine the members of the FYC making this journey every day, despairing at the signs of social collapse.

On arrival, I'm offered a seat and some pamphlets to read: *The Condom Controversy*, *Sex under Sixteen?*, *Deconstructing the Dutch Utopia*. The office is one open room, full of computers and files. A bookcase crammed with titles: *The Loss of Virtue*, *Catholic Directory*, *Reclaiming Education*. The people seem earnest and friendly, with slightly shabby, badly fitting office clothes: slacks, blouses, suits with jumpers underneath. I wonder at the difficulty of communicating with a fashion-sensitive generation when you so obviously signal your difference.

Robert Whelan, the director of FYC, is smartly dressed and softly spoken. Normally, I find men who wear cartoon ties with expensive suits somewhat bizarre, like they're trying to convey that beneath the business-like exterior there is a wacky guy, but in this context, the *101 Dalmatians* tie is plaintive, almost touching. Here is a man who wants to save the lost children.

There is no rant from Robert, nor an insistence that everyone live according to the codes set out by the FYC. Instead, he focuses on the lack of impartial information that is available to children, as well as the fact that people don't choose to be single parents, to get divorced or to have abortions. These are things that happen to people. He identifies the factors that we often see as giving us a certain lifestyle freedom – the pill, abortion, quickie divorces, etc – as causes of family breakdown.

'The whole of modern culture is saturated in sex. Very sexually oriented, and that's why it's difficult for parents: you're bringing your children up in this culture where they are going to be bombarded by sexual imagery, and you're trying to work against that. Public authorities should be supporting the parents, doing the best for their children. Sex education can be a form of pressure, because if you give youngsters the idea that everyone is doing it, then they think there is something wrong if they're not doing it.

'Everyone's free to live as they want, but real freedom only comes when it's based on full knowledge of the different choices. And the trouble is that kids get into these relationships very young and they're too young to know what the outcomes are, and they need the guidance of the older generation. But they are increasingly being separated from them.'

Robert firmly believes that parents, and responsible members of the older generation, are the people who should be telling young people about sex. That it should be coming from limited and controlled sources. In our information-drenched culture, I find the idea of controlling where kids find anything out – especially something as tempting as sex – an unlikely situation.

FYC describes the sex education that is provided in schools as amoral, because it explains sex without attaching consequences to it.

'There are no moral values attached. They deal with relationships as if they happen in a moral void, as if no arrangement is better than any other arrangement. They don't give you the full facts. They give kids the impression that it's okay to sleep around, just use contraception, you'll be fine. Apart from physical problems, there are emotional problems, starting relationships at an age when they are not mature enough to handle them.'

As he says this, I think of my own string of relationships, which in Robert's eyes would be failures because of their temporariness; I think of the chaotic nature of so many adult couples, and wonder if we ever really become mature enough to handle them.

The FYC is unhappy with the way that sex education has been taken away from the parents. So that even if parents do not want their kids to undergo the form of sexual education practised in their schools, there is little they can do. The health authorities now run clinics in schools, and they are not subject to the restrictions of educational activities.

'The clinics in schools just assume that children are going to have sex, and therefore the only thing you can do is give them contraception, but actually children are not necessarily going to have sex. It's not the same in other areas of health education. You don't say children are going to smoke anyway so let's give them free cigarettes.'

So, is there an alternative to this laissez-faire attitude? I ask Robert about teaching abstinence before marriage, and whether it is a practical or possible strategy for today's sexually aware youth. In 2002, FYC had arranged for a Canadian group called Challenge to visit schools in the UK and talk about abstinence. One of the pamphlets I take away with me trumpets the success of the visit.

The response was tremendous. The message was clear and simple. Over 5,000 pupils in England and Wales aged 13-plus heard that sex has consequences. Being a young single parent is not fun. Contracting a sexually transmitted infection is not fun. Contraception reduces risk, but does not eliminate it. Sex is special — it is the most intimate gift that a man and a woman can give to each other. Saving sex for a future marriage partner increases the chances of that marriage being happy and lifelong. Teenage audiences sat in rapt attention as they listened to the team. You could have heard a pin drop. Students responded to the presentations with words such as: 'wicked', 'really cool', 'I really respect them', 'I'm glad I'm still a virgin', 'I'm going to wait till I get married from now on', 'It really made you think'.'

Robert is keen to point out that the views of the Challenge teams were fresh, unheard of. A different possible way of viewing sex.

'Well, they ought to know it's an option. At the moment it's just not being presented. That's why the Challenge team are doing so well, because people are saying they have just never heard it … a new radicalism. It's new to a lot of people. In the sixties people were rebelling against the standards of their parents' generation, but now youngsters haven't got anything to rebel against because they didn't grow up knowing any standards.'

A couple of months later I talk to Vicky Hamburger, a TV producer/director who had made a programme called *The Joy of Teen Sex* a couple of years back and had more recently been researching abstinence in the States. Her take on abstinence is somewhat different from Robert's.

'The STD rates and the pregnancy rate in Texas, which is where one of the big drives for abstinence is, are going through the roof. All they are taught is not to have sex. No one talks about sex, apart from the abstinence educator, who puts quite a lot of fear in them. Yet, these are kids with hormones and they are going to explore. So it is pretty clear that it is not working, because they are still getting diseases, and getting pregnant. I don't think that is a result of abstinence education, but it does turn a blind eye to all of that, so it doesn't address the fact that kids are going to be sexually active. They think that if you teach kids about sex, it is going to encourage them to have sex. Which is rubbish, because kids are having sex anyway.'

Open access

I am fascinated by Robert's attitude towards sex. Not merely his belief that abstinence could return in full force as a source of youth radicalism, but also his hatred for sex education and the clinics that hand out contraception. To meet the beast, I go to visit Paula Currie who works as a locality manager for Brook Clinic in Euston.

The five-minute walk from London's Euston station to Brook Clinic gives me a quick hit of explicit sexual imagery and language, as pervasive and normal as road signs and cracked paving slabs. The first flyposter I see appropriately screams out 'Sex is everywhere' in bold black and red lettering. It's actually promoting a film called *Roger Dodger*, but the title takes second place. The fly type reads: 'It's all around us, it's not some distant destination. It's right here. You have to attune yourself to it.'

It's hard not to attune yourself to it: right next to it is a row of posters for Machine Gun Fellatio's EP, 'Impossible Love', featuring hits like 'Mutha Fukka on a Motorcycle' and the more surprising 'Not Afraid of Romance'. The poster shows a picture of a rabbit mounting a chicken, or more accurately a rooster, so the impossible love in this case, rather than referring to some tragic love story, seems to be all about the mechanical difficulty of cross-species homosexuality.

The walls on Chalton Street are, of course, covered in pen. 'Black boys rule', 'Becky is my girl', 'Debbra sucks cock'. The clinic is a few doors down from the Cock Tavern. As I ring the bell, I imagine teenage boys lingering outside, distressed by strange and painful changes to their genitals, staring angrily up at the pub name.

Paula is at the reception, where there is an A4 list of the reasons for visiting (smear test, pregnancy test, STI, etc). This means that visitors can just point. This sensitivity to the potential shyness of sexually active teens goes throughout the clinic. There are leaflets in the toilets so that nobody has to see which ones you are picking up. They are trying to get artwork from local schools so that the clinic loses some of the feel of an impersonal hospital. Certainly Paula has little of the NHS about her. In her mid-twenties, she has one of those zigzag centre partings and short tousled blond hair at the back. She dresses neatly.

The Brook Clinic is a national centre for sexual advice and education, aimed at younger people. It has a waiting room, a doctor's room, a nurse's room and a counsellor's room. The counselling is an important part of the service, Paula explains.

'For many of the people who come here, sexual health and activity is just one of the many issues that they are dealing with: parents in prison or on drugs, family violence, poverty, etc. Often, the counselling is as important as the health advice that is given, and is one of the factors that makes Brook more approachable and useful than hospital GU clinics or the local GP. If you're very young, going to a huge hospital, you're probably having to tell four strangers what you're doing or at least where you're going and that puts people off.'

For Paula, access and ease of use is everything, which is why you don't need an appointment and why Brook is open after school and on

Saturdays. Yet the amorality that Robert had mentioned to me seems exaggerated. Rather than just handing out pills and condoms, the centre offers more holistic support for young people. I ask Paula about the perception that clinics hand out contraceptives thoughtlessly to anyone who comes in.

'There is a reality to the services that we provide and we're very aware that young people need access to contraception. They are having sex and 90 per cent of our work is providing services that are in demand and are needed by young people. We have a really sexualised society but the information behind that is not put across very well. There are young people who still need to be informed about access; there are others who need reassurance and help to put knowledge into their real life.

'If there's a perception that some judgement is being made about them or their attitude or lifestyles, then they don't actually access services,' she continues. 'The apportioning of blame is irrelevant. The fact is more young people need to be attending STI services, so how do services make that happen? The wider moralisms are a separate political opinion. My interest is in helping people to act in a way that they can access, and find more about how to protect their sexual health.'

For critics of these sexual health clinics, accessibility is the cause of our current sexual crisis. For Paula, who readily admits there is a crisis, accessibility is the one thing that might help. This is in marked contrast to people like Robert or Dr Trevor Stammers from St George's hospital, London, who believes that saying no is the only way to 'reverse the tide of sexual infections engulfing young people'.

These opposing views remind me of the differing attitudes towards entertainment that I have encountered. At the core of both is the issue of teenagers' ability to deal with unmediated information or entertainment. Or whether there should be stricter controls. Certainly Paula has little time for a message of abstinence.

'The debate around sex education encouraging young people to have sex is a redundant one. The more information you have around any choice – whether it's your mortgage, your dentist or any aspect of your life – the more ability you have to control your own destiny.'

In Paula's world, sexual behaviour is one more lifestyle choice. The question is not so much whether you should be doing it, but that if you are, you are doing it as well and as responsibly as you can. This stretches beyond simple contraceptive choices into the areas of how you conduct relationships.

She paints a picture of teens who are genuinely interested in coming into centres, finding out about STIs and negotiating relationships. The best that a service can do is support that interest, and make it as easy as possible for them to access information. She gestures around the waiting room. There are posters about gay Asians, abortions and love stings, posters featuring young black males being friendly to each other, a poster of a happy couple cuddling on a bed with a condom packet in front of them.

Paula is adamant that sex education should happen before people are sexually active. As she says this, I consider what other leisure activities that are so tied up with people's emotional and physical health are embarked on without any prior information, or only gossip and guesswork. You wouldn't start driving lessons after you'd taken a car for a spin.

'Can you be too young for sex education?'

'The perception around sex education is that it is about intercourse and actually sex education for very young people is not necessarily about that; it's about awareness of being touched; and that's important for young people: to know what is appropriate behaviour, and what you should do and say and who you should tell if those situations ever come about. From a very young age, being able to say no, stop, I'm not comfortable, I'm telling my mum, or whoever, is actually really important. It's about whether you can negotiate when and where and if to have sex.'

Robert believed that parents were being excluded from the process of sex education, while Paula feels it is essential that they are brought into the debate. So, on this point at least, there is some common ground between Robert and Paula.

'It's the information that is important. Withholding that is never going to be a solution. To either party. Young people are curious. Moving the debate forward to include parents is really important. Most parents might not want it to happen, but if it is they want to know that their son or daughter is safe. Given the reality of their son or daughter feeling so isolated, you want someone to help them. Many parents are supportive of us. The relationship between parents and their kids is quite complicated around sex, so that's why it is important that they have somewhere they can go.'

This makes me think that it's not only sex where parents have less of an influence on their kids' lives. As the number of available information sources expands, so the number of occasions when parents are the best source of advice or information decreases.

Perhaps the clearest thing to emerge from my conversation with Paula is the fact that teenage sex doesn't have to be problematic. That it can be responsible and pleasurable. And that sex education can help teenagers to do sex better. More safely and with more mutual respect for their partners.

'We see on average about fifty young people a day. Sex is a part of young people's lives. Brook can allow young people the confidence and the practicality to enjoy their sexuality in a safe way. Safe for themselves and safe for the people they are having sex with. There's something key about Brook being able to support young people to enjoy their sex life, which is different from other people who come into the debate about the pros and cons of sex. We want them to be able to explore it, but safely. I think it's fine if young people don't want to have sex before they are married, but the reality for most young people is very different.'

Starting young

Magazines like *Sugar* add to the whirl of sex info and chat out there. *Sugar* is for 13- to 16-year-olds, but 21st-century sweetness is a million miles away from candy and all things nice. It claims over a million readers, putting it head and shoulders above any other teen girl mag. As well as providing entertainment, in terms of celeb news, fashion and music, assistant editor Charlotte Blackburn likens it to an elder sister, passing on wisdom about 'dealing with bullying, family problems, sex, all the sort of things that are happening at that time'.

And there's obviously a need for this elder sister. Sugar 'gets a sackload of mail every single day' asking for advice and direction (she assures me that all the problem page letters are genuine), which she attributes partly to the inadequacy of other information sources.

'We did some research recently, and 85 per cent of the respondents were too embarrassed to talk to their parents about issues like boys and sex. However, 70 per cent of those wish they could talk to their parents. And a lot of them felt that they did get a lot of their information from magazines like *Sugar*.'

While Charlotte makes no claim for *Sugar*'s superiority to more official sources, she tells me that they do have regular meetings with the government to discuss how to get a responsible sex message across, and that they've worked with the Teenage Pregnancy Unit, who were looking for 'advice on how to phrase things in sex education lessons'. When I ask why *Sugar* works so well, the answer is unsurprising.

'We speak to the readers on their level. A lot of the stuff that the government does talks down to them.'

'What about the accusations that *Sugar* encourages girls to think of themselves as sexual beings before they're ready? And encourages them to have sex?'

'That couldn't be further from the truth. All teenage magazines are bound to run by the TMAP [teenage magazine arbitration panel] guidelines, which were drawn up a number of years ago in conjunction with all the teenage magazines and the Department of Health. We have not been ruled against for a number of years. The guidelines are all based around informing and educating, and empowering teenagers. The main *Sugar* sex advice is: "Never have sex unless you are 100 per cent ready." "It is illegal under the age of 16." "Every time you have sex, always protect yourself against diseases and pregnancy." "If you are in any doubt whatsoever, slow down, there is no rush. You don't need to do this now. You shouldn't be doing it because all your friends are doing it, you shouldn't be doing it because you think your boyfriend will dump you, and unless you are happy." We don't talk about sexual pleasure, we don't talk about technique or anything like that.'

I check out an issue and have to agree with her. *Sugar*'s tone is informative and helpful. The problem page, entitled 'You and sex', covers everything from contraception to wet dreams.

A thirteen-year-old reader writes.

'I overheard one of my older sister's friends saying she doesn't like foreplay when she has sex with her boyfriend, but I don't know what foreplay is. Can you tell me?'

'Foreplay is a term for the touching and the kissing people do before they have sex. Some people find it gets them "in the mood" but others, like your sister's friend, don't enjoy it. But the important thing is to

make sure that you don't ever do anything that you're not happy with —
and not to have full sex until you are legally old enough.'

In the txt SOS, the communication is minimal, but still helpful.

'Me & my boyf have neva had sex bbt we laid on top of each
other wiv our clothes on. Now my period is 18 & Im scared im
pregnt.'

'u cant be pregnt if u haven't had sex or tuched each other
intimately. There r reasons why u r 18 so C ur doc.'

Reading through *Sugar* I get a similar sense of the curiosity and hunger for
information that Paula had talked about. Clearly sex is an area of
fascination and attraction. To be able to contain this in any way seems
unlikely and naive.

Jokes about paedophiles

Near Guildford, a few miles from the M3, I drive through calm suburbia,
neat gardens, Jeeps in the driveway, cutesy street and house names, into
a circular cul-de-sac where weeping willows protect a semicircle of
seventies detached houses, men wash their cars and three eleven-year-old
girls talk happily to me about paedophiles, slasher movies and snogging
boys, while one of their mums sits and laughs with them.

Becky, Hannah and Livie marry young excitement with occasional adult
sensibilities and awareness. When I ask them what their dreams are, the
answers swing between the practical and the cute. Livie aims to be a
fashion designer and has it all mapped out: 'I'll probably go to college for
two years and when I'm eighteen I want to go to America – to the
California Fashion College to learn the designs.'

Hannah's reply is more simplistic. She laughs as she tells me, 'I like tills.
I like pressing buttons on tills so I want to do something like that. And
then I want to do something magic … like David Blaine.'

The three girls sit on the sofa together, constantly touching and looking
at each other. Livie's older brother watches TV the whole time I'm there

and hardly speaks. Angela, their mum, perches on a chair next to them, and so they form a row of swishing blonde heads. In the couple of hours I spend with them I notice how far parental disapproval has disappeared. Angela seems to collude with the girls. The mum starts to tell me how much 'the girlies love the high life'. After that one-liner the rest of the story is told by four voices, each cascading over the other, replaying a story that is clearly well worn.

Livie begins the tale. 'For my birthday we went to Brighton, and we went on all the rides. We were in a limo. It was Becky, me, Hannah, Laura and Milly and Rose. We had a great time in that. We were waving to everyone out of the window.'

'We went for tea to the Grand Hotel and we were exploring the Grand Hotel and we were in the lifts.'

All through the story, the girls who aren't speaking are giggling as Mum looks warmly on.

'We went down to the swimming pool and we really wanted to go swimming … '

' … so we jumped in with our clothes on … '

' … and we needed an adult to supervise us and so we had to get our driver and pretended he was our father, and everyone believed us and we were wearing our tops and jumped in and it was so funny. It was kind of embarrassing because we were in a really grand hotel.'

'Because the driver came back to me and I'd had quite a bit to drink by then, and he said, "The girls are swimming," and I said, "They can't be, they haven't got anything to wear." "Oh, they've taken their clothes off." '

'No, we weren't naked.'

'They had their knickers on.'

'We had our T-shirts on.'

'Well, some of you didn't have your T-shirts on. So I thought he was winding me up, and then I thought of the staff and the other guests watching this one man and these girls all going "Daddy". If that wasn't a case for paedophilia, then there would never be one. I was actually waiting for the police.'

Everyone explodes into laughter.

I'm slightly stunned, although I manage to smile, thinking how it becomes almost impossible for any situation not to have a sexual element. How every action is loaded with sexual potential. This is something that

Stubley had suggested when he told me about his socialising on Face Party. That in the heightened atmosphere of the site, every contact is potentially sexual. Livie's story suggests that this pervasiveness has drifted offline.

If paedophilia is such an easy subject to talk about, then admitting to a degree of sexuality is completely unproblematic.

Livie laughs, pointing at Becky. 'She is a boy maniac. Hannah and I are so normal; we haven't had a boyfriend, we're only eleven.'

Angela adds, 'And she's on number nine by now.'

'This year!'

Becky is not happy with the number. 'Ten actually.'

' … and she kissed them.'

'But I've gone off them now because this last boyfriend called Tony was really out of order, he was really overprotective and he wouldn't let me call any other boys and so I broke up with him.'

Angela adds a bit more detail. 'She got lost in the woods not so long ago.'

'Yeah, I got lost in the woods with Tony.'

'It isn't really serious boyfriend and girlfriend I love you; it's just like a little play, like experimenting.'

Despite the openness of the conversations, a sense of stranger danger has seeped through to their personal experiences. There is an awareness of bad behaviour in chatrooms, and the girls are keen to distance themselves from them. Livie presents them as dangerous spaces.

'At school we have this little group and we always talk about chatrooms, but never actually go on to chatrooms and do these things that thirteen-year-olds do.'

'I don't go on them any more,' Becky tells me. 'A girl I knew went on a chatroom and she didn't think it was a paedophile and it was and she went to meet him and she got raped. And so now I don't go on any chatrooms. And I went to see her one day and she was like completely white. She's about fourteen, she's still not over it. It was about a year ago, and she's really shaky everywhere she goes.'

'I'm so freaked out about all this rape thing,' Livie tells me. 'I don't go in chatrooms. I don't like even being in the house alone. I never walk my dogs on my own cos I'm scared.'

Following this shocking story Angela says: 'One night when Becky and Olivia were sleeping down here and I came down in the early hours, the television was still on, they were asleep.'

The three girls start giggling in anticipation.

' … and this monkey' – pointing at her daughter – 'had been watching *Temptation Island* … she'd gone on to Sky and she was watching *Temptation Island*.'

Becky and Livie accuse each other of having done it.

'It was really funny because they were walking around topless.'

Angela gestures towards the TV. 'Her little face was there and *Temptation Island* was there … '

'Didn't I say I liked being tempted?'

'We didn't know what it was at first until we saw the humongous bosoms coming on the screen. I fell asleep with the channels still on, so when my mum came down, there were tits everywhere. And she was like … my daughter … what has she done?'

Hannah, Livie and Becky's openness is refreshing. They are smart, thoughtful and seemingly untraumatised by their level of sexual awareness. It feels a happier state than one where words or activities are shrouded in shame or ignorance. Coupled with this easy awareness is the burned-in sense of how dangerous sex can be. The flipside of its pervasiveness is its inability to exist in a pure form, without being contaminated.

Before I go I ask to take their photos. They take me up to Livie's bedroom. On the door above the Avril Lavigne sticker is the sign: 'I want to be just like Barbie. That bitch has everything!' Inside it's like a boudoir: tiny and pink. Before I take the photo, Livie puts on some make-up. The three girls pose on a four-poster bed drowning in heart-shaped pillows, looking like little princesses or pop stars. The make-up, the poses, the lack of embarrassment and the sense of all taboos covered before you hit your teens points to a burgeoning sexuality … which vanishes immediately when Hannah races my car as I drive out of the cul-de-sac.

Young mum, evil baby

At Homelands, Ursula is bobbing from toe to toe. She is tiny and slender, with big hair and big pupils, wearing a wasted grin. She tells me her name is Nicola ('I always say that when I first meet people … just in case') and that she has left her eighteen-month-old baby ('evil but lovely at the same time') at home.

'I used to come to a lot of festivals but I got a daughter now so this is the first one in about two years. I've come because I like jumping in the mud. I come because it's a release, innit? It's a release of everything. You get away from everything. I come to escape everything. And just have a good time. Get away from reality.'

When I ask her about drugs she says: 'Bit of everything. Anything. I'll try it once.'

The second time I meet her, it's at her cousin Lydia's home. I sit in the back garden with Ursula and her boyfriend, Ryan. Her baby is sleeping upstairs. I have come expecting to talk with a carefree mother whose child hasn't prevented her getting high in fields.

Ursula was twenty when she got pregnant and gutted when she found out.

'Cos that's not what I wanted to do. I wanted to work a bit more, have a bit more independence. I just didn't think that was the right thing for me at the time, but … she's proved me wrong.'

Despite the fact that neither of them had expected or wanted a child, they decided that they would go with it, and Ryan would stick by her.

Ursula looks over at Ryan and smiles. 'He said it was cool, everything's fine, we'll like … might as well work at it now we've been irresponsible.'

Ryan smiles back and agrees. 'I wasn't really too sure what to do about it … not sure if that was the right thing to be doing at the time. Still kinda young, still had loads of things to be doing. It wasn't really something I jumped to at the beginning, but after we discussed … '

'When it happens you make the decision and whatever the decision is, you just stick with it. That's what it is: you just live with it. It's not something we chose to do, but yeah we went with it once it had happened. And that was cool.'

Having a baby has transformed their lives. Everything has changed.

'There's not one thing that's the same about our lives.'

'Everything revolves round the baby now. It's not the same time … '

'It's like if you want to go raving you have to like plan it two weeks ahead, you have to find out the event … '

Ryan starts laughing as Ursula outlines how much more responsible she has become.

'No, but I'm being serious. Before I'd just jump up. Before, I'd go to work say Monday to Friday, Friday I'd come home, find out what rave's happening, get ready, have a drink with my mates, go out, come back at whatever time in the morning, wake up whenever, do the weekend, go back to work on Monday. Now if you want to go raving, you have to find out two weeks before, get a baby-sitter, you know, make sure you've got enough money to be able to get there, get a drink and get home again. When I didn't have Rianne, I still lived at my own flat but you know, silly things, like if my phone bill come and I didn't feel like paying it, I wouldn't pay it and I'd just go out. Now it's like a responsibility. I have to pay it. She's changed everything.'

'Do you think it's hard to leave the good times behind?'

'Don't get me wrong. I'm not saying it's easy. I'm not saying it's an enjoyable experience by any stretch of the imagination, but when you come down and see Rianne digging in the garden and she turns round and says thanks, just the fact that she said thanks is cool, is all right for me.'

Ursula and Ryan have no plans to get married.

'I think it's right for some people and I think it's wrong for others,' explains Ursula. 'It's like religion, it's like everything: it's right for some people and wrong for others. I've seen cases where marriage works really well, but then I've seen really bad examples of marriage that goes wrong. Where I was brought up I kind of lived on a rough estate in Wandsworth, so lots of people that I grew up with take drugs and do lots of different stuff. If you haven't been to prison by the time you're twenty-one and you're a boy, it's like something's missing. Somewhere like that, marriage isn't an issue. I was the only person at my class in school that had a mum and dad that lived together; that's the only way I can explain it. Some of my friends haven't even met their dads.'

I could imagine Robert hearing this and visibly blanching.

But Ursula and Ryan have had to determine their own level of responsibility and, in doing so, have become judgemental of the way their friends have dealt with similar situations.

'I got a friend who's twenty-three – she had a baby when she was twenty-two, she's got a five-year-old daughter and basically she spends her whole time taking Es. We went to her daughter's birthday party and she came out and said, "Oh, thanks for coming."' Ursula does a wide-eyed impression of her mate. 'And I just thought: that's just not what should be happening at a child's birthday party. We ended up taking the kids home. I look at some people that I know and they don't appreciate their children and they expose their children. And I can see why the press give young people such a bad name because those people are disgraceful.'

I am reminded of Cordelia's criticism of her ket mates, or even Outlaw and Wize's feeling of superiority to other pirate stations. In a world with very few moral codes – or at least moral codes that seem in any way relevant – rather than an anything-goes attitude, there exists a personal conservatism as many kids seem to be creating their own limits.

As young parents, Ursula and Ryan are very conscious of how they are seen by the world. That because of their age – and possibly because she's mixed race but looks white and he's black – they attract comment.

'It's just like anything,' Ryan adds philosophically. 'There's good and bad in anything. If you only ever show the bad, it's a stereotype. All young mothers are all bad cos they all have children young. Even the sound of it is repetitive. It's hard for people who aren't living the generation, who aren't here doing it for themselves, to understand, because the times that they lived aren't the same as the times are now.'

'And I'm really aware of conforming to that stereotype, you know,' adds Ursula. 'I don't think in any way that I conform to that stereotype but I'm talking about when I walk down the road from an outsider's point of view, I'm really aware of looking like that single mother. I don't smoke when I'm outside any more. You can see people looking at you and you can see what they're thinking. Look at her: young single mother, walking down the road with a black man, a white man and a Chinese man.'

'Don't think,' says Ryan wisely, 'just because we live in the modern times, certain things from old times still aren't very apparent.'

Calmly expecting twins

Lorna is about to become a mother. It's a bright Sunday, and on Tuesday her identical twins are going to be induced. We're sitting in the garden of the small semi she shares with her mum on the outskirts of Leicester, drinking diet Coke. Parts of her uncle's motorbike lie scattered along one wall. Piles of branches and weeds take up the garden. She tells me they've been getting it ready for the children, so they'll have somewhere to play. Lorna is seventeen. She found out she was pregnant three months ago.

'I hadn't put much weight on, but Mum said I was putting a bit on, and it was all-over weight, and she was like, "Are you sure you ain't pregnant?" And I'm like, "I'd tell you if I was" – but that put a thought into my head, and I thought: best check.'

'And was it a surprise when you found out?'

'Just a bit. I was like that … ermm, don't know what to say. It was mixed feelings. In one way, I was like, oh … okay. But I was trying to think of every option possible before I made the final decision. But I looked at all the other options and they couldn't work for me.'

'And did you tell your mum straight away?'

'I couldn't at first. I told my cousin and she come round with me, and as soon as I seen Mum, I just told her. My mum was kind of expecting it, but she was still shocked. She just gave me a cuddle cos I was upset, and said it's all right: we'll sort it. Then I had to tell my brother.'

'What did he think?'

'All he said is: "Where's my fags?" and sat down.'

As Lorna talks to me, squinting slightly in the sun, her hands cup her enormous belly. She plays with the hem of the loose white smock she is wearing. To have gone from a seventeen-year-old girl to a six-month-pregnant woman must have been a dramatic upheaval, and yet she seems unfazed by what's happened. In fact, it seems to have given her a focus that she suggests was lacking beforehand.

'How do you think your life's going to change when you have your children?'

'Well, I'm going to have two other people to look after, so I'm going to have to fit my school work in as well. I don't want to stay at home. I want to get out there and get myself a career and do something with my life. I've always wanted to do something, but it's a matter of what, so if I get my GCSEs and A levels, and see where it can go from there. They'll be in the nursery during the day, so the spare time during that day I'll have to do revision, cos obviously when I'm at home, they'll need my attention. But I'll manage because I want to do it. It's not just for me any more. It's for these two as well. If I don't do anything, they're not going to get nothing. That's what I said to Mum, one good thing, when I was at college before I'd feel that I couldn't be bothered to get up, but now I'm going to have to get up.'

'Do you think it will be difficult?'

'Yeah. Looking after babies is hard. They need a lot of attention. My family's really close and I've got enough support around me to be able to cope. Well … that's when I thought it was one. I found out it was twins about a week later when I went for a scan. She went, "Yeah, there's definitely two in there," and I went, "Pardon?" She went, "Didn't you know?" I was really upset. I just thought: how was I going to cope with one, and then she told me I'm having two, but after I sat and thought about it, it was okay.'

Whenever Lorna talks about her future, she uses 'I', suggesting that she's already accepted that most of the work and responsibility lie with her. I can't tell if her certainty and determination is borne of considered reflection or is the result of not quite understanding what's in store for her. Either way she refuses to be daunted by what lies ahead, however unstable it might seem.

'What about the father?'

'He doesn't know. When I went to tell him, because I wasn't seeing him for that long, I don't know if he'd heard from someone else and then disappeared, or had just left anyway. But he's not in Leicester now. I went to see him at work, and they said he hadn't turned up for three weeks, and that's when I found out.'

'And how did that make you feel?'

'Upset in a way, cos I want them to know their dad, but I'm going to cope if he's there or not. But when he does come back, or if he does, I'm going to tell him. It's going to be a shock for him, and he might say, "They're not mine" or something like that. That's what I'm expecting anyway. But at least then I'll have told him.'

'Do you think that's a strange situation? Most of the time, people are into it, or they're not into it, but you don't really know. Had you fallen out of touch with him?'

'I hadn't seen him for about six months, I'd see him if I went up town with my friends, and we'd say hi, but there was nothing, no conversation or nothing like that. We hadn't fell out. There was just not time … we drifted apart. That's the weird thing: me not knowing, does he know or not? I'd like to know if he knows, because if he does, and he don't want nothing to do with it, then that's fair enough, but if he doesn't know … '

'You seem calm about the father not being around. Do you think you'll want a partner at some time?'

'I think I'm calm about it cos I was brought up without my dad, and so I just see it as I don't need him if he doesn't want to be here. If he wants to be part of their lives then that's fine, but he's not going to be coming in and out of their lives. In the future, I'll have a partner, but it depends when. These come first now. If this bloke don't like the kids then he's not going to be part of my life. The kids are first.'

Lorna didn't intend to become pregnant, but puts this down to an accident, rather than carelessness.

'When you were seeing this bloke, were you using contraception?'

'Yeah we were. I wasn't on the pill. We was just using condoms. And I was. I don't think my mum believes me.' She laughs. 'But I was. With condoms, the way that they express it is that it's always safe. But it's not.'

She goes on to talk about the sex education that she received at school, where it seemed to have been an incidental subject, rather than one where not understanding it can have such a profound effect on your life.

'At school, you did get taught about contraception, but not as much as you should. I was about fifteen when I was taught. I think I was in year ten, so fourteen, fifteen … and people are already having sex by then. I must admit when I first slept with my previous boyfriend, I didn't really know much about contraception, but I found out about it. I did use it. People seem to think that teenagers don't know about all these STDs, but you do. Nobody wants them. That's why I use condoms.'

'Is the sex education helpful at school?'

'Not really. I think the teachers get more embarrassed talking about it than the students. They quickly show you what things there are; you must get a half-hour, an hour and that's it. They try and tell you as little as possible. They say what's available but don't tell you what it's for. And if you're not there that day at school, you've missed out. That's your chance gone. There's a lot of websites as well which offer advice about it. But a lot of it is what you hear from other people. You speak to your friends. So you get information from each other. You should get more education.'

Throughout our conversation, I'm struck by how easily Lorna seems to have adapted to her life-changing situation. When she shows me her swollen hands and feet, and tells me she can hardly write at the moment, she laughs. Her eyes shine as she talks to me and strokes her belly. She seems excited about the idea of becoming a mum. In many ways, this is a normal situation, because many of her friends are going through or have gone through the same thing.

'I've got quite a few friends who have had children already. Quite a few, yeah,' she says, laughing. 'Everyone seems to be pregnant at the minute. My best friend, she's pregnant. They're all fine about it. They're all dead excited. They're like, "Hurry up and have it." I keep getting phone calls from them: "Haven't you had them yet? I wanna bring the dresses round for them. I wanna dress them up."'

The problem of being a teenage mother is not a problem in her eyes. It's what's happening, and she's prepared to deal with it, actually suggesting that there are benefits to having a kid young.

'We're put across as really irresponsible people, and some people – older people – when they see that I'm pregnant, they give you like funny looks. You can see them thinking: that's disgusting. I feel I could do as good a job as a person who had a child at thirty. I'll have more energy. Everyone brings up their children different. A lot of people say I don't want to have children, I want to get my career sorted. But you get your career sorted and sometimes there's not the time left to have children.'

Lorna is no victim, no tragic tale or symbol of irresponsibility. She is totally dismissive when I ask her about the pressures on young people to have sex.

'I didn't feel pressured to have sex. I just … ' She breaks off, laughing. 'It was just one of those things. A lad I was going out with.'

'Cos that's one of those things that you read about … '

'Peer pressure,' she sneers. 'That gets me. It's like, if they don't want to do it, they won't do it. They always say it's hard to say no, but it's not. If you don't want to take drugs you won't take them. If you don't want to sleep with someone, you won't sleep with them.'

For all her serenity and acceptance, as we're standing up, Lorna looks over at me and smiles shyly.

'It does seem really strange, you know. This week's gone so fast. It's weird to think that in a few days' time I'll be home with two babies. It's a bit scary.'

Before I leave the small terraced house, Lorna takes me upstairs. Her bedroom awaits the twins. Two cots line one wall, so there's less than a foot gap between them and the end of her bed. Her wardrobe is bursting with pink, yellow and white outfits. Two crates of toys and sterilising equipment are wedged in one corner.

'They've taken over already,' she laughs.

As I say goodbye she asks in a practice motherly way, 'Are you sure you don't want to go to the toilet? It's a long drive back to London.'

We've seen most things

I'm sitting in Benji's bedroom, with his friend Ben. They're seventeen and sixteen and it's a familiar teen set-up. On the walls, the obligatory posters jostle with one another for attention: a huge I / beer poster; an image of a chess piece holding a spliff and a gun, titled 'Hardcore Pawn'; an out-of-focus message: 'No sex causes bad eyes'. There are piles of CDs, DVDs and computer games on the floor, mixed up with clothes and school books. A Gamecube peeks out of the mess. Pint glasses and empty beer bottles are scattered around. There's a computer on the desk, a stack hi-fi in the corner, and widescreen TV with video and DVD. As Benji puts it, he's made sure that he doesn't have to spend a lot of time in the rest of the house.

If young mums are one easy target, then teenage boys are another. Would Ursula's or Lorna's unexpected sense of responsibility also be found among young blokes?

They're lounging on a crumpled sofa, still in their school uniforms. Benji has short brown hair and full lips, an expressive face and a slight stutter. Ben has shorter hair, wire-rimmed glasses and a more serious demeanour. He plays with a pen the whole time we're talking. They're both doing A levels. Benji's studying double maths, politics and physics. He's planning on a gap year when he's finished school and wants to study engineering at college. Ben is studying art, psychology and politics. He has no clue what he wants to do afterwards.

We start talking about how easy it is to see sexually explicit imagery. Ben tells me that he's grown out of it now, partly because it's something he associates with childlike curiosity.

'When I was about eleven, me and my mate started looking online for pictures of naked women. For something to do. It's so accessible.'

'It's incredibly easy to get hold of,' Benji agrees, although for him the appeal hasn't worn off. 'I still use it a lot. I think it's great. It's free and hassle free. Just use a search engine.'

But the pictures of oversized cocks, fisting and dwarves aren't just for solo consumption.

'A lot of stuff that is sent to you is from girls. The funnier or stranger stuff. Lots of sexually explicit material, tied in with jokes.'

This kind of stuff is freely accessible, endlessly circulated … and completely normal, it seems.

'Most people our age have seen hardcore porn,' Ben assures me. 'I don't think there's much porn you could show boys our age that would shock them, or they'd say, that's too much.'

'Most people have seen most things. The ones you get sent by e-mail, the ones that shock you, are the ones you haven't seen.'

The two boys acknowledge the distance between their fun porn and real-life sex, and perhaps because of this easy distinction can't see why it could be considered problematic.

'Porn is very removed from actual sex and the way that people think about sex.'

'There's definitely a big gap between the two.'

'I don't think it's harmful. I suppose what could be harmful is if you get into the mindset that it's normal and that the outrageous things that you see on the internet are the things that people do every day in their bedrooms.'

'Anyone who thinks that an eleven-year-old boy is not interested in sex or is not interested in getting as much information as they can about it, and is not having a wank as well, is completely wrong. To say that it shouldn't be going on is missing the point. Because it is going on and it's natural.'

Benji and Ben both feel that the sex education they received was useful in teaching them about the mechanics of sex, plus the things to watch out for: diseases, pregnancy, etc. They knew all of this before they started getting off with girls. And for them, the sex education worked. When we're talking about the crisis of teen sexual behaviour, they are surprisingly critical of other teens. As far as they're concerned, the information is easily understood and available to everyone. The problem is whether you choose to take note.

'I don't know what else schools could teach people to make them less promiscuous or have less diseases,' Ben says, somewhat dismissively. 'I don't think it is an ignorance thing.'

'Most people do know and they choose to ignore what their mind tells them. I'm sure most people receive the same education that we do. It's how you choose to apply it.'

'And do you always choose to apply it? Are you responsible?'

Ben has a slightly horrified expression on his face as he imagines the consequences of being irresponsible.

'To me, the risk of anything going wrong as in getting someone pregnant or anything like that would just be too ludicrous for me to even consider.'

'You think double maths homework is hard, you get a girl up the road pregnant and see what that's like.'

Benji has just started seeing a girl, while Ben is single at the moment.

'I had loads of girlfriends when I was younger but I have had one since I was fourteen. At the moment, I prefer not to be in a relationship.'

He obviously misses his ex. When he tells me they split up recently he immediately corrects himself and admits it was months ago. And in a further dig at perceptions of non-stop promiscuity, he is passionate when I ask him if it's important to be faithful when you're going out with someone.

'Damn fucking right. I think it's damn important.'

Both Ben and Benji have had sex with one person ... someone they were going out with at the time.

'I didn't have a big conversation with my girlfriend,' says Benji. 'We consulted each other.'

'I talked about it with my girlfriend before I had sex with her,' Ben tells me. 'I was fifteen. Sex was more of a big deal than sexual experiences in general. Having sex itself is still something different from everything else. But I wouldn't have a problem having sex with a girl one night and not being emotionally involved. I wouldn't think that was bad.'

'Often teenage culture is portrayed as just that all the time. Which it's not. There's nothing wrong with it, though.'

'It's not one or the other.'

'I wouldn't consider anything wrong.'

'I think that everyone's own lives are their own lives and they can do whatever they want with them. And I will do whatever I'm comfortable with.'

Part of the boys' calmness about sex seems related to the fact that it has never been an issue in their homes. It sounds like their parents have sat back and let them get on with it.

Ben tells me his parents have never said you should do one thing or you shouldn't do the other.

'They've never told me I couldn't do anything,' adds Benji.

'What if they did try to tell you what to do?'

'I'd be unhappy about that. That would cause a serious argument.'

This laissez-faire attitude goes further than not interfering. It seems both Benji's and Ben's parents are happy with their kids' sex lives starting young.

'My girlfriend was allowed to stay in my room. Before she was sixteen. Although I wasn't allowed to stay at her house.'

'The same for me. I was sixteen and she was a year younger.'

'And will your new girlfriend be staying over?'

'I'm sure of it, yes. My parents are pretty good about it. They're like: it's your own life. If I came back every weekend with a different girl, I think they might say something. But they're pretty cool.'

'If they think you're responsible in general in your life. My parents know that I've got my head screwed on. So I don't think they're thinking, by stopping him with his girlfriend sleeping in the room, it's gonna make a difference to whether I have sex.'

'A lot is based on trust from other areas,' Benji agrees. 'People certainly assume that because people are young they are irresponsible. Also a lot of people who have the power to make decisions decide that all teenagers are one big group. They don't ever split it into smaller groups.'

My conversation with Ben and Benji is one of the strangest I've had. They are two of the most reasonable, balanced kids I've met, with very considered attitudes towards their sexual activities. At times they appear old beyond their years with their complete rejection of risk or thoughtless behaviour, the pride with which they present the fact that their heads are screwed on, the fact that Benji 'consulted' his girlfriend before they had sex. At the same time, they talk happily about getting off with girls, drinking, surfing porn. If diseases, promiscuity and unwanted babies are one future for young British sex, I wonder if Benji and Ben offer an alternative outcome.

Over to Amanda

Despite the lack of shame that most people seemed to feel when asked about their sexual habits, I felt my gender would prevent me from having a truly intimate chat with girls about their attitudes towards sex. So in December I ask Amanda, a friend of mine who works as a researcher, if she'd mind helping me out by coming to Manchester on a rainy Friday night to talk with teenage girls about sex. She kindly agrees, and so she takes over for this section.

I ring the buzzer of the sturdy Victorian block, with wine bottles in hand. The front door is opened by a wholesome-looking Catherine, whose fresh appearance bears little resemblance to the gravelly voice I'd heard on the phone. She wears plain black trousers and T-shirt, with dark brown, shoulder-length hair pulled back in a ponytail. Catherine's friend, Selena, is on the sofa. She's an attractive, mixed-race girl, with pale skin and an unruly bleached blonde afro. She's in beige corduroy jeans and a blue V-neck top, her shoeless feet crossed beneath her. While the same age as Catherine (nineteen), Selena has a look in her eye suggesting a quiet confidence.

Catherine is the middle child of three to Christian parents and moved to Manchester two years ago to study acting. Selena never knew her dad, and is one of two daughters to a four-times married 'flamboyant' woman. Neither of them currently have boyfriends.

'I don't have a boyfriend. I'm supposed to be seeing someone at the moment, but it's … ' she trails off, eyes to the floor.

Catherine lost her virginity at seventeen and has had just one other partner since. 'When it came to it I felt totally comfortable. It sounds so pathetic and wet, but my boyfriend totally respecting my wishes made it nice. But it certainly wasn't great. It was one of those horrendous moments when you realise you have absolutely no idea what you're doing.' She makes me smile as I recall my own fumbling foray into teenage sex.

Selena claims to be 'very different', having lost her virginity at fourteen and had twelve partners since, eight of those in the last year. 'I just really like boys,' she giggles. 'I was so ready to lose my virginity. I'd been involved in sexual things from quite a young age. Not intercourse, but fumbling, groping, hand jobs and blowjobs from thirteen upward. The guy I lost it to was twenty-one. He stayed over and we only got to sleep at about six. I remember having this weird feeling of "I've just lost my virginity". It was like a strange day. I didn't have any expectations about would it hurt, would it go soft, that was all out of my mind. It was like, let's do it! There was loads of foreplay for about two hours and around fifteen minutes of actual sex. It didn't hurt, but I didn't have an orgasm or anything.'

The girls' different backgrounds and approach are becoming increasingly apparent. They shift slightly as I persevere, mentioning this fact to them. The liberated Selena speaks first. 'My sexual orientation is a bit complex. I was sexually abused when I was younger and again when I was fifteen.'

Everyone in the room automatically reaches for a cigarette at this point and Catherine's protective arm on Selena's shoulder makes me wonder if this is something they'd discussed, or if it is a revelation for her too.

'I hadn't had a dad, so there were all these different factors. I'm looking for something I haven't had with any of my sexual partners, because I've never been in a secure relationship. If I want to have sex, I want to. I'm very spur of the moment and haven't got much control. You'd think that with my past I'd go about things a bit differently. But it affects me the way it affects me. With the middle-class views and values I have inside me, I see what I do as not particularly acceptable. But I'm doing it and am aware of the modern age we're in and how liberal we are.'

Selena's ability to both mention and then rationalise her abuse in such an upfront way impresses me. Her body language says she is comfortable with it if I want to continue, but I don't feel I want to pursue this particular confession. I change the subject by asking them about living in a sexualised society as I refill our glasses.

Catherine leans in. 'Our generation is quite broad-minded sexually. My parents are different. They worry about all these teenage girls getting into trouble – and we are! It's just that we're okay with it. A lot of children are over-smothered and protected. Sex is treated as a subject that's taboo and secret. I was very lucky; my parents openly talked to me about sex all the way through childhood. I must've been about eight when I plucked up the courage to ask my mum what a blowjob was. My friends had been talking about it in school and I felt left out. I clearly remember it; we were in the car. My mum took a deep breath and then just matter-of-factly told me what it was and I was like, "What? You do that with it!"'

'I go with the motto you're never gonna know unless you try,' says Selena with a wry smile. 'It's an awful thing I'm about to admit, but most of the time I'm totally done in with alcohol or whatever else and I'm so charged up. I'm doing what I want to do at the time. I'm absolutely awful when I'm drunk. There's just no stopping me. Whatever I decide goes. The atmosphere in the room bends around me when I'm pissed.'

'But it's safe sex?'

Selena nods. 'All the time.'

'Unfortunately not all the time for me,' shrugs Catherine. 'I've never had any problems. I've been worried, but it's never been a major issue.'

'This "getting it out before" stuff; I nearly lost my virginity on millennium New Year. I was really up for it but said no because he didn't have a condom. I was unbelievably drunk and still was like, no. At the end of the same night there was another bloke and with this guy I wasn't even asking for a condom. He couldn't keep it up. Thank God.'

'It's very naive of anyone to think that rules are somehow going to curb people or stop them doing anything,' Selena continues. 'It's making people aware of things, not scaring them off sex. Saying sex is taboo before sixteen, or sex involves getting pregnant or getting STDs is useless because it's also pleasurable and fun. At the moment it's a very one-sided view. Things are gonna happen the way they happen. People have different views; there is no right way. Rules are just boundaries to keep us in check. Things go on whether the rules are there or not. Everyone makes their own choices; you have to make your own rules.'

I notice we've drunk nearly two bottles between us. We all have wine-flushed faces. It feels time to move things up a notch so I ask if they feel pressured about having sex.

'There's pressure to be good at sex. It's like: "Have you had a threesome?" "How good was your orgasm?" "How many times did you do it in a night?" It's gentle competition. It's interesting to hear how other people do it; it helps you explore your horizons. If they can do it you can find something better,' giggles Selena.

'What's on your list of things you want to experience?' I ask rather brazenly.

Catherine appears flustered by the question. 'Actually, to be honest with you, mmm, well,' she says, clearly uncomfortable, 'I actually quite fancy women at the minute. It's a very particular sort of woman ... okay; it's the one woman. Everything is sexy about her. There's something about the way she is with everyone; she's obviously sexually charged, even her walk shows it. It's not like "I fancy you", it's more a fascination. The worst thing is I didn't know how to go and talk to her; I've never felt like that about a woman. I work with her. Everyone's always made up and well turned out in the shop where I work. She has really full lips and is very womanly … Oh my God!' She covers her mouth to stop herself saying any more. I notice Selena has turned to look at her; this is one confession I'm certain hasn't been shared previously.

'Do you think you'll take it further?'

'No. This is the thing. I could easily kiss a woman; that's not a problem. I have a problem with going down on a woman, that's not somewhere I want to go. I think women's bodies are beautiful and I think that's why women are attracted to other women. I'm very emotionally aware of myself. I can understand why women choose to be with other women, I know lots of girls who do, but I'm not attracted to that area of a woman.' She gestures slightly disdainfully below the waist.

'I permanently fancy women!' Selena interjects in a high voice. 'I'm sure people think I'm bisexual, but I'm not. I'm just a very loving, fancy-everyone type person. I've had snogs with women, and I've had a threesome with two girls and a guy. It was unfortunate for him cos we were really pissed. The poor bloke was so overwhelmed that it didn't go very well for him. I was very vodka'd and he just kind of shrivelled up. He didn't know what to do with himself. So, yeah, I fancy the socks off some women. I fancy the pants off of Kylie, but I also just love her, I think she's great.'

'I'd do Britney Spears. If she were to come up to me in a bar or club … I would, I'd have sex with Britney Spears,' Catherine adds dreamily.

'A girl on me, doing whatever they want to me is absolutely fine,' continues Selena. 'Me touching a girl is fine, but there are limits. I reckon I'd go down on a woman … but it just squeams me out. I love a boy to go down on me though.'

'I've told my parents about my fancying women and the fact that I've kissed girls. They didn't have a problem with it. It's acceptable to just be who you want to be,' says Catherine.

'You change throughout life and may have different partners. Marriage is just a block really. I read an article in the paper that it's so unreal to think that we are monogamous. Divorce rates are so high,' continues Selena.

'I don't think marriage can work fully. Inevitably one of the two decides they're not as happy as they want to be and goes off with someone else,' Catherine agrees. 'It's not as simplistic as that, but you find other people *who satisfy other parts of your personality. So you stray and then end up questioning your relationship anyway. I honestly don't think it's possible. I trust myself to be honest, and to get out if I'm not happy.'*

'There are going to be more possibilities that will decrease the amount of people who'll get married,' concludes Selena. 'My rules are safe sex, as long as I'm willing. If I have a one-night stand it's because I want to.'

I'd come to Manchester expecting to feel older and wiser by comparison to these girls. I leave Catherine's neat and tidy flat struck by how more sexually aware and at ease with the subject they are than I had been at their age. I'd spoken to two very different girls, from vastly different backgrounds with contrasting views to sex. They are up for it, but also aware they're still learning the ropes and have plenty of mistakes to make. They are open about what they don't know and emotionally equipped to find out about it. In a morally abundant world, one with few defined rules, both had a pragmatic approach to taking the choices that would make them happy.

When Amanda told me about her evening, much of what she said seemed familiar. The willingness to share intimate details of their sexuality, Selena's insistence that you have to make your own rules, the eagerness to explore new areas, the hunger for more, for different – all fitted with the self-determining, sensation-hungry attitudes of the people I'd been speaking with. Catherine and Selena's views on the unreality of monogamy and the idea of different people satisfying different parts of your personality matched the fragmentation of identity and endless quest for new that Face Party encourages.

In addition, there was a mischievousness about Selena that had parallels with the disobedience of graf artists and free party people. As she put it, they're okay with getting in trouble. Like drugs and graf, sex without limits – or only the limits that an individual decides are relevant – offers a way of embracing behaviours that other generations feel uncomfortable with.

Where watching fucking is normal

Esme lives in a mansion block in Bethnal Green. Compared to the rude boy garages and the sixties estates, it looks grand. But of course like most big residential buildings in British cities, it's been carved up into neat little flats. In Skin Two, I've seen Esme dressed in a rubber nurse's outfit, as a forties vamp, in intricately designed latex that looks like lace. But when she opens the door to me, the only clues to her fetish existence are the pierced tongue and the distressed gun design on her T-shirt. Although, these days that could mean anything.

There is little in the minimalist apartment that she shares with the more heavily tattooed and pierced Jake to suggest what they get up to at weekends. A Mac with the achingly desirable transparent speakers; the slim soundsticks; the sub that looks like some underwater creature, or an ancient valve amp. A David Lachapelle book. A hook-nosed mask on the wall. Only the jar of dentist tools on the mantelpiece suggests any kind of strange hobbies. That and the slender pale scars on their arms.

Esme is twenty-one and has just graduated from Goldsmiths College, studying drama and theatre arts, doing modelling and part-time reception work. She's relieved to finish college and ready to mix with people who aren't students.

The fetish scene had interested me because it seemed to point towards a world of sexual expression and experimentation that is more colourful, more playful, and unconstrained by any morality or shame. Within fifteen minutes of meeting Esme, she's happily showing me pictures of herself semi-naked. We're eating peanuts and drinking tea, as her pet rabbit flops about on the floor. She talks me through her portfolio, where she poses in rubber top hat and tails, complete with walking stick and surprised expression. Or sits coquettishly in black panties with two hearts covering her nipples. There's no embarrassment, no blushing, just pride at how great she looks in the pictures.

'Before I went to uni I lived in Liverpool and I was really into the goth culture and hung out with a lot of goths and metallers, listened to Cradle of Filth and that kind of thing, and their artwork is very blurred between fetish and goth. The Torture Garden is like this kind of mecca, so I got into looking at websites and checking out the Torture Garden site before I came here.

'I got into the modelling after me and Jake were hanging out on the fetish scene. We met two of the people who were working at Torture Garden and they said would you like to do some fetish modelling and I was like whatever, great, so did one thing and it went on from there.'

The fetish scene is another space in the UK where extreme behaviour can take place. And as with any scene that is united by a powerful activity, it sets up its own behaviours.

'It's got its own little world and its own little culture. It's the look, the lifestyle, the clubs. From my point of view it's about the dressing up and the music. For others, it's the playing and the bondage. For some it's the swinging aspect.'

Despite Esme's nonchalant way of chatting through fetishised versions of herself, this sense of easy acceptance did not extend to her parents.

'They were absolutely horrified. My dad's a scientist, my mum's a nurse and marriage-guidance counsellor. She's just started doing sex therapy, which I find hilarious. They're very nice, but they're very middle class. They've got their ideas of what's what and they're pretty protective. I'm the youngest in the family.'

'How did you tell them?'

'I wrote them a letter. My mum hated me being a goth; she hated Marilyn Manson. She used to freak out about it. Once she found *Bizarre* magazine ... they had a photo of a woman covered in blood with big spikes coming out of her body and plastic hair extensions. It was hilarious, over the top. But my mum freaked out, was like ra ra ra, so I was like, I know not to mention that any more.'

The reaction to *Bizarre* magazine is telling. For Esme, in the new sexual world, blood, spikes and nudity are something to laugh at. For her mum, the images still retained a sense of shock and depravity.

'It got to the stage where they'd come and visit me in my halls in uni and I'd take down all the pictures off my walls and hide all my rubber clothing and it was just stupid. So I was like, fuck it: I'll tell them. But I didn't tell them I was modelling, they just thought I was hanging out there. So I sent them another letter, and they reacted very well. My dad phoned me and said, "Fair enough; I'm worried, but it's your life." My mum didn't like it at all and was really upset. She thinks because I've got a university degree that modelling is wasting my brains. To her models are bimbos.

'But the reason I do fetish modelling is it's a lot more interesting than normal modelling. I tend to do forties and fifties stuff and it's fun. At heart I'm a performer and I like getting all tarted up and showing off. For women it's really quite empowering. In the fetish scene, lots of women have strong sexualities; the whole mistress thing is admired. It gives you a chance to express yourself in ways you can't usually in normal clothing. It's for big kids, people who want to dress up and play out fantasies. I've got friends who have a persona for the whole evening.'

The way Esme talks about fetish makes me think of the Face Partiers who construct their entire online identities as a way of expanding their personalities.

'People are frightened by the whole S&M thing … to a lot of people it's really weird. It freaks my mum out because I'm her little girl and she thinks it's dangerous and seedy and has the impression that it's an underground cult. People who go for the first time can't believe how friendly everyone is. You can go up to pretty much anybody and start a conversation. Everybody is there for the same reason.'

'Do you think your attitude towards sex has changed? You talk about some pretty wild stuff as if it's normal.'

'Well … it's certainly an exposure to a lot of different ways of doing things. I was kinda into S&M in my private life when I was younger. Which I suppose is one of the reasons it attracted me. But I've gone away from that element. When you're hanging out in a fetish scene and you know most of the people who work there, it's a bit funny to be down in the dungeon, playing, getting on with whatever and then one of your friends walks past. So for me it's not really about that any more. I used to beat the crap out of men and trample all over them with stilettos, burn them with my cigarette, do all kinds of things, poke them. I'm not particularly into being submissive myself. Not in public at least. I used to have a stereotypical mistress persona, hard-faced and bitchy, and I used to really enjoy it.'

As with cruising or squat parties, the fetish scene sounds like another piratopia: where acts and behaviour deemed unacceptable by normal Britain are carried out in private spaces. Within fetish clubs, the most private of these is the dungeon.

'In the dungeon it's always ambient and quiet. Loads of people just sitting around, having a drink, whatever, and it's very surreal the first time you experience it. It looks like everyone's just sat there chilling out, but then there's big wooden crosses and cages and people tied up against the wall and being beaten and whipped and having needles stuck through their backs. Everything under the sun going on. But everyone's acting like there's nothing weird going on at all. It's a very voyeuristic thing. There's a dark room where there's no lights and people just go in there and it's usually just a big mass of body parts and fluids.'

Esme describes how quickly the norms of mainstream society – the ones that say sex is a private act – are replaced by an alternative set of principles. Fetish clubs sound like the logical endpoint of Selena's view that you make your own rules – a place created by the multiple and variable desires of its audience.

'It's like a weird parallel universe. You go in there and nobody cares if you've got no clothes on, you see people having sex chatting to their mates next to them. Before I went to a fetish club, I'd never sat and watched two people having sex live in front of me, but when I saw it didn't seem like that much of a big deal. In that environment it doesn't seem weird. It makes sense somehow. It doesn't seem out of place.'

'Do you think it's healthy?'

'Nothing has ever happened to me in TG that I would be upset about. You hear about so many rapes from normal clubs. I've had cases where I've been followed around and hassled in normal clubs and you go and tell the bouncer and he's like, "Whatever. Go and get on with it … you're a girl in a short skirt … what were you expecting?" Whereas in somewhere like Torture Garden, if something happens that you don't like, you just have to say one thing to a member of staff and they're out.'

Esme's remark that fetish clubs are safer than 'normal' clubs reminds me of Natalie's comments about feeling perfectly happy buying any kind of drug at a squat party. She has found her own safe house in a place that looks dangerous, even depraved. A place where behaviour that is illegal or at least frowned upon is safer, more friendly than the places where they are forbidden. She also believes that exposure to the extreme is liberating, almost comforting, rather than corrupting.

'If you're given that much freedom you have to accept that no means no. And there's posters everywhere that says TG is a safe environment. If you're going to feel comfortable doing those kinds of things you need to know that something will be done about it.'

Esme goes to make me another cup of tea, and as she's doing so suggests that I come check out a fetish night. It's the Rubber Ball in a couple of weeks – a three-day extravaganza of leather and whips, chains and corsets. She thinks she can sort me out with a press pass, which will allow me to take pictures.

'You have to make an effort, though. You can't turn up in jeans and a T-shirt.'

An image of myself trussed up in a gimp suit, being beaten by some giant dom, flashes through my mind and the uncertainty must reach my face because she laughs and reassures me.

'Don't worry. I'll look after you.'

Torture Garden

The place where anything goes is round the back of Angel tube station in London, down a dark cobbled street. It's the weekend that the roasting revelations about the Premiership footballers hit the headlines. The difference between the two portrayals of and reactions to sex is staggering. From acceptance and enjoyment to shame and recrimination. When the *News of the World* gets hold of the story, judgement inevitably creeps in.

I go with a friend, Martin, and his new girlfriend, Amba. They've only been out a couple of times, and Martin's not sure that it will be a great third date, but I persuade him it might impress her. The three of us visit Paradiso Bodyworks in Old Compton Street. Martin and I have decided on pervert businessman for our look. This lets us get away with suits worn over a mixture of leather and rubber. So, we're having fun, putting together a mixture of chains, manacles and masks. In the changing room I can hear Amba moaning to the helpful assistant about some tiny rubber skirt, and I wonder if I'm going to mess things up for Martin. But she emerges happy and our shopping is done. As a final thought I buy a pair of leather underpants with a zip from front to back just in case things get messy. I don't like the idea of my more regular boxer shorts being sneered at by purists.

Amba's initial hesitance decreases in relation to the amount of eye make-up she puts on and the height of her heels. Once we're inside the club she's in her element: leading Martin and me around on chains. We exchange nervous looks, although later on he tells me that he's never seen her looking so hot.

As Esme had promised it's a mixed bunch. Aged from early twenties right into their fifties and sixties. But mostly around the twenties and thirties. A strange mix of the comic, the beautiful and the depraved. Men in full gimp suits with their hands bound into paws. Women dressed as nurses. Lots of sharp military outfits. Infinite combinations of rubber and leather. A female alien, a nun, a pair of naughty schoolgirls. A woman with a metal brace round her neck that curves gracefully over her face.

It feels like a slightly dark fancy dress party; there's a lot of laughing and pointing: mutual respect for other people's costumes. A sign on the wall reads: 'Torture Garden is a safe environment. Please report any form of harassment to TG staff, TG dungeon monitors or TG security.' Underneath someone has stuck a sticker: a white cross on a black square with the word 'Porn' in the cross.

A fashion show takes place in one of the rooms and Esme is transformed from the polite and helpful girl I interviewed on a sofa to a larger-than-life pink rubber version of a forties vamp, complete with black Bakelite phone and pillbox hat and veil. Her lips are bright red and she strides up and down the catwalk like she owns it. A girl wearing a gas mask and holding a machine gun guards the stage. This is comic-book fetish – brightly coloured and playful – and the crowd love her.

The festivities continue when a stream of girls are strapped to a car with a speaker jutting out of the boot like a rocket. A bass note fills the room and rocks the car. It's meant to be the magic frequency 33Hz, which will bring a girl to orgasm. The girls enjoy it, but none of them appear to go all the way.

Downstairs, a man is suspended from hooks through his knees and spun around. Then he attaches a series of ropes to hooks in his back and dances maniacally above us to the Butthole Surfers 'Satan'. During the choruses he takes a knife to a rope each time, until he is suspended by just two ropes and the skin on his back is stretched taut. Blood drips down his back, which is covered in a tattoo, and looks like his skin has been torn open to reveal a mechanical or alien skeleton within. By the end his dancing becomes so frenzied that the remaining two ropes snap and he falls to the floor. I stare fascinated, enthralled by his ability to damage himself so energetically, but Martin looks slightly queasy and I notice him leaving the room.

We get talking to a couple. He has a shaved head and lots of buckles. She has long dark hair and is poured into a rubber catsuit. Noticing our chains, she asks Amba if she can borrow me. Amba hands over the chain and I stare back at my new owner with what I hope is a look of defiance.

She slaps me hard across the face. I try to keep my disobedient expression, but my cheek stings. Another slap, harder this time, and then one more. I feel my jaw move sideways. Much as I like the idea of being hit around by a beautiful catwoman, it hurts, and I flinch and duck the next blow. Disgusted she hands me back to Amba.

In the dungeon, the play is getting more serious. A man lies on the floor, with a woman's toe stuffed into his mouth, while a second guy masturbates him. A woman is tied to a metal frame and beaten. A guy squats in a cage on the floor while a woman hurls abuse at him. A woman lies on a leather swing, her dress torn open as a man stands between her legs, fucking her. People stand around watching. Catwoman and the guy with the shaved head turn up. He lies on the floor in a cage while Catwoman, Amba and another woman all grind their heels into his chest. I see him take Amba's heel and suck heavily on it.

Of all the disconnect/zones I'd visited, this was the most radical. A place where sex is transformed and made public, accessible and new. Rather than a sex club, though, it felt more like one more club where people happened to be fucking. While the audience was older than most of the places I visited, the Torture Garden operates on the same rules as clubs, skateparks, cruises and marches. Normal rules are irrelevant; life works differently inside here.

I say goodbye to Esme and walk out, trying to hide my leather trappings from the cab driver. It strikes me how rapidly something that is beyond acceptability becomes normal. I had just watched several people having sex – something I'd never seen live before – with little more than a tremor of curiosity. When everyone is complicit, then extreme acts become normal. When there is none of the outside world to bring its different morals and codes, you get places where you can stretch your experiences and try stuff that elsewhere would not be allowed. Where different rules apply. This ability for these kinds of extreme scenes to flourish and exist within a more conservative country seemed to be one more sign of the disconnections that exist and are growing within the UK.

Dogging, spit roasts and a happy finish

One reaction to the pervasiveness of sexual imagery is exhaustion and wear-out, rather than a continual sense of arousal. Certainly the kind of stories that make the headlines towards the end of 2003 rely on the freakish or the absurd for their currency. How far we've come, or how little shocks us, is clear from the *News of the World* headline in November: 'Is Charles Bisexual?' The idea of the future King of England getting a happy finish from one of his valets is presented semi-comically, coupled with a picture of Charles looking unusually fey. Other sex highlights include a feature on the growing popularity of dogging – watching people have sex in car parks – and the fascination with footballers' penchant for roasting or spit roasts. This latter practice – which either involves passing a woman round like a piece of meat, or a man in each end of a woman, depending whose description you go by – quickly becomes another joke, so rapidly normalised that Mars is happy to run an ad in *FHM* describing spit roasts as pleasure you can't measure.

Wherever you look, there is a simultaneous heightening and diminishing of sexual power. By bringing it into the open – via posters, via promiscuity, via its pervasive presence in all things musical – sex loses one of the things that has kept it so potent for so long: its privacy. As more of sex becomes public and normalised, so the extremities come into play. The mythic status of sex – as representing transcendence, as being the most magical act that you can share with somebody – is questioned and it teeters on its pedestal. Nights like the Torture Garden, or events like Gay Pride where sexuality becomes the catalyst for a flurry of colourful and vibrant activity, point towards a more disposable, playful, version of sex. Just another leisure activity.

SM play has been described as a sexual contact sport, which reminds me of Paula's comparison between finding out about sex and mortgages. Sex is just one more consumer choice or physical activity, and out in the open it conforms to the same logic as any other activity in our culture. We constantly need to find ways of doing it better, different, making it new. Fetishism is to do with obsessing about certain images and constantly seeking a new version of that image.

And of course, it's two-way. Sex is just one thing to be fetishistic about, but as a culture we have developed many fetishes. Perhaps the growth of sexual acceptability is part of a much bigger, inevitable movement towards seeing, experiencing and owning endless variations of products and activities. Modern culture is fetishistic, not just in a sexual sense, but in the endless reiterations of familiar designs: the sequels and prequels, the version 7.2.3, the updates.

Martin Amis says: 'The world is getting less innocent purely by accumulation of experience.' This is often seen as a negative effect. But is a loss of innocence any different to gaining knowledge? There is no reason to see an increasingly fast succession of experiences as blunting or numbing. Surely the more we see and know, the more we are expanded.

Children, teenagers and young adults are often treated in the way that God treated Adam and Eve: as innocents who cannot deal with the truth. Perhaps in the old world, when knowledge was only available through an apple, or via your parents and teachers, such a narrow approach was viable. But now, with so much info floating around for anyone to tap into, the most important skill for anyone is how to travel usefully through the endless flow.

What we have among younger people is a far more relaxed attitude to sex. Behaviour still needs to catch up. Rather than seeing the explosion of STIs and pregnancies as one more sign of a decaying society, is it possible to see it as a blip, a temporary readjustment, where people are coming to terms with a freedom that has been denied them for too long?

The Mates website says it best. Like the brand, it is a combination of explicitness and sexual celebration underscored by responsibility. There is a new, practical morality at work here. A morality that says: multiple, unattached, pleasure-seeking random sex is just fine … as long as you wear a condom. No one expects fidelity or monogamy.

Like drugs, sex in the 21st century is about personal pleasure, just one more way of entertaining yourself and it's up to you to decide what you're into and how far you want to go. No one wants to be told not to do it. The only acceptable advice is about how. And like drugs, while the media adopt a serious, we're-all-fucked tone, the kids are far more carefree. It's another area of amusement. So Face Party's agony aunt, Grim Rita, a dominatrix version of the more traditional figure, promises to administer 'inappropriate advice to the youth of today'. The letters show a lack of any embarrassment and talk about sex as a simple, amusing leisure activity.

There are no moral issues here, just questions about how to do things better.

> Dear Rita,
> I have slept with over 50 women — and that's just the ones I remember the names of! So am I a legend, or just an easy lay?
> **Compared to me darling, you are a fucking amateur.**

> Dear Rita,
> I met a guy last week and we had great sex. Afterwards, he asked if I knew what felching is. What is it?
> **It's when you suck sperm out of your partner's arse. If you're slightly sophisticated, you can use a straw.**

> Dear Rita,
> What's the best position for two girls to have sex? My girlfriend and I have been trying for weeks, but there's nothing to stick in!
> **You've got oral sex and mutual masturbation. If you want to get flash, then get yourself a strap-on. Oh, and if you can work the bloody thing, invest in a double-ended dildo — tricky, but fun.**

If you carry the logic of Rita, Mates or the Torture Garden through to the rest of the world, the bombardment of our public spaces and awareness of sexual explicitness is an entirely positive thing. From Paula to Esme, the belief is that more exposure equals a more responsible and more playful attitude: oversexed is a positive state.

'The reason all these things exist,' says Esme, 'is not because someone sat down and decided how to make some money. It's what people want. To be able to express yourself in a safe way.'

'Duno wat a book is'

More than 200,000 seven-year-olds are not learning to read properly because the Government's national literacy strategy has left teachers 'confused' about how to teach reading, Ofsted said yesterday. Another 50,000 seven-year-olds could not write properly because their teachers did not know enough grammar to teach it effectively.

Daily Telegraph, **November 2002**

Pupils are told to pick A levels in soft subjects.

Evening Standard, **August 2003**

Almanack editor-in-chief Lauren Simpson said: 'We are a nation obsessed with celebrity culture.'

Ms Simpson said everybody needed to 'escape from real life' once in a while. 'I would like to see more people putting down their celebrity gossip magazines ... to keep abreast of current affairs and the world around us,' she said.

The level of knowledge was worse among younger people, with just 27% of those in the 16–24 age group able to name Tony Blair's deputy.

BBCi News, **November 2003**

Stupid art

I see two things on screens at the beginning of 2003 that make me consider our attraction to stupid.

The first features a guy sitting on a bed, explaining that he's about to sew pieces of wood onto the soles of his feet. He talks factually about something that is going to hurt, citing ancient African tribes as his influence, and explaining that 'some areas of the foot are going to be easier to sew into than others'. All the time, the grainy video rolls on. You can't see who he's talking to, but you sense it's a friend.

Then he begins. You see him forcing the needle through the toughest part of his skin first, as if that's going to make it easy.

'Oh, Jesus,' he exclaims on the first stitch. 'Christ!'

At times you can see the thread inching its way through his semi-transparent skin. Throughout the short film, the man alternates between dispassionate commentary and surprised agony.

'There's obviously going to be some blood, but once you start you might as well keep on going … There's quite a bit more blood than I expected … This foot's actually a lot more sensitive than the other foot.'

After doing both feet, he limps painfully to bed, telling the camera that his legs have gone numb.

Cut to the morning; him waking up, the wood still there, dried blood crusting over. 'It's even sorer than it was last night. It's the sorest thing I've ever had to deal with in my entire life.'

A handful of people watch this in the room with me. They are laughing. There are a few groans in empathy, but no one is horrified.

The second piece: a man wearing a bulletproof vest stands in a shooting range. Beneath the vest someone has drawn a target on his stomach. His hands are tied behind his back and he looks faintly ill. We pull back to see a stocky man with a buzz cut taking aim with a rifle. There's a bang and the guy falls to the floor, groaning in pain. Two days later and a deep purple bruise the size of an orange glows from his skin. A cinema full of people watch. They are laughing so hard that many are crying. There are groans of disgust, but everyone loves this. And this is just one of a plenitude of gross painful stunts. Compared to woodfoot man, the frequency and magnitude of pain is greater. And there is less commentary. Just a few screams, sniggers and oh dudes.

The two stars of these short pieces are David Sherry and Johnny Knoxville. One is a finalist in the Becks Futures Awards, the biggest cash prize for artists in the UK. The other is one of the stars in *Jackass: the movie*, a film that cost about $5m to make and grossed over $60m in the States in 2002 and took a further £4m in the UK in 2003.

For anyone who thinks that art trickles down to more common entertainment, forget it. Jackass got there first by a long way. Mass populist stupid television, idolised and adored by millions of kids, leading the way.

Since the show's inception, Johnny Knoxville, Steve-O and co. have fired taser guns at themselves, been lifted by a crane in a Portaloo and emerged covered in (other people's) shit, dropped fake babies in busy streets, crashed shopping trolleys, thrown up eggs and had baby alligators attached to their nipples.

David Sherry didn't win the Beck Futures prize. If he had done, he would have walked away with twenty-four grand, not bad for an artist, but peanuts compared to the kind of figures Knoxville and team are pulling in. The ability to fool around creatively has become a valuable talent.

Steve-O, one of the *Jackass* crew, has his own video out. It's more of the same, just different: darts are thrown at his ass, till one hangs there shaking; he sniffs curry sauce until he pukes; shoots firecrackers out of his ass; has firecrackers shot at his ass; jumps off buildings into swimming pools while his hair is on fire. All the time laughing. None of Sherry's pained explanations. He just keeps on hurting himself in increasingly stupid and creative ways.

'People ask me why I do all this stupid shit, and it's such a simple answer. I don't like work and I don't like school. And I want to be remembered for ever, dude.'

A bad influence

The *Jackass* DVD is advertised on sickbags and promises '32% more stunts than in the cinema'. It carries the warning: 'The stunts in these videos were performed by professionals, so neither you nor your dumb buddies should attempt anything from this movie.'

Not everyone takes note though. Websites spring up showing British boys getting up to their version of stupid. On crippleproductions.com, coming out of Brighton, you can watch paraplegic boxing (one contestant with his hands and feet tied getting beaten to shit by his mate), or Jamie's bag (where a kid of the same name is thrown down a flight of stairs in a sack). Tricks on other sites include somersaults from house tops, and games with petrol and matches. Every few months you can find stories of serious burns and sprains. Although the real shockers seem to be elsewhere.

In May an eighteen-year-old in Florida jumps from a five-storey condo into a pool, catches the edge and shatters his pelvis. The disaster is captured on video by his friends, and soon makes it round the internet. And in September, an Australian sticks a firework between his butt cheeks, and falls over just as it explodes. Leaving him incontinent and impotent.

Stupid entertainment is everywhere. From Bumfights (filming tramps who have apparently been paid to kick the shit out of each other) to *Vice* magazine's 'cum vs moisturiser' feature (Nick and Lisa rub both substances into their faces for a month to see which is better for your skin).

And of course Backyard Wrestling: US home movie-making at its best. Insane battles in which kids jump from roofs onto their prone friends, smash metal chairs and road signs over each other's heads, and stand round in circles chanting: 'Fucking kill him, fucking kill him.' So stupid it's inspired the Playstation game 'Backyard Wrestling – Don't try this at home', a video game featuring the group Insane Clown Posse. Compared to the shiny, stylised and fake videos pumped out by record labels, this kind of film feels raw and dangerous. Replacing music as the most rebellious and violent art form or pastime.

Stuart – boyfriend of drug-taking primary-school-trainee Cordelia – explains the attraction of imitating *Jackass*. 'You know when you go out and you're really rowdy and pissed and you've been drinking Stella and then someone's like, oh it'd be really funny if we had a fight to see who'd give up first if you punched each other in the face a couple of times? It's all loads of stuff like that … it's been quite disruptive since we've watched that, there's been so many injuries … '

'When we were at Reading festival walking along, me and my mates, and I was beaning [on ecstasy] and my mate was just pissed and we found this big fire in the brown campsite, which is the one where all the troublemakers go, and there was a big fire on the walkway and there's like lines of people either side, like all queued up either side of the walkway, big fire there and everyone's going "oi, oi, oi, oi" and I was like, what the fuck's going on?, and I stand to the side and they turn round and then I realise they're actually all going "trolley, trolley, trolley" like that and they've got a shopping trolley, right? And they get in – they're putting people in it, pushing them as fast as they can into the barrier through the fire, and there's loads of people there watching it all, chanting.

'We got real pissed up one night and my mate accidentally punched me in the face when we were having a play fight and I was like, right, I owe you a punch in the face. Later that night, absolutely paralytic, I ended up wearing a tutu and some really big flip-flops and a cowboy hat and nothing else and I was outside. I said, oh, Alec, I owe you a punch, and my other mate got the video camera out and we had it on the video tape of me punching Alec flat out in the face wearing all this gear, and his parents found it on the video and they were just giving me such fucking funny odd looks. "We thought you were such a nice young man." It was so funny.'

There's no doubt that stupidity is celebrated. Behaviour that is far from logical, that often brings with it the possibility of physical pain or material damage. That upsets and disgusts people.

And the fear is that this stupid behaviour is the sign of a more profound mental decay that is sweeping Britain. The fear goes something like this: kids are dumb. They know nothing about history or politics. They leave school unable to spell correctly and with no grasp of maths. They would rather play computer games or watch inane TV shows than think about important subjects. Ignorance is celebrated and mean, humiliating entertainment has taken over.

The accusations come from many sources. One of the more interesting in 2003 is *Whitaker's Almanack*, a reference book whose sole claim is that it stores lots of facts, unrelated to any application. Trivia for the sake of having trivia in one place. A survey found 73 per cent of 16 to 24-year-old respondents could not name the deputy prime minister. While 24 per cent of all respondents could recognise Gordon Brown, 30 per cent were able to name at least one *Big Brother* winner. 'We can only conclude from this report that Britain is dumbing down.'

Over the year, I talked to kids who loved *Jackass* (nearly every bloke), who preferred celeb mags to books, and whose punctuation and spelling were looser than Johnny Knoxville's underpants after they were used as a bungee cord. None of them seemed stupid. What was the appeal of stupid, and did the abbreviated and distorted language that seems to characterise young communications represent the grunts of a dumber generation, or a new set of smarts?

School's out

If not liking school is a criteria for dumbness then the UK certainly has a problem. Few of the people I spoke with had good things to say about school. These were largely energetic, interested, creative kids, who wanted to make and do something, and yet there was an almost unanimous feeling that school had little to do with preparing them for the world. In conversations about their dreams, their hopes, their role models, school didn't figure highly. Of course, this is nothing new; school has never been a favourite choice for kids. But as Disarm's Bill Brown pointed out, these days there are so many other things – whether it's music videos or modified cars, building websites or hanging out in chatrooms – that capture their imagination and passion better.

The criticisms are varied, ranging from boredom to bullying, but often centre on the fact that they feel that an old model of discipline, learning and even social conduct is being forced on them.

While I'm at the ICA, browsing through their very consciously unstupid book shop, I pick up a postcard with a black and white line drawing of a husband and wife chatting to their child's teacher. The punch line goes: 'So you see, Mr and Mrs Smith, our education system works. The little fuckers are just dumb!' As I talk to more people, I begin to wonder if it's the other way round, and if Britain's kids have grown out of an education system that was built for another time.

Speaking to Charlotte, Majahid and Amanda about why they joined the bridge course at their sixth-form college, they are critical of the way they were treated at school. Amanda spells out the difference.

'Here you get treated like an adult. At school it was in the classroom, take off your coat, sit there, be quiet, that was it.'

'They treat you like babies,' Majahid adds.

'They didn't teach us. They just said here is some work, do it and didn't explain it.'

Carina and Lucy, the girls from Thurrock service station, ambitious and confident, are equally critical.

'My teachers were wankers. They couldn't control the kids, innit.'

'The teachers used to come in and we would blatantly tell them to go away. Mr Smith, he was our head of year, and he used to go, "Earrings, girls, blazers," and we used to go shut up.'

'He used to make us wipe our eye make-up off.'

'Yes, he used to say wipe your make-up off, and we used to say go away you pervert. He used to go, "Blazers," and we used to go, "Erh, get off me." And he used to leave us alone.'

Gemma, a girl I meet in a Birmingham club, is absolute in her criticism of school: 'School was a complete waste of time. I never went because I got bullied a lot and then I failed all my exams. I didn't get any at all.'

The more kids I spoke to, the more people kicked back about both the method and the content of what they were being taught. Perhaps the most common criticisms were around issues of practicality and relevance. There was no implicit belief that knowledge by itself has any use.

Old words, nu wurdz

I only notice a shared characteristic of many of the houses, flats, bedrooms that I visit after several months, because it's an absence. Very few have bookcases. VHSs, DVDs and video games easily outnumber the books. And they rarely come up as subjects of conversation when I ask people for their favourite entertainment.

You only have to look at some of the 'favourite author' lines on the Face Party site to realise that reading books is not high on many young people's list of priorities. Lauren121 writes: 'Whoever Writes 'Ok' Mag =)'. Stubley45 writes: 'pardon? say that in me gud ear.' And rapfan (Lee – 17): 'yer rite.. duno wat a book is exept kama sutr.' Rather than simply ignorance, this seems to reflect something approaching scorn for an old way of doing things.

This rejection of books does not go hand in hand with lack of creative expression. This is how lauren121 presents herself.

```
In My Own Words …
^v^v^— *Ummz* ~ I'm Dizzy · Bubbly · Happy · Confident ·
Cheeky · Fun Loving · Outgoing · Smirnoff Sippin' · McFlurry
Munchin' · Off Her trolley · ChatterBox · Fashion Obsessed ·
Music Mad · Clubbing Crazed · Addicted 2 Hugz · Gossip Luvin
· Girly Girl · with … Vª Vª V°°m! =_ (So Dont Judge this
Girlz Book By Her Cover) _·· _ Im a Quality Drunken lass! .
<3 ·BRING ON tHE BACARDI· [Grown>A<Liking>4<SmirnoffIce] I
Kick Butt @ Doin tha >> 'MoonWalk' \\ :. [jacko-stylee-
baybee] Cant WAIt till I can start learnin2 drive! Gonna be
a Girl Racer™ ~ Y e a h … B a b y! <3 *Loz Knows* ^v^v^—
PS.. SHOUt Out 2 Si [trippin trout] ~ ACCESORIZE™ (Boy! I
can SOO Kick u @ Checkers!) Hu da Laydee!!!?? OMG!! I Have A
'Loz~Wannabe' *Grrr* ~ Copied All My Profile! ~~>
candy_floss_21 >> stoopid faker ~ Get a LIFE!!
```

Likewise stubley45 is not reticent.

```
hey, ive got a gr8 sense of humour n i play about alot, any1
who listens to HIM, then look at my pics cos ive met Ville
Valo :P i also got a signed cd! woohoo RATE ME n MSG ME,
cyas 18as lv ya \m/
```

Whatever you think about this, you have to admit it's a complex and highly personalised form of expression. This is why Lauren gets annoyed at candy_floss copying her style and so nicking bits of her personality. At Face Party, where the aim is to encourage people to get in touch with you, the language needs to be accessible. It needs to be friendly. And most importantly it needs to help you stand out from the other, equally visible, million-plus members. Being different, distinctive and playful is more important than being perfect. With the increase in the forms of textual communication, writing has become less formal than speech. So, even if you're feeling down, like Kayla claims to be on Face Party, at least you can have some fun with the way you tell people.

```
:-( Kinda sad, im totally screwin with sum1's life bcos of
this nd it aint fair x im sorry bradley x Im a confused lil
```

```
girly at ze momentum … im totally completely 100% in love
with some1 i aint allowed 2 b in love with :-( SUCKS …
HELP!! … please … :-( so i can 'turn my frown upside down'
:-) O well!! Tis true guys..IM PAST SAVING …
```

The signs of linguistic creativity are everywhere: on the back of album sleeves, on the walls surrounding estates and schools, on bags and T-shirts, on the music channel text-ins and the chatrooms and forums. These people can't spell. Or rather, they spell very differently.

Language is never static; most of us have come to terms with that. The first dictionary only struggled into being in the eighteenth century. And even then it was out of date. Shakespeare and Chaucer managed without one. We know that any attempts to keep checks on language are bound to fail. But these days there is an unprecedented involvement in twisting language and an explosive ability to record and distribute these mongrel forms. Check out urbandictionary.com, which doesn't try to restrict a word to a tight definition, but invites multiple submissions, people's own interpretations. The verbal equivalent of time-lapse photography, where you see a plant grow, flower and wither in the space of seconds. You can't help thinking that you are watching evolution.

Are we happy with this? In many ways it depends on whether the egalitarianism, accessibility and democracy of modern communications bothers you or not.

It certainly bothers people like Martin Amis, who have made their money and names distorting language, but from the privileged position of someone who has been taught how to. I go to hear him read from his book *Yellow Dog*, a novel within which language degenerates at the hands of everyone from his satirised royal family to a transsexual e-mailer, whose abbreviations and new combinations are far more extreme and illogical than any teen chatroom. The reading takes place at the Cecil Sharp House in Regent's Park, which serves as the headquarters of the English Folk Dance and Song Society. It's a regular bookish crowd: the serious, bespectacled males in jackets and bad-fitting cords who ask fervent and personal questions at the end, revealing two decades of Amis adoration; the mid-forties couples on their second cultural wind; the stylised frump and chaotic hair of late twentysomething women. There are a couple of younger kids with their parents. But no teenagers on their own.

We sit in one of the dancing halls. I read about sprung floors and splendid acoustics. A couple in front of me remarks on the quaintness of English folk dance; they're surprised that it still goes on. As Amis takes the stand, about to read from one of his most criticised novels, I wonder how long it will be before the novel joins folk dancing as a slightly comical, antiquated art form.

Unlike the flow of a proficient texter or messenger, where words are used to make reading more simple, or more fun, transsexual k8's mails just make everything more tricky:

```
I've got a new str@agem: not washing. Let's c how long he
can st& the s10ch! …
```

At the talk he bemoans the death of distance, how the egalitarianism that is sweeping the nation affects his art, because there are more people who claim (inappropriately) to be artistic. 'You can get rich without talent, you can get famous without talent,' he says, 'but you can't get talent without talent.' It seems to me that Amis believes that only a select few can mess around with words. But most of young Britain isn't taking any notice.

Seeing kids constantly texting, e-mailing, chatting and blogging flies in the face of an idea of an explosion of illiteracy. It looks more like the spread of a sort of individual literacy. People deciding how they want to use language at a certain time for certain audiences. This distortion doesn't have a solid basis in the correct rules of English grammar, but is there something wrong with people learning their craft at their own hands? As long as the people who receive the message understand it, what else is language for?

We know that people don't need grammar or a fixed form of spelling to understand stuff. We can see this from the flexible spelling everywhere, and just in case you didn't believe it, an e-mail doing the rounds in October and purporting to refer to a Cambridge University study backs this up.

```
Hlelo
Aoccdrnig to a rscheearch at Cmabrigde Uinervtisy, it
deosn't mttaer in waht oredr the ltteers in a wrod are, the
olny iprmoetnt tihng is taht the frist and lsat ltteer be at
```

the rghit pclae. The rset can be a total mses and you can
sitll raed it wouthit porbelm. Tihs is bcuseae the huamn
mnid deos not raed ervey lteter by istlef, but the wrod as a
wlohe.

Tanhks vrey mcuh

Basic skills

Another of the British media's favourite subjects is the lowering of
standards in schools. Mickey Mouse university degrees, easy exams,
incompetent teachers, teachers fixing exam results, and so on. And of
course, these exist against a wider background of the endless articles about
the dumbing down of modern society. But the core message is the same,
however it's told: more kids are stupid, they can't spell properly, they can't
do their sums, and you might as well forget about grammar.

The Basic Skills Agency exists to improve the UK's numeracy and
literacy. As I try to enter the building where its offices are located, I am
reminded of a cartoon where the front door to the Hang-gliders Club
opens thirteen floors above the street. I see the name 'Basic Skills'
through the glass and wrestle with the door for a few moments until I
notice the smaller writing: 'Please report to the West entrance.' When I
finally reach the correct floor, I'm greeted by a big sign in the door:
'Please do not leave deliveries blocking these doors.' Beneath the sign are
a few cartons of milk, and to the left of it are two large taped cardboard
boxes, hurriedly discarded. I wonder at the level of literacy among
delivery men.

Alan Wells is the director of the Basic Skills Agency. He's in his mid-
forties with short, dark grey hair and metal-framed glasses. He is friendly,
and most definitely not the precise academic: I am pleased to hear him
pepper his conversation with less-than-perfect English. His office ends
in a point. It reminds him of a ship's prow, he tells me, and when he has
a tough problem to figure out he stands at the apex, gazing at St Pauls,
seeking inspiration. Throughout our interview, I have a vision of him
sailing his Basic Skills vessel to the corners of the UK, searching out the
innumerate, the illiterate and the unlucky. Although according to him, a
true illiterate these days is hard to find.

Alan has little time for the endless doom-laden reports of the media. I ask him how many illiterate people there are in Britain, quoting a few of the more extreme headlines at him.

'The press tends to say millions of illiterates. I've been doing this kind of work for thirty years. I've met probably five people who I would say were illiterate, and largely they were travellers who had never been to school. What we've got is people whose skills are not good enough because the goalposts have moved. Fifty years ago their skills would have been perfectly adequate. Your skills have to be better because the nature of the world has changed. That's why it's really difficult to compare literacy standards over time.

'Standards in primary schools have been going up since the mid-nineties. Every time you say that, someone brings out a piece of paper saying they haven't. I've been to about twelve hundred schools in the last three years. Of those, over a thousand are primary schools. You've only got to go to a lot to see that standards have risen, children are better.'

As with so many of my interviewees who actually worked with young people, government reports and media portrayals are seen as inaccurate and damaging.

'It's politically popular to claim high illiteracy, but the research here does not demonstrate that. You have to understand that politicians see things in short-term ways. They want headlines, they want big sums of money thrown at particular problems. There's no great joy in saying "country literate". That's not a headline. And no money's going to be produced.'

Perhaps part of the hysteria that surrounds the transformation of English is more to do with adult than youth illiteracy. In the *Telegraph* in March an article appears about a teacher who was horrified when a girl handed in an essay in text shorthand.

'The teenager's essay began: 'My smmr hols wr CWOT. B4, we usd 2go2 NY 2C my bro, his GF & thr 3 :- kds FTF. ILNY, it's a gr8 plc.' Translation: 'My summer holidays were a complete waste of time. Before, we used to go to New York to see my brother, his girlfriend and their three screaming kids face to face. I love New York, it's a great place.'

Her teacher, who asked not to be named, said: 'I could not believe what I was seeing. The page was riddled with hieroglyphics, many of which I simply could not translate.'

Horrified partly because here was a language, a version of English, that this teacher had no ability to understand. Language is one more strategy of disconnection, and youth languages are creating vast swathes of culture that are unintelligible to people who like to think of themselves as literate.

As with the scorn that Stubley displayed for books, there is a more general rejection of inherited, and correct, language. As if to say, we don't want your fashion, your music or your laws. Why should we take on your forms of expression when we can make our own?

On the side of so-called proper English, you've got the weight of history, where English matures gradually, under the watchful eye of its approved guardians – the poets, newspaper editors, the BBC. On the side of mongrel English, you've got speed, variety and volume. Too many different sources of different language changing too quickly for one set of rules, for a standard form, to triumph. And of course, these variations bleed into the everyday. When Dizzee Rascal, a nineteen-year-old rapper from east London, picks up the 2003 Mercury Music Prize, it's a sign of how quickly incorrect language makes the leap. In the track 'I Luv U', he separates correct language from stupidity:

right im not articulate
im not an idiot

And of course, his fans are as creative as he is with language. Following news of his victory, message boards are lively with enthusiasm and abbreviations.

```
i lv his nu vidio is shabby!!! big up!!!! anyways lets get
bk 2 dizee ma hubby well keep up all da gud work an dnt let
no1 let u dwn an stop u frm doin ur thing coz der jus hatin
on ya cuz they cnt get ur voice or hav all da gyals u hav
there aint no point hatin really ur jus wastin ur time an
der isnt any point u peeps jus aint got a life so go GET 1
an stop hatin please an dis is 2 da person dat shot him FCUK
YOU STOP HATIN wot did i jus say gheese any1 eles wnt 2 hate
him aint no point
```

This clash of old and new languages, of standard and variations, is demonstrated nicely when Mr Justice Lewison is asked to rule in a copyright case involving the Heartless Crew. Describing terms like 'mish mash man' and 'shizzle my nizzle' as a foreign language, he confesses to being at a loss even after consulting an urban dictionary on the internet, which seems relatively farsighted for a judge.

For Alan Wells, literacy at its most basic is about being able to communicate appropriately, and that doesn't always mean using perfect English or conforming to one set of rules.

'Most people have more than one language. They have more than one spoken language. Most young people know that the way you write an application form for a job is not the same as the way you text your friends on a mobile. It's insulting to think that they wouldn't know that.

'We should give people a bit of respect and acknowledge that these things will always be there. I think you have to live with realities ... there is TV, text messaging, the internet. The idea that television's wholly bad and reading's wholly good is simplistic: it depends on what you're reading. You can't take choices away from people. What you can do is to give them the appropriate skills so they know which choices at which time and which appropriate language at which time.'

Certainly the kids I meet have many languages. When I talked with them, as with anyone, they tended to speak more formally and thoughtfully than when they spoke to their friends. I would get texts from someone I was about to meet that wouldn't contain a proper word. Just abbreviations and numbers. But this is in itself no indication of illiteracy. Critics mistake one characteristic of communication for its entire truth. Kids slip between different versions of English like they slip between different realities and different identities. They choose what they want to use and when.

As English becomes the world language – at least in terms of entertainment – so its role becomes broader: it has to work for many more people, and many more types of people. English is almost a meta language ... a source code for thousands of regional and cultural variations, of which 'proper', 'correct', grammatical English is just one version.

Mark, Bart and Charlie Brown

I was curious about the people at the front line of the transformation of British kids' intelligence. From the incompetence of teachers, to the supposed irrelevance of new courses – Sheffield Hallam university offers a thirteen-month MSc in entertainment software development (sponsored by Sony and dubbed the PlayStation degree) – the falling standards of exams to the growing problem of pupil-on-teacher violence, schools have frequently been accused of contributing to the overall decline of British youth.

Mark Yelland is assistant head teacher at the London Nautical School. I wait for ten minutes in the reception, looking at the display cases of cups, the annual photographs, the bells and model ships. Despite the naval setting, Mark tells me that the school is mainly for working-class kids from estates in south London.

His office is tiny and cramped. There are piles of books and papers, a life-size cut-out of Bart Simpson leaning against one of the windows. There are clothes hanging from the bookcases. He speaks very clearly and plays with an elastic band the whole time. Afterwards he tells me that the microphones make him nervous. He's the only person I speak to who ever mentions the tiny minidisk that generally sits between my interviewees and me.

He talks about the importance of bringing the outside world into teaching.

'You have to make sure you plan something that's effective and accessible and relevant and fun and structured. It's important to include stuff from outside of the classroom, from real life, from TV and music.'

He nods to the fact that outside school kids are exposed to a far greater range of stimulation and experience, and acknowledges that this should affect the way that school works.

'The way things are done in the classrooms is changing. We're going to have an interactive whiteboard in each room that links to the computer, it plays CDs, you can show images on it. If you capture people's imaginations, they're going to be more focused on things.'

But despite this influx of tech, he admits that the basic way intelligence is measured has not changed and remains firmly in a time of learning by rote.

'Examinations haven't changed. I do feel that it's a failure of the education system that we examine memories, not skills. A written answer doesn't really test very much except the use of grammar, punctuation, spelling, quality of handwriting and memory. You see amazing learning going on in lots of schools: kids from different community groups working together on a long-term project, and what they take back is greater than the memory of a fact. But how you would examine that I have no idea.'

Mark feels that his experience of kids varies greatly from the way that British youth is portrayed in the media.

'It annoys me and frustrates me immensely. When I tell people I'm a teacher, they are surprised that I'm enthusiastic. The idea is that teachers complain and don't like their jobs. And aren't very good because of media representation. There was a programme called *Gangs* on the night before and it was pure media propaganda. Yeah, there are these gangs and they've been stabbing and robbing people, but it's part of social dysfunction and alienation. I haven't seen a documentary that shows teenagers in a positive light ever. I haven't seen anything about the kind of teenagers that grow up to be positive influences in their community. Every year we have a prize giving, and there's one community award, and the things that kids have been working on out of school range from working with the elderly, the physically and mentally disabled, volunteering, to sports coaching with primary school kids. And you look at their lives and their difficulties – poverty, deprivation, divorce, bereavement – all the social issues that are not addressed in the media and they are doing fantastic things – inside and outside schools. And yeah, sometimes they're little buggers.'

'Are the kids aware of how they're portrayed? What kind of effect do you think it has?'

'Oh God, yeah. Yeah. They see the same things on TV that we see. They see the stereotypes of what a youth is. They're a lot brighter than people understand. It's like the Charlie Brown cartoons – they are adults, they're just smaller. I don't think media shows the breadth of experience of teenagers. The front page is only ever "Head Teacher Stabbed" ... not anything else. Sometimes my parents worry about me working in London, in a school in the inner city. They read things and I try to explain that that's a tiny part of it. And I stopped watching the programme on gang culture because it was annoying me.'

When we leave, he asks me to wait outside while he changes from his suit into sneakers, T-shirt and slightly tight trousers. We go to the pub. The teachers sit and chain-smoke, making up for the nicotine-free days. They speak with slightly exaggerated gestures and facial expressions, making-the-point-very-clearly. What strikes me is the passion for their job, and their interest in their pupils. They talk about them fondly, by name, aware of certain issues at home, recounting conversations where they talk to them, not quite as equals, but certainly not as morons.

Teaching teachers

Mike Smith presents me with another view of school. He is older, and slightly more cynical, but still seems convinced of the overall goodness and smartness of his kids.

It's a sunny afternoon, and I walk past the Adidas-sponsored basketball course. A few customers (that's how the pupils are referred to here) are strolling home, but the school is empty. It's exam time, and Mike is down to a few hours' teaching a week. He's the director of IT at the ADT school in south London, a former city technology college where much of the funding comes from private companies. There are 1100 students aged eleven to eighteen here, at all levels of academic ability, but also with some degree of technical aptitude.

We sit in the sun next to the Thames Gas and the Unisys buildings. He's spent the day deleting downloaded games from the school network. Gigabytes and gigabytes, he tells me.

'They have no problem being amoral. Copyright isn't even on their radar. The ones with broadband download entire films and sell the DVDs in the playground.'

Recently he asked the Federation against Copyright Theft (FACT) to send stern letters to the more persistent entrepreneurs. But despite his immediate nod to their criminality, he laughs off the suggestion that schools are full of mini-gangsters.

While Mark had turned off Channel 4's documentary on gangs because he was so annoyed by it, Mike is less upset. 'It's play-acting. It's cowboys and Indians. It's how the eleven- and twelve-year-olds act. Those things do exist but not for most kids.'

And he is unwilling to toe the 'kids are more stupid' line either.

'I don't think that's true. They might not be so good at the old-fashioned skills, but they're very media savvy. They know when they're being bullshitted. Very perceptive. Very good at learning new skills. They've got amazing IT skills. The kids who have been through the Key Stage Three strategy and the literacy and numeracy in primary schools, they're a lot better than they were ten years ago. Kids are better at basic English and basic maths than they used to be.'

Mike then goes on to suggest that they are considerably better at working problems out for themselves. Rather than just receiving pre-prepared nuggets of wisdom.

'They're very open, they're prepared to have a go, sit down and figure it out. The internet's just the internet. It's nothing new; they just accept it. It's part of their lives, like text messaging, instant messaging and down-loading games, videos, trailers. Communication is not even talked about. It just happens.'

He also suggests that learning and teaching have become more of a two-way process, with kids contributing to the overall class.

'My background's in maths, and I've never been taught maths by a kid, but every day I might get taught something in IT. Something that I've not seen before, or a new technique. A new way of doing things. And teachers have to embrace that. Some teachers aren't very comfortable with that. And some of the kids aren't that comfortable either.'

Nevertheless, it's still the traditional notion of passing on welcome knowledge that makes him enjoy the job.

'The best day for me is coming in in August, when you get a good set of exam results. But also every day when you see a kid's face go from being puzzled to their eyebrows going up and them saying, "Ah, I never quite understood that," and then they get it. Those are nice warm moments as well.'

Education through music

'I think that schools are the biggest destroyer of our youth. I think they should be replaced immediately. They are a bastion of traditional pedagogy. They should be taken away. It's a waste of money when we could do it cheaper.'

I'm talking with Alwyn Pereira, CEO of YES (Youth Entertainment Studios), to get an idea of a positive alternative to school. It's a charity/company that he has been running for two years, offering 'hard to reach' kids a different model of learning. The charity is in a converted house in an area that Alwyn describes as 'the ghetto'. There is a recording studio, a video editing suite. When I go in, there are groups of teens huddled around computers, a buzz in the air, and people laughing. It doesn't feel like school. Alwyn tells me that they've had up to three hundred kids wanting to use the facilities. Currently they have a waiting list of ninety people, and they can only take on ten at a time. As Beverley Thomas had pointed out, if you get expelled from school, there aren't a lot of alternatives.

YES offers a different model of education … not just in terms of the enthusiasm, but in the erasure of lines between teacher and pupil. The people who start courses here go on to become mentors for newer students.

As Alwyn explains, 'YES is a new kind of education system. When young people come in here they're challenged to make a product that is marketable and they can sell so they can engage in the marketplace and the economy which is all around them.'

Despite the fact that many schools might offer courses in web design and other contemporary media, Alwyn feels that YES presents it in a very different way. There is a focus on tangibility and output, on making something that can work in the real world, beyond the classroom.

'It's not being taught in schools in this way. For example, we do web design or we do music editing or video editing. But it's about making products. The young person will produce a film or a CD, and we will help them do it. We bring in coaches from different industries, mentors, they tell us how to do it, and off we go.' This immediately addresses one of the criticisms of school that I'd heard from several kids. That it was pointless, because they could see little practical application for what they were learning.

'The official term for the kids who come to YES is "hard to reach". What does that mean?'

'That's because they don't attend other facilities or they're marginalised. They've caused trouble there before. They won't go to school, or they're excluded from school. Or they have criminal records. They're the ones who would be hanging round. They're a silent group, but they could cause lots of trouble. They're perceived as causing trouble; they're very difficult to engage.'

Alwyn believes that part of the reason that schools can't engage with these kinds of pupils is that what he calls 'normal systems' are too rigid.

'There's so much bureaucracy and paperwork in schools, it's difficult for teachers to teach in these ways. And there's a set style – I think it's political – which appeals to a certain group of Middle England who say, if we get all these SATs, then that's a good measure, and it's just not true. If you're too structured and inflexible, you're not going to be able to adjust. And we don't want to teach young people to be inflexible when the reality is that all businesses are always in a state of change. It's continual learning. We are a new education system for a new age. The age of transformation. Here everything is customised.'

'Do you find it hard to work with them? Is it difficult to manage or engage them?

'No. I enjoy their company. I want to build a rapport and support them. But they enjoy it here because this is what they want to do. This is where their passion is. We profile them all the way through, and you can see when they come in the first week, it's like, "Uhhh, another college," and then you follow it up in two to three weeks and you see the change. "I've got hope, I've got vision. I don't want to leave. I want to stay because this is going to get me where I want to go. If I don't do it, it's my own fault."

'There's a lot of responsibility given to them; they just feel this is their chance: "If I don't take it, I can't blame the school; it's me."'

While music is the most popular course here, Alwyn tells me that the kids also have ideas for film, fashion, photography. He waves a bit of paper at me.

'Here's a guy who's just done a business plan for his start-up. If you look at his educational background, he's been written off; there's no way he can do that. In ten weeks, these guys who aren't meant to be computer-literate are learning how to use Avid DV and Pro tools. How's that possible? That's a remarkable transformation.'

'And what would your students be doing if YES didn't exist?'

'They would be hustling. They would be bored. They probably would be doing crime. They don't want to grow up and be criminals. They definitely don't. They're pushed there. And I can see that progression from a young age.'

Alwyn's describes these 'hard to reach' kids as passionate and motivated. They are the same kids who are presented as surly and difficult when in a school context, and yet, somehow, in this crowded and underfinanced building, he has managed to unlock a stream of energy and creativity. This is partly due to the fact that he is helping them get closer to something that they care about, rather than forcing some random way of working and learning on them.

'They want to be doing this. Half of them want to be doing their business. They want to be self-directed. In charge of their own destiny. Not someone else controlling it. And what's really sad is that given the money they would make it. Because they work so hard. I've worked with lots of different groups, I've worked with nice kids, kids at private schools, but these guys have got a determination because it's the ghetto.'

Despite the obvious benefits of Alwyn's scheme, despite the plaudits he has received from local police and some of the professionals that he has brought in to do courses, it has been difficult to keep the funding coming in, partly because of the application systems which mean you have to reapply each year, partly because most education funding is geared towards exam results and so YES is not credited, but also because of the perceptions that he is running a school for criminals.

'It's very difficult to get any venture capital. As soon as I say a black TV station, it's like: what do black people want TV for? When my potential funders saw black youth on our photographs, I had some saying to me, "If you get some white kids, some little girls, it's more appealing. This picture is not appealing. As soon as you look at it, you go, 'Muggers. Why should I fund muggers? Why should I let muggers have a good time?'"

'But we know this thing works. We use the energy of youth to get stuff going in a way that schools can't. People team up and form their own companies and they employ each other. It's like So Solid Crew, so you'd work within that crew. Lots of different skills and they'll pull in people at certain times. It's a fantastic model. So we can work with different gangs, and get the whole gang to be part of a company. And not feel left out.'

Be your own catalyst

Lionel, Romano and Daniel are the trio at YES who talked to me about being street poets and helping the blind man to see how life really is.

They echo Alwyn's sentiment that it's about mixing different skills and working as a team. Daniel is engineer, producer and DJ. Romano is the vocalist and A&R man. 'I look for talent and come up with mad ideas.' Lionel is a lyricist and producer 'as well as being on the business side'.

'We're making music and trying to make shit happen. We all a team right here. Everyone in here is actually a team.'

Romano echoes this: 'A team.'

'Yeah, working together, man.'

The first principle of teamwork – equality – seems burned into them.

'We divide as one, you get me?' says Daniel.

'There's no "he's higher than that one" cos everyone can do their own ting, innit. We just come together, bring all our different talents together. See what we come out with. A lot of these places don't really get funded because they feel that people are not going to get nuttin out of it. Again as I say, idle hands make the devil's work, so if I'm in here, I'm not going to be outside robbing. I'm gonna be inside making music, get me?'

One of the attractions for them is the lack of traditional teaching, of being told how to do stuff. Instead, they have been left to get on with it themselves; it's about tools, not rules.

This freedom seems notably lacking from their experience of schools.

'In school I was always doing the music ting but it was in my own time, I make tapes of them tings for my bredren,' Lionel explains.

'I don't think schools are equipped for the music thing,' Romano adds. 'If you're saying you want to do something on the creative side, I don't think they're equipped. Their thing is teachers and books. They're not equipped for the creative side when it comes to showing you how to do music or do whatever we want to do. Know what I'm saying?'

'In my school they did have a studio, but when I went to the music teacher to try and get on it, they were going kinda funny, like they didn't want to let certain people on it. When I did want to go in and do music, they didn't allow me.'

'Is that because they didn't like the kind of music you wanted to make?'

'Not only that. They think I'm going to steal the equipment, you get me?'

There is a strong feeling among all three of them that if you don't follow a prescribed course at school, there's nothing else.

'They'll just leave you,' Daniel tells me. 'Certain time teachers think that if kids are rude and that, that they're dumb, you get me? They don't know what they're going through at home or nothing like that. Certain teachers need to sit down and talk to pupils individually, see where they're coming from, what they wanna do.'

'School's a dictatorship, not a lot of people can hack that,' Romano explains. 'You can't just sit there and be told when to get out of your seat. When to talk and when to do this or do that.'

'That ain't teaching you nothing,' affirms Daniel.

'There's only so much of that you can take.' Lionel joins in. 'But in here it's like everything's just there.'

'This is real life. You gotta be your own catalyst. You got to be self-motivated. That's what this place teaches you. If you don't do nothing, nothing won't get done.'

I can't help thinking that Margaret Thatcher would have been proud of these boys. And that their fierce ambition and independence are the results of immersion in a country where you don't expect others to help you out. I had noticed a latent conservatism in many of the kids I spoke with, even as they were taking part in non-conservative activities. The creation of powerful, local communities in isolated territories, the lack of tolerance towards difference, the personal codes and rigid moralities, the importance of appearance and possessions seemed to have more in common with the certainties and isolationism of the Second World War generation than their liberal, tolerant, expansionist offspring.

Lionel, Romano and Daniel are quite sure what they want from YES, and the education it provides: visible, material success.

'We're hoping to get to the top of this shit,' Lionel tells me with assurance.

'Yeah, knocking Warner Brothers, all of them out,' Romano joins in.

As he says this, all three burst into laughter.

'Once one man gets his foot in the door,' adds Daniel, 'then everyone goes.'

'Trust me.'

'We just knock the door down.'

'We ain't stopping at music. If the shit's successful, films, clothes, cologne.'

'Hell yeah, we come with the bombardment.'

'Kitchen utilities, everything.'

Everyone laughs again.

Natural learning

The creativity and passion of Warfare Records is representative of a broader hunger and talent that is forming a new type of learning and intelligence … fuelled by computer games, the internet, by music editing programs and bits of software that let you mix images, words and sounds with a few mouse sweeps.

I find Saru through someone else's art. A painting catches my eye at a warehouse sale, where a bunch of artists are offloading their spare work. An image of a kid watching TV. The kid's eyes are square, and he drools from the side of his mouth. The screen is tuned to KUNTV, and shows a man and woman fucking, as the woman beheads her lover with a giant axe. The legend '50 channels of sickness to give me bad ideas' is repeated in the background. I'm drawn in by this visual response to the same world I'm exploring and get chatting to Chimp, the artist. As I explain why I like it, he suggests I should talk with Saru, describing him as an example of self-motivated and intelligent creativity. He also gives me a good price for the picture.

This clichéd image of a vacant, violence-seeking generation, beaten into Mogadon-esque catatonia by overexposure to modern culture, comes into my mind when talking with Saru … because he offers such an alternative outcome to the absorption in a hyperactive, colourful entertainment world.

Saru is sixteen and doing A levels. He has the same piercing eyes and quietly confident stare as the kid in the Orange ad. He describes his passion as street art and since first learning to use a computer a couple of years ago has put hundreds of hours into creating and maintaining a website that documents his photography, stickers, clothing and painting.

We're sitting at a table and Saru pulls a Mac out of his rucksack and immediately opens up a stream of picture files. These are to be the backgrounds for the updated version of his site, www.saru-saru.co.uk. They are a mixture of photography, painting, illustration and computer design: a teddy bear holding a machine gun, a tagged CCTV camera, a woman sporting one of Saru's trucker hats. The exit frame is a photo of a figure stood on the roof of a rusting car skeleton. The car is covered in spray paint and half submerged in a sandy beach. The figure on the roof is drawing shapes in the air with a torch or a fire brand.

Saru talks me through the different frames for his website, and explains how it will all flow together.

'I'll load these backgrounds up to Dreamweaver, and type will come here – and you'll be able to click and then a new window opens and it will just be an image. Just the images will come up. I like websites that are simple to manoeuvre around. I can't stand all the Flash things bobbing up everywhere and it just gets on your nerves. My site will be easy to use so anyone can navigate.'

While Saru's current site documents the stickers (mainly ape heads) that he has put up in London and New York, his ambitions for the relaunch are broader.

'There's going to be more graphics. Not just my street art. I want something that reflects all my interests. I'm processing black and white photos in the lab. And this is the page for the shop. I'm going to make T-shirts, and hope to get them out. Which will hopefully fund the work, cos I'm aiming to get a screen-printing set-up, and there's posters, stickers, graphics and photography.'

Despite his laid-back manner of speaking, his eyes and hands don't stop moving. When he's talking with me, he's also looking towards the screen, flicking through a stream of images, indicating a particular design, or gesturing towards a photo as he gives me the story behind it. He burns me a CD of his work while talking me through his customised trucker hat – with Saru rudely painted above the peak. When he's not playing with the computer, he spins the ring on his right hand.

'How did you learn to use the software to put together a website?'
Saru smiles and shrugs.

'It just came naturally. For Photoshop, I just opened it. I don't really read manuals. I've never read a manual for anything. It usually comes spontaneously to me. You learn from errors and mistakes. If it looks good then you know what button to press. With Photoshop you can just press undo, and everything is so easy to change. If you don't like it, you can delete it.'

'How would you figure out how to do something new?'

'I'd try it a few times, and see which worked better. I think Photoshop's an easy programme. I can do anything graphical but as soon as it comes to writing code, I can't do that.'

I wonder how this intuitive method of learning compares with school. While Saru's thoughts about school are among the least negative of anyone I've spoken to, compared to the vibrancy and visible results that his website delivers, school to him, seems unrelated to any practical use.

'It's not that bad. A little bit repetitive after a while. It gets a bit annoying. All the teachers care about is the grade. It just seems that you're working towards one exam, for one grade. And you're not really learning anything. You're learning how to pass an exam. I use the website and my street art as a break from homework.'

Of course, Saru does learn from other people as well, but in a far more fluid sense. He says that most of the artists he hangs with are considerably older than him – in their twenties – and he sees them as a source of inspiration, and sometimes support. When he gets stuck with web design, he talks to a mate who makes sites for companies.

Additional inspiration and learning comes from the web. While the stereotypical response to our overloaded culture is that it blunts its viewers through repetition and volume, Saru sees things differently.

'I'm always searching the web. Everything's an inspiration. It all accumulates and I have hundreds of sketch books with everything stuck in. You end up looking through them over and over again. It all just merges. I end up printing out everything that I like, and put it up on the wall, in folders.'

'What about the links on your site? Is that a good way of finding stuff out?'

'Yeah. It's the way that you find out about different things. For example: woostercollective.com. They're a couple in New York that I met when I was there, and they update it every day with interviews of artists, and I've been featured on there once. I found wooster by clicking on a link randomly, and then from wooster, I found different sites. It's the way that you navigate.

'You have to navigate yourself into this web, and you've got to circulate yourself, and new websites will come up, and you add that to your favourites, but you can't really venture outside of this mesh that you've created. Because then it becomes irrelevant. I can't stand Google, because it brings up totally useless topics.'

This controlled chaos is also reflected in his approach to art.

'I'm producing these jellyfish. Or squids. I nicked the To Let signs made out of corrugated plastic. Cut all these squids out, sprayed them and stuck them up all round London. I didn't intentionally create it to be like this. I used an inkjet printer – cos that's all I've got – and it's not waterproof. So I put acetate over the top, and it bled from underneath. It just created these mad colours. And you could never have planned for that.'

He flicks through a stream of photos of squids, clicking image after image, hands flying over the keyboard and mouse.

'Here I found a car on a beach and sprayed all these squids on it. Every time the tide came in, the paint was eaten away by the salt, so it actually looked like a sea creature by the time it had finished.'

Half an hour, and hundreds of images later, I ask Saru if his passion and productivity are common among his friends.

'Not really. In my school, there's pretty much no one. They take the piss out of you for doing all the street art, and they just sit on their arses all day, playing computer games. And I tell them to fuck off.'

When I say goodbye to Saru he gives me a handful of stickers, produced by a friend in Germany. Teddy bears with machine guns, a godlike figure proclaiming 'Saru: your last hope'. He's got thousands of them done, and is looking to spread himself around. He tells me to put a few up.

Once again, I'm struck by the multiple types of youth contained in one person. In his Stussy hoodie, low slung, scuffed denim and knowing Nikes, his look is pure renegade artist. And the images he has stickered over his part of town point towards someone with a blatant disregard for property laws. But that disregard is backed up by a more altruistic desire than pure vandalism, or even self-promotion. As he says in a post on the woostercollective site, 'i feel that everyone should be able to see art wether they be rich or poor, street art is for everyone and i want to make a contribution'.

Saru is doing four A levels, and has every intention of getting into Central St Martins, one of the country's best art schools. When we're talking he's keen to make sure I understand the intricacies of his web design and painting techniques, even as he's showing me absurd images of jellyfish attached to lampposts. At home, I'm listening back over our conversation through my headphones, thinking how polite and helpful he is. There's a point where I leave the room to go get a blank CD. I hear my footsteps in the distance. There's a moment's silence, a rustle, and he's obviously picked up the mic because a cough explodes in my ears. It really hurts. I can hear Saru sniggering until I return to the room. It reminds me of *Jackass*.

Me without wearing a mask

Saru has the talent to create his own website, but for the less web savvy, the internet offers many opportunities to publicise their thoughts, their creativity, their opinions.

Whereas Face Party lets you present a snapshot of yourself, weblogs allow for a deeper, ongoing personal presentation. Brands like 20six act as hosts: they give you a framework and some storage space and you fill it with your personality. The framework is porous, so you can select colours and fonts, upload graphics and sounds to make the site yours.

Many weblogs revel in the mundane, the quotidian, the tiny details of living, learnt from the attention that celeb mags pay to every element of stars' lives. They represent a democratisation of expression and fame, where everybody has the ability and right to be published.

> I'm a girl of 16, 17 in May and I'm a Gemini. I live in Mansfield in Nottingham, UK. My real name is Clair, but my friends call me Mouse or Mousey. Physically, I am 5'2' (short), have dark blonde hair with pinky red streaks and blue eyes (see 'groovy pics'). I'm open minded, random, Bi-sexual (but prefer guys), I sometimes get very angry and depressed but am usually a very nice and polite person (to some of my friends dislike), however, I can't stand people that are racist, sexist, shallow minded or attention seekers.
>
> **The Year of Fulfilled Dreams/Broken Ambition**
> **(Following The Year of Broken Bones)**

Just told Rhian that Schism have split up, she didn't know …
maybe she was better not knowing but I guess she'd find out
somehow anyways. Got quite a lot of homework done this weekend,
got study leave on Tuesday, and might come home Monday
afternoon cuz we don't have to go to Sociology, just have to
revise. Dad all of a sudden has decided that he is proud of
me … he's never cared before so I don't know why he does
now. I bet he couldn't even tell anyone WHAT I was studying!

Life of a Teenage Weirdo

When I ask Babydragon, author of 'Life of a Teenage Weirdo', about her reasons for having a weblog, she explains it in terms of a space where she can truly express herself.

'If I need to say something that I don't think I can say in my own life, my weblog is where I can say what I need to. I'm not bothered about people reading what I have to say, my weblog is somewhere I can be ME without wearing a mask.'

Despite not being bothered whether people read her weblog or not, she proudly tells me that: 'People come and read my weblog and leave comments about it, and I have became the 38 most favourite blog.'

Looking through these weblogs, which displayed inventiveness, self-deprecation, humour, sadness, but rarely stupidity, got me thinking about the easy equation of celebrity fascination and dumbing down. *Whitaker's Almanack* lays the blame for Britain's idiocy firmly at the feet of our celebrity-obsessed culture. I wondered if it was that simple.

Celebrity worship syndrome

'Just cos you're interested in high heels doesn't mean you're not interested in politics. Just because you might sleep with your new shoes in bed doesn't mean that you haven't got a brain. I think we're so past that myth that you're either a bimbo or a brain.'

One rung up from the gossipy pages of *Heat*, *Now* and *New!* is *Glamour* magazine … just as celeb-fixated, but without the bitchiness. Of all the magazines, it seems the most likely to offer me an intelligent point of view about why celebrities are so important.

The *Glamour* offices are appropriately above Dolce & Gabbana. They appear to be peopled almost entirely by women, apart from a pretty male receptionist, and an older man with his own office, wearing a shirt and tie. The rest of the staff look like they've just strolled in from some classy drinks party. I sit on the sofa, surrounded by purple velvet *Glamour* cushions.

Deborah Joseph looks as perfect as anyone in the pages of *Glamour*. Lustrous dark hair, deep brown eyes, smooth tanned skin, a graceful pink suede coat. We go to a cheap Italian across the road and I feel like I'm having lunch with a celeb, rather than the lifestyle entertainment editor of Britain's favourite celeb mag. She describes *Glamour* as 'real mixture, everything a woman wants', carrying features from beauty tips to women in Iraq. She has no time for people who dismiss celebrity as shallow, and sees no contradiction in the mix of articles that the magazine runs.

Deborah talks about the details of celeb lifestyles that are now laid open for the public: from celebrity make-up artists' tips to exercise regimes and stars' favourite bars.

'Previously you wouldn't even compare yourself, nowadays you actually find out what diet they're on, where they shop.'

Celebrities are life's winners, and magazines are the means by which the trappings of this success are transmitted. Our fascination with them is partly about learning how they do what they do. They represent a better, more successful version of humanity, and we look to them not just out of adoration, but from a desire for our own improvement. Tips to do life better.

'Anyone can be famous for fifteen minutes, or five minutes these days. By going on *Big Brother* or *Changing Rooms* or shagging a celebrity. People want to do it because they associate money, glamour, sex, cars, sexy men, big houses, travelling. It's loads of money for what seems to be not very much work. It's the lifestyle that people want, and also to be adored by the whole world.'

Deborah suggests that the level of intimacy people feel with certain celebrities translates into more profound social influence – and that contemporary celebrities perform a role once reserved for priests and teachers.

'People talk about celebrities like they're friends. So I'll sit and discuss David and Victoria's marriage as though I'm talking about Jo and Steve.

There's no difference. They're part of your extended family. A lot of it is to do with the fact that communities don't exist in the way that they used to but that gossip element is just part of the way that women share information. You don't discuss your neighbours any more because you don't know who they are, but you do talk about a complete stranger who you're never going to meet. If David and Victoria divorced I think it would affect the way Britain thinks about marriage. People would think … if it doesn't work for you, then I might as well give up.'

An article in August in *New Scientist* magazine backs up the theory that we look towards celebrities as a means of improving our own lives. Our brains have learnt to copy our role models. Which helps us to lead more fulfilling lives. In the article, Kate Douglas identifies it as a key element in human evolution. 'Humans are born to imitate and our success as a species is largely down to this talent.'

And evolutionary anthropologist Francesco Gill-White from the University of Pennsylvania in Philadelphia adds: 'It makes sense for you to rank individuals according to how successful they are at the behaviours you are trying to copy, because whoever is getting more of what everybody wants is probably using above-average methods.'

So, while *Whitaker's Almanack* might criticise teens' preference for celebrity over political knowledge, it seems an entirely practical life strategy. A smart choice. Despite the myth of superficiality, it's clear that successful people live better lives. And through magazines like *Glamour*, shows like *Pop Idol*, and as a result of the sheer velocity of modern entertainment, celebrity has become less distant, more democratic, more touchable, potentially achievable for anyone.

Busted

Reading a few mags a week is one level of celeb interest … chasing limos and waiting at airports to catch your favourite star is another. I bump into Leigh Ann, Bridget and Marika when they're waiting outside the BBC in White City. It's a Thursday and they're hoping to catch a glimpse of Busted – a trio of good-looking boys who claim to write their own songs and play their own instruments – when they arrive for *Top of the Pops*. We get talking and they tell me that they're Busted's greatest fans. When I ask them if they'd like to explain to me what being a fan is all about, they nod enthusiastically.

We get together a week later in a nearby coffee shop. They're wearing short denim skirts with thick leather belts hanging loose, and chains dangling from the belts. They've all got long light-brown hair streaked with other colours – blondes, pinks, greens. They wear sweatbands and are clutching a book that has the familiar skull and crossbones on the cover, with a halo and wings added to it. It's their tribute book to Busted, they tell me. The second one.

They're about to do their GCSEs, and moan about the fact that a Busted gig lies right in the middle of them. They plan to stay at college: Bridget to study drama, Leigh Ann to do business studies and Marika sociology. But they know what their special subject is. As Bridget says, 'If we had an exam in Busted we'd definitely get an A star.'

Leigh Ann, Bridget and Marika are three lively girls. But they talk like one fan. United by their passion for Busted, they speak collectively, regularly using the first person plural. As soon as one girl draws breath, another starts talking, but this isn't interruption, it's a seamless flow of fan anecdote.

As befits their three-into-one status, each of them conveniently has their own favourite in the band. Leigh Ann who claims to have been into them first likes James best. Bridget goes for Matt. And Marika prefers Charlie.

As she says, 'It's kind of worked out that we've all got our favourites.'

'We didn't plan it like that.'

'We all went for the one we liked best.'

'We all suit each other's look and personality.'

'And you say you're good fans of Busted?'

'We're better than quite good fans. We are the best. I know everyone says it but we really are.'

'We are their number one fans and they know. If you ask them they will say we are their number one fans.'

'What lets you say that?'

'Okay, once we went to the airport at seven in the morning,' Bridget begins, 'and we didn't leave until half ten in the evening cos we thought they were going to be there.'

'Fourteen and a half hours.'

'Fourteen and a half hours and they weren't there and we were still happy at the end of it.'

'We got an invite to their video shoot. They put fans in their video. So if you're part of the website then they will send you out an invite.'

'They send you an invitation if you're over a certain age.'

'So we went to Birmingham.'

'Were you in the video?'

'Yeah, yeah, yeah.'

'Yeah, but you can only see us if you know where we are,' Bridget says, a touch mournfully. And Leigh Ann comes in with 'know where we are' for the second half of the sentence at exactly the same time, like an echo. I get the sense that these stories have been told before, that between them they have created a Busted folklore.

'Before the video, we started making them a book. We stuck loads of photos inside and we wrote things about them and about the album.'

'One thing we did was write a review on the album and they didn't know which one to release and after they read our song review they've decided which one to release. So their next song, it was chosen by us.'

'What song?'

'"Sleeping With the Light On",' say three voices in perfect unison.

'Someone might think that we see them differently because we go out of our way so much.'

'Because it's nice being in their company: there was one point they stopped for half an hour and were late for something else to chat to us.'

'Capital FM: they were asked on Capital Radio Live what was one of the best things a fan's ever given them and they said, "Well, there's these three girls … "'

'"Hardcore."'

'"Who come and see us a lot. Hardcore fans, and they made us this book, and it was so good, and it had loads of stuff in it. And we thought that was so nice."'

'"Nice of them."'

'Maybe if there's a lot of fans they won't stop but if it's us three there they will try their best because they know we do so much for them and they appreciate it.'

'The amount we spend on them as well.'

'And they don't always see us as fans, because there was a signing with loads of fans and James was talking to her, and their managers tried to pull him away and he was like, "No, it's different: I know her." And we thought that was really nice.'

'We actually feel more like friends.'

Both Leigh Ann and Marika chime in together, 'Friends than fans.'

Not only do they see their relationship with Busted as deeper than average, they believe that their devotion has given them a certain visibility among the other fans; that, relatively, they have become famous.

'The weird thing about it is that other Busted fans know who we are.'

'People always recognise us but we don't know who they are.'

'The stuff we do for them,' Bridget concludes. 'If we felt it was going nowhere then we wouldn't do it but because they do nice stuff back, it's like ping pong, a two-way thing.'

This two-way thing is important. Leigh Ann, Bridget and Marika believe they are part of Busted's world, that they are valued and recognised by the three band members.

I ask them to talk me through the book they have prepared for Busted. They giggle and apologise for what they call the 'bad language' inside the cover as they show me their 'amazing, peaceful and totally fucked world of Busted angels'.

'That's like our nickname ... we're Busted angels.'

The book is a sign of their devotion to and involvement with everything that is Busted. Every 'o' on the intro has a devil's horn scribbled onto it. There are bios of all the girls, where half the answers relate to Busted; a section entitled '10 things I would like to jack from Charlie/Matt/James', including items like 'his baby blue shirt with the rocket' and 'his number'; pictures of all three with their band favourite. In their '10 things I love about ... ', they've all written 'his ass'. Then there are the illustrations: Nicola from Girls Aloud having her hair blowtorched, Louis Walsh, manager of Westlife, with a noose round his neck. The representatives of manufactured pop getting it.

Despite such adoration and effort, Leigh Ann and friends aren't dupes, and display a practicality that might seem at odds with their devotion. I ask if Busted are different to regular people.

'To us it's only a job,' Marika says coolly.

'It's just a job.'

'They're not famous, it's only a job. They're just doing a job that they like.'

'Their job is to entertain people.'

'So we don't really see them as famous.'

Talking with Leigh Ann and friends, I realise that a simple fan/celeb split is oversimplistic. These fans slip between different levels easily. They like, even adore, Busted as fans. But they understand they are real. And they are fans of Busted, but celebs to other fans. Their passion for Busted is not just directed at a distant band, but acts as a social and creative force for the three girls. It has also let them participate – however briefly – in the world of celebrity, via appearances in the video and namechecks on the radio. They are an active audience, keen to play a role in the success of their chosen band. This didn't seem dumb to me.

Active fanatics

This active fanaticism is highly visible online. Type in any band name and a plethora of sites as well as the official site will spring up. These tend to be similar: news archives, photos from gigs, band info, track listings. But the energy and time put into each of them suggests that the kind of devotion that Leigh Ann and friends displayed is common.

I get in touch with Owen Richards, who has been running his Hell is for Heroes website since 2001, after teaching himself Dreamweaver. He's nineteen and studying photography at Exeter University. And he feels that running the website has helped in his course.

I e-mail Owen some questions about his site and his affection for the band. Like the Busted fans, Owen feels that they are receptive to his attention. I ask him if they're a good band to support.

```
definitely. they really care about their fans (HIFH don't
like that word they prefer supporters) they used to sell
their own merchandise so they like interaction with people.
i am naturally biased though. also the people surrounding
them (managers, tech guys etc) are really friendly and
accommodating.
```

This friendliness has translated into useful contacts for Owen.

I have met them quite a few times. they are really
supportive of the site and they actually want to talk to you
about stuff other than music. I am into music photography
and they have some contacts which have helped me. on a
personal note I have made a lot of friends through them.
such as other bands and people in the music industry like
photographers etc. I get a few free tickets to gigs and they
have sent me some promo records. i also get to meet the band
as they know me. my photographs have been in their official
fanzines, i think that was as a result of the site too. I
have also made friends through it.

Owen is keen to distance himself from the 'fan' label. In the same way that
Leigh Ann and co. place themselves above the average Busted fan, Owen
describes a more active role, even taking responsibility for some of HIFH's
success.

a fan is someone who buys the records and goes to the shows.
a supporter is a person who helps establish a band be it
through a website or word of mouth. I was known as their free
PR man for a while. i have helped create the online fan base.

I get a similar sense of active involvement from Christina, who is
seventeen and has been running a Busted site since 2002. Previous to that
she had run one devoted to Mattie-Jay. She learnt how to do it from 'just
little things I have picked up over the past few years'. She likes the fact
running the site has given her contact with the band as well as respect
from other fans.

other fans visit and appreciate the work that you do. Also,
Matt knows about my website I run on him, and its nice to
get his comments on what he thinks of it. I think as well,
the fact that we feel as though we have made a contribution
to busteds success … that feels really cool!

When I ask her about her level of commitment, I feel fortunate that Leigh
Ann isn't there. 'Do you think you're their best fans?'

Lol yeah in a way i do! We have been there for Busted since before they made it big so we have seen them grow into what they are today. We helped to spread the word when they were first starting out, and we are still with them today.

DIY

When you've got Google and mobiles who needs memory? When Spellcheck is one click away, how important is it to truly know words? Much of the unease expressed around kids' intelligence seems to be a nostalgic attachment to a 'proper' but less effective way of finding and using information. The YES boys and Saru are representative of a more practical model of learning and creativity, where the process is only important if it leads to some useful or entertaining output. Owen, Leigh Ann and Christina show how the so-called superficiality of fame can be the catalyst for inventive and productive communication.

All these kids represent the amateur creativity and self-expression that is sweeping Britain, erasing the line between producer and consumer, between artist and audience, between instructor and pupil. More and entertainment requires audience input – from the TV shows whose result depends on the viewers to more engaging forms like PlayStation's MTV Music Generator. This provides the user with beats and riffs that can be used to create original tracks. A much more active form of leisure.

Modern intelligence is not about spelling or taking exams. It's about the relevant combination of many forms of media to form fast multiple messages. It's about participation and improvisation. Brands, computer games, websites, mobiles have learnt these new ways of presenting information and entertainment much more quickly than schools. More important than the ability to remember is the ability to find, absorb and move through vast amounts of information and stimulation. This is about discovering what is useful, rather than adhering to a prescribed or inherited canon of knowledge. A shift from being taught to working something out for yourself.

Our model of education is from another time. A time of single information sources, a bank of finite and manageable knowledge and built on a model of intelligence through the acquisition of 'facts'. The lack of enthusiasm for schools that I encountered is hardly surprising when you consider what they are up against in terms of stimulation and mental development. Kids are certainly not too stupid for school. Perhaps school is too stupid for them.

Too stupid, too slow, too uncolourful, too mono for a bunch of kids for whom speed, excitement, words, pictures, sound and film are all parts of acquiring and passing on information, all ways of telling stories.

At some point, decisions about the way we educate kids will have to take a much more radical stance than arguments over whether A levels are too easy, or if vocational subjects have the same value as 'proper', academic subjects. The form, content and method of knowledge delivery within schools is out of sync with the way that people learn elsewhere, with what they value, with what counts in this world.

These days it's about a far broader set of skills, about wider knowledge. Contact with the real and the useful. Ryan, Ursula's boyfriend and father of their child, expresses it clearly: 'You can't be taught by one person. You have to be shown different views.'

Rejecting books, spelling loosely, following celebrities does not equate with stupid. Or illiteracy. Just a different kind of literacy. When you consider the many ways that information and stories can be communicated via pictures, music, film, photography, pixels, where the order is controlled by and responds to the user, reading a set of words in a particular order, repeating the same physical motion page after page can seem a poor choice. A reduced option.

Dumbing down is one way of describing educational priorities for British kids. Another might be to consider that Britain is looking elsewhere for the things that are worth learning about … and that for most people knowing who the deputy prime minister is, or how many wives Henry VIII had, is of very little use.

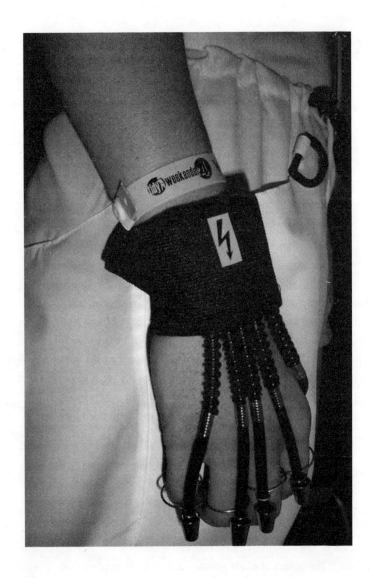

'Being someone different'

The Royal College of General Practitioners is urging the fashion-conscious to avoid piercing altogether and opt for stick-on tattoos because hepatitis B rates have doubled in the past 10 years. Dr George Kassianos, a GP and spokesman for the RCGP, said: 'The risk is too great that the (tattoo) parlour has cut corners by re-using tattoo needles or not sterilising equipment. If you want to decorate your body get a transfer – they are usually better quality anyway.'

Observer, **September 2003**

Indeed, sheer handsomeness is likely to be one of the earliest aims of genetic intervention. Once you accept the idea that our bodies are essentially plastic, and that it's OK to manipulate that plastic, then in the words of Silver, 'there's nothing beyond tinkering'. There's not a feature of the human body that can't be enhanced in some way or another. The vision of one's child as a nearly useless copy of Windows 95 should make parents fight like hell to make sure we never get started down this path.

Bill McKibben, *Observer*, May 2003

I wanna be a ball

It's drizzling. You move through a landscape of wet rock and giant trees. The rain clouds up your visor and it's hard to see very far until you enter a tunnel burrowed into the rockface and your visor clears. The tunnel walls are etched with strange markings, the signs of another civilisation. Spooky, discordant music plays and your own breathing echoes in the small space: asthmatic, metallic, nervous. The tunnel opens out into a cavernous room. A tree rises up through the floor. Its trunk is laced with fluorescent green filaments. The room's walls look like circuit boards for transmitting ancient alien data.

A white flash, and blue static fills your vision. As it clears you're just able to see a figure disappear. Some sort of space pirate spirit. You've encountered them earlier; they're difficult to kill because they keep vanishing, and their white energy bolts do a fair bit of damage. But you're better equipped now, packing a wavebuster, flamethrower and near-invincible armour. The fight goes on for some time; each time you hit them they disappear only to descend on you again. But they do die, at least for a while.

Once the spirits are out of the way, it's time to move on. The only way to leave the room seems to be via a tiny shelf, cut into the wall, far too small for your broad-shouldered, gun-toting character. A flick of the thumbs, and you flip into a glinting metal sphere, which rolls with ease along the shelf, gold puffs of smoke emerging from the back as the ball picks up speed.

Becoming a metal ball may not figure highly on anyone's list of body modifications, but that's just one of a whole raft of desirable additions that Metroid Prime offers. In the game you play Samus Aran, a powersuit-enabled female bounty hunter, hired by the Galactic Federation to eliminate the metroid threat.

It's a first-person game which means you see the world through Aran's eyes, or more specifically her combat visor, which is equipped with features like a mini map, radar, threat assessment, lock-on reticules, energy gauge and missile count. The screen is convex to reflect your enhanced vision, becomes misted with steam if you pass broken pipes, or splattered by alien guts when the fighting gets nasty. As the game's endline promises, 'Immerse yourself'.

The better you play, the better your suit becomes. You can upgrade to a heat-resistant Varia suit, or a visor which lets you see better underwater. There is also a scan visor that allows you to read and download information about your surroundings. Chozo ghosts can only be seen with X-ray scanning, and shriekbats are easy to spot if you have thermal imaging.

Once you can see better, it's time to move around. The Grapple beam lets you cross large distances, and even latch on to slow-moving creatures called Gliders. And of course the ball is upgradeable too. If you don't want to depend on gravity, the Spider ball lets you ride grooved tracks, clinging to surfaces and rolling up walls. If you drop a morph ball bomb, the force catapults you into the air, while the boost ball lets you ride half pipes and operate complex machines known as Spinner Devices.

And then there are the weapons: plasma beam, arm cannon, charge beam and the chilling ice beam which emits a sub-zero attack. Once you've frozen an opponent, you can fire a missile to shatter the body.

The game's mission is to locate and destroy the range of vicious aliens: the talon crab swarms, the war wasps, and of course a whole family of metroids, from the hunter (with energy-draining tentacles) to the fission metroid (ability to split into two tough but unstable forms). But half the fun is romping through the luscious graphics, finding power-ups, weapons and other extras for your suit. Because this game is all about transformation.

It's about improving your performance: in terms of perception, changing the way that you see the world, or take in external stimulation; in terms of movement, defying gravity and speed limits; in terms of appearance, becoming a different size, colour and even shape. It's about becoming a better person.

In many cases it's also about changing sex. First-person shooters are still a male-biased genre (although this is changing), and it is no coincidence that some of the most compelling and popular games have female heroes – Tomb Raider (Lara Croft), Dead or Alive Volleyball (a whole host of bikini chicks) and of course Metroid Prime. These virtual sex changes just underscore the identity fluidity that is at the heart of gaming: the assumption of another character's name, appearance and skills. And in many games the human body is never enough. If you want to win, you have to change. The motif at the centre of Metroid Prime is one of addition, of improvement, of physical and sensory upgrading. And so, Metroid Prime represents a powerful desire at the heart of British contemporary society, that of personal transformation.

Create yourself

Metroid Prime is not the only game to play around with ideas of physical and sensory adaptation. Computer games offer thousands of identities for you to assume. Whether it's Primal ('Civilisation is only skin deep'), where the lead character looks fairly normal except for one mutant green arm, or Tiger Woods Golf, where you can play as the legendary sportsman, or create your own Mohicanned swinger, the process is similar … you play (and in many cases compose) a character who looks and behaves radically different from you.

Not all of the games are as fantastic in their offerings. The Sims 2 (Simulations) takes place in a hyper real version of this world and indicates how detailed role-playing and transformation has become. In this game, you guide a family of Sims through the course of their life. There are no talon crabs or morph balls in this game. Just jobs to get, meals to cook, home decorating to be done, parties to go to. The kind of stuff you'd do in this world, but on a screen. While Metroid Prime is about superficial transformation – add-ons and plug-ins – The Sims is all about letting you play more intimately with the human form.

The Sims' developers have done everything they can to add verisimilitude to the game: both in terms of the 3-D world the Sims inhabit – the lighting, the presence of real-world brands – and in terms of the responsiveness of the characters themselves. Decisions you make early on in the game will affect its personality and actions throughout the game, and eventually determine how successful you are as a person/Sim. Beyond the expected signs of ageing, there are more subtle physical changes. If you keep your Sim well exercised, it will stave off the paunch that a layabout, burger-muncher develops. The characters respond to each other's behaviour and personality and can distinguish between family and friends, romantic and platonic love. On a more profound level, the Sims brings genetics into the gameplay, so a character's DNA is passed on to the kids. Add to this the 'Create a Sim' feature where you can sculpt every facial feature of your character, and you've got a human factory.

In the world of the Sims, there are ostensible goals – build a bigger house, make friends, keep your happiness quotient high. Just like in this life, there's no one way of doing things. Much of the gameplay is about human and social experimentation, about seeing what happens if: you try to seduce the next-door neighbour; you set fire to your house; you make babies with that alienish-looking kid from down the road. The Sims lets you play out possibilities that aren't allowed in this world.

While the transformations that computer games allow are perhaps the most extreme, the urge to tamper with appearance and physical performance crosses much of young British leisure. If fame desire is one gene that is present in an entire generation, then transformation would seem to be another. From fashion to fast cars, there exists a desire to play with the normal, or basic form, and make it different.

In mainstream entertainment, this urge for human modification and improvement tends to be presented as superficial, undesirable, even evil (think *Terminator*, think *The Matrix*). But in the clubs, at the car meets, in the clothing stores and festivals, it's clear that that the current version isn't enough. Everywhere I looked, kids were modifying themselves, upgrading, improving.

Approaching the ideal

'I've got both ear lobes stretched up to 16mm holes. I've got a Prince Albert (pierced penis) and a librette (lip piercing). I have had my nose pierced twice and my nipple and my belly button but I don't have those any more. And I've got about six or seven tattoos.'

Jake is Esme the fetish model's boyfriend. He comes into the room when we start talking about body modifications and shows me his various tats and piercings. While Esme's transformations are from demure student to louder-than-life vamp, Jake's are more subtle and more permanent. He's slender, with dark hair and thoughtful eyes. He talks me through his body's marks and holes and also shows me some of his tattoos: a Chinese-style dragon on his shoulder, three stars in the crease of each elbow, a solid circular design above his left nipple. He strokes them as he talks about each one.

For Jake this decoration is more than fashion. It's about improving the basic version of his body, upgrading it visually. He talks a language of addition and ascension. The opposite to a Christian point of view, which views the human body as the perfect form: the closest representation of a higher force. For Jake, his body is wanting, in terms of appearance, but also in terms of his hold on it.

'With piercing and tattoos I feel like I'm adding to my body. More than distorting it. Making it into a closer approximation of my image, what I want to look like. It's not a feeling that I'm unhappy with my body. Mine is about improvement. It's a sense of claiming my body for my own. It's an act of rebellion in a way. There's a normative idea of what your body ought to look like and by changing it into something else, you're reclaiming to a certain degree your own body. It's like sticking a flag in it.'

The language he uses reveals a drive that I see in so many kids: to do something that projects their personality, makes them stand out. That signals their difference.

'It's like customising,' Esme adds. 'Because everybody has a body which is to a greater or less stage the same … the basic prototype is we're all cast from the same mould. It's like individuality from the clothes you wear. It's the same thing.'

She's right. It's all the same thing. It's all normal. T-shirts with slogans, piercings, hair colouring, make-up, tattoos. They're all options: ways of making your body personalised, more beautiful, closer to your mind's image rather than the image you have been given. The Sims works because it offers in virtuality what is wished for in this world: the ability to sculpt your features and your appearance from birth. To be present at your own conception. As control and influence seep away from many parts of our lives, the areas that we can affect are subject to a growing intensity and attention.

Despite Esme's willingness to place tattoos and piercings on the same line of identity and self-improvement as clothing, she balks at cosmetic surgery. For her, it's the intrusiveness of the procedure rather than the effect. For Jake, though, cosmetic surgery (in its present form) is not interesting because it tends towards the normal, the same, rather than delivering the difference and uniqueness that his body modifications provide.

'In the vast majority of cases, plastic surgery is to do with working towards a norm, to making people look more normal and more like the archetype or prototype.'

In other words, it's going backwards … back towards the identical human source, the basics, rather than embracing the possibilities of human transformation.

Jake touches on another theme of transformation. It is a continual activity, whose meaning is not about reaching a final destination but having a lively and beautiful journey. Tattoos signify events that have happened to Jake, so image and personality are totally bound up in one another.

'It's a continual process. I take piercings out as often as I have them done. I don't have a fixed image of what I want to look like … it's quite instinctive … getting closer to that ideal.'

Of course, there are limits to how far you can go. The dream of endless, creative mutation is tempered by a more practical awareness of how such change can be viewed. As Esme puts it, 'In the real world there are some things you just can't do if you've got a tattooed face.'

Crack fashion

Esme had drawn parallels between clothing and tattoos: both offering ways of transforming appearance. And Jake's restless desire for ongoing change reminded me of an article that had run in the *Observer* in May, taken from a book called *Fashion Victims: our love–hate relationship with dressing, shopping and the cost of style*. By Michelle Lee, it introduces the concept of speed chic. 'McFashion, like fast food, relies on speed chic. One of the realities of fashion is that we fall hard for a trend, then not only tire of it but begin to despise it. So we're stuck in an endless cycle, trying futilely to hurry up and be cool. To make matters worse, the giant hamster wheel of style continues to accelerate, so we grow weary of trends much faster than we used to. Speed chic is the crack cocaine of fashion: cheap, fast and addictive.'

Predictably the article looks at contemporary consumer culture and makes a rash of negative observations. The article accuses fashion chains of eroding individuality, while at the same time bemoaning the endless choice that is constantly being made available. Similar critiques arise regularly … brands like Gap or Nike have often been accused of stealing individuality by clothing everyone the same. Culprits in the identikiting of a generation.

As with critics of computer games, fashion pundits like Michelle Lee are judging an area by their own criteria, rather than trying to understand the appeal of 'the giant hamster wheel of style'. For people who know sneakers, who understand the subtleties of their hues and shades, sneakers aren't all the same. Sneakerholics see the constant iterations of colour and fabric, sole and style as an ongoing seduction. Where new figures emerge blushing into the store windows. Echoing a design from the past, or, more rarely, displaying a radical leap in sneaker chic. To the untrained eye one pair of trainers looks very much like another, but to insiders it's all about nuances. Not just sneakers but Nike. Not just Nike but Air Max. Not just Air Max but Air Max 97. Not just 97 but the brown ones. That only came out in 2003. Twists and turns. Variations. Same but different.

Check any crowd of young shoppers in any mall or store. They are anything but uniformly dressed. Structurally there are certainly similar looks, but within these looks is a myriad of variations. Stores like H&M and Gap may sell lots of identical clothes but their young customers do not wear them identically. Instead there is a stream of combination and distortion … vintage jeans worn with a smart jacket, sneakers accompanying a suit. Bags that have been hand-drawn on. Pants that have been mutilated. I look at the clothes young people are wearing and see endless variety and colour.

At the core of the *Observer* article is a snobbishness, almost a distaste for the masses who are being fashionable. What Lee really seems to object to is that stores make it easy for kids to buy lots of clothes, to move through them like fast food. She seems disconcerted by the speed with which one look is discarded and another assumed. As a 'leading fashion writer' she clearly believes herself to have developed a fashion sense and you can feel she might resent the fact that being fashionable is now a mass activity. People are doing fashion without the proper qualifications! She writes nostalgically about the fear and self-doubt that a proper clothing store should engender in any shopper, as if consumption should be about confirming insecurities rather than pleasure and self-expression. 'At a McFashion store, it doesn't matter how cool you are. Chain retailers encourage shoppers to touch the clothes, they invite even the fashion illiterate with open arms. Meanwhile the glamorous designer and gauche mass market worlds have collided, so consumers can believe they're engaging in high style on the high street.'

While Ms Lee might criticise this explosion of choice, nobody else seems to bother about it. Certainly the stores aren't ashamed: they playfully draw attention to the ranges they offer. The Brent Cross Shopping Centre runs a campaign in the autumn featuring a washing line with numerous pairs of jeans hanging from it, and the strapline, 'Feed Your Addiction'. An ad for Foot Locker shows a guy fleeing a black cloud of sneakers, pursuing him like angry bees … 'the agony of choice'. And French Connection runs a series of giant back-lit posters showing a girl looking toughly out at the world, with the words, 'Apparently there are more important things in life than fashion. Yeah right.' They can only make these jokes because they know how happy their shoppers are with the situation.

And while the French Connection ad might appear trite, I began to see that it points towards a far greater truth. There is nothing more important than fashion, because the dynamics of fashion – freshness, variation, individuality, imitation, transformation and distortion – have spread way beyond clothes. From software to furniture, phones to politics, all categories have succumbed to a restlessness, to the belief that you are only interesting as long as you are new or different.

Talking with Becky, Hannah and Livie, all eleven, I get a sense of how quickly kids move through clothes and looks.

'How often do you go shopping for clothes?'

'Probably … sometime every weekend, or every other. Sometimes I go shopping and don't really buy anything.'

Mum makes a noise of disbelief at this point.

'I don't! You buy me things.'

'This child has more clothes than I do. I spend a fortune on her clothes. It just happens.'

'I get bored of stuff so easily.'

'I can't wear things once they've got just a tiny bit too small.'

This attitude transfers easily to other areas of their lives.

'How long was Tom your boyfriend?'

'Two months. I get bored so easily with boys. Cos there's only like Luke,

Adam, Babyface and Tony … they're like the only boys in our group really, and I've been out with all of them.'

But it's Carina and Lucy, both seventeen, the girls who are up for sex in car parks, who confirm the speed of chic.

'I love clothes,' Carina tells me, grinning.

'You have got to look nice, you can't be seen in the same clothes.'

'My dad spent £1000 on me the other day. And all I got was a coat, a Prada coat – all my clothes are designer, innit.'

'That is my focus, my clothes, and, because I am in that sort of industry, you know what I mean, you have got to look good, you know what I mean.'

'We are not like normal girls, like around here, like Burberry and Louis Vuitton.'

'Yes. We were out the other day, and I had on like pink slouch boots, with black patterned tights, they had diamonds all sort of here, and a denim miniskirt, a Diesel one, it was a Diesel matching denim jacket, and a pink top and it went, and I was like Burberry, it ain't the normal check by the way, I don't do that. It is Burberry, it is baby pink, and it is beige and baby blue. All stripes, and I had my scarf on. And her mate went, oh my God, what has Carina … '

'Yes, what is she wearing?'

'We mix colours. Obviously we wouldn't do stripes and flowers. Because that don't go. But we do different colours, just to look different, we want to be different.'

'I don't want no one else to have what I wear.'

'Plus by the time we are rich, by the time we have earned our money, we are going to go shopping in Oxford Street every day! We love shopping in London.'

'How many pairs of shoes have you got?'

'I don't even know. Loads. I have matching, can I name them all, these red ones, red matching bag, I have got Gucci pointy ones, Gucci matching bag, the only things I ain't got is Dior shoes, but I have all the latest Dior bags out. I have the Louis Vuitton shoes. And matching bag.'

'You can get a Louis Vuitton bag for £3000 … '

'One in my car is £1200, that one is £1200. But it is well nice. And I have little ones that are about £300 like the Dior ones and stuff.'

'I have loads of trainers, got red ones, blue ones, I have got Prada trainers. I have Adidas trainers. Nike, I have loads.'

'Can you have too many clothes, do you reckon?'

'No, of course you can't.'

'You can only wear the certain item of clothing for three, four times.'

'Then you don't wear it for ages, and then you … '

'Put it in the boot fair, or … '

'Charity or something.'

'I bought this dress right, D&G, I think it was £190, something like that, my dad bought it. And it was well nice, but I tried it on, it looked all right in the shop, but you have to have a certain sort of bra with it, and I tried it on and I was going to wear it the other night, but it makes it look like you have got no tits. And it makes your tits really flat. And I am thinking, I am never going to wear it. And I don't know where the receipt is. So I've got it. But I don't think I am going to wear it.'

'We have to have them things. Up to date.'

Shop till you drop

'You can't put people in boxes. We like to think that Top Shop is about reflecting British culture. It's different from everywhere else in the world. It's street, eclectic, it mixes styles. Vintage, designer, basics. It's like one big dressing-up box.'

As an emblem for contemporary Britain, Top Shop is pretty close to having it all. It's about speed, quantity, choice, individualism, entertainment, simple personal transformation; the victory and power of mass, popular, accessible style.

250,000 fashion-conscious shoppers pass through the flagship store on Oxford Street every week. On Saturdays it feels like they all are there at the same time. It is chaos. Three storeys combining shopping with eating, with entertainment, with model scouts, with Top Shop TV. Here, they change the mannequins' outfits every day, so there's always something new to look at. They sell jeans for £20, so you can buy a different pair every week, so you only have to wear them a few times to get value out of them. There are racks of shoes, socks, pants, T-shirts, handbags, bangles, stretching from floor to teen-girl head height. There is a whole wall of hot-water bottles – shaped as hearts, as stars, as lemons.

Top Shop might be crack fashion, but it's not lowest common denominator stuff. There are young designers – with names like 'Love you long time' and 'uncouth youth' – who would seem more at home on some urban market stall. Clothes with attitude: underwear sets with 'On the pull' branding; pants with Kapow written Roy Lichtenstein-style across the crotch; Emily Strange's red-and-black ghoul gear. For the sexually adventurous, there's an Ann Summers-esque corner, featuring whips and scanty lace undies. And thumbing its nose at any accusations of repetitive, bland fashion, the Top Shop Unique section offers a small selection of upmarket designer-style dresses and tops.

Jo Farrelly is the marketing director for Top Shop. We sit among rails of clothes, piles of boxes and a stream of fast-talking, kookily dressed women in their offices above the flagship store. It's scruffy and energetic. She looks at the same landscape as Michelle Lee, but sees completely the opposite: a world of choice and individuality. And playfulness. She describes Top Shop as 'a shop for women of all kinds of ages. The interesting thing is that you'd think it's for fifteen- to nineteen-year-olds; in fact, it's for anyone who's interested in fashion. Everyone from seven to seventy. And we aim to embrace all those people who are interested in fashion.'

Her view of Top Shop customers bears little resemblance to Lee's picture of a nation of mugs, blindly buying identical clothing. Jo is very clear about who's in charge.

'Big brands are so out of control when it comes to kids. Your customer controls you. You've got to be in touch with them. Students and young people today are very cynical about brands. The customer will decide what we sell. We don't decide. We're constantly looking at moving things, and constantly trialling things so they're very very reactive to the customer.'

And for her, speed is everything.

'We do very short runs. So things will sell out – if you don't buy it on that rail it will be gone. If customers are buying something and they want more of it, we will take that T-shirt and do it in twenty different varieties, with different motifs. We have three hundred new product lines that go on that floor in Oxford Circus each week. It is phenomenal. The store is open twenty-four hours a day behind the scenes. There are deliveries going on twenty hours a day. They cannot get it out on the floor quick enough. The stock turns so fast. You can go down there in the morning and when you go back down in the afternoon, you're like: "Where are those trousers, where are they gone?"'

There is almost a temporal distortion going on here, a new calendar being created, to respond to our need for ongoing change.

'In terms of stock turning over so fast, we will bring in autumn/winter stuff in June. In January and February some of the spring/summer stock is coming down the floor. Young consumers, they want things now, they don't want it tomorrow. They want things fast and they want to be able to choose, they need a huge amount of choice. Many of our customers are in every week, even twice a week. It's about disposable fashion. They want that choice, variety and boost.'

Talking to Jo, I wonder about another side of disposability. Whether it has to be a bad word. Disposable culture is one that leaves a lot behind, but this is simply the flip side of continual improvement. It can also be seen as a sign of progress, of positive transformation.

'In order to make our customers happy you need to constantly bring them new things.'

Famous cyborg

If you want to go further than surface transformation, Kevin Warwick, professor of cybernetics at Reading University, is your man. Or perhaps your cyborg. I remember seeing him on the cover of *Wired* magazine a few years ago after having implanted a chip under his skin, the first time that implants had been used to improve human performance rather than repair defects. This seems the closest we have in real life to Metroid-style enhancements, so I get in touch with him to fix an interview. He tells me he prefers to do it by e-mail, which I guess is appropriate after he explains how the implanted chip offered a different channel of mediated communication.

'I have a passion to find out how far we can go in linking humans with machines, ultimately linking the human brain to a computer. Apart from implants (e.g. heart pacemakers) to help people, before 1998 no regular person had had an implant looking at the possibility of upgrading humans.'

He describes how quickly his body became used to the additions.

'I also had an extra (ultrasonic) sense which allowed me to move around, with a blindfold on, and detect objects – rather like a bat would. I was amazed that my brain tuned in to the ultrasonic signals and made use of them directly.'

More profoundly he was linked to another human – his wife – via a computer so that it became a medium for rudimentary communication.

'My wife received microneurography – electrodes were directly placed (from the outside) into her nervous system. When she moved her fingers, neural signals were transmitted, via the computer, and played down on to my nervous system. When I moved my fingers, my neural signals were played, in the reverse direction, on to her nervous system. So if I moved my fingers 3 times, my wife (Irena) received 3 pulses & vice versa. So we communicated in a basic (telegraphic) way from nervous system to nervous system.'

They had hoped to go further and transmit not just motor neural signals, but physical and emotional signals as well, and this is still his dream. When I ask him about his longer-term dreams, the reply is audacious.

'In a ten-year time frame – I would like, via implant, to link my own nervous system with a computer. I would like to be part of the first thought communication experiment.'

Kevin understands that the idea of man merging with machine can be off-putting.

'I guess upgrading humans is bound to frighten some people. Many would like things to stay just the way they are now. The possibility of Cyborgs (upgraded humans) having Superhuman abilities is bound to be worrying.'

But while recognising the uneasiness, he sees it as an inevitable development.

'Why not upgrade if we can? If we can have extra senses, upgrade our mathematical and memory abilities and even understand things in many dimensions then this is a very exciting potential experience. I think it is inevitable because the potential positives are enormous. It also appears to be a necessity if we are to get machine intelligence to operate for us rather than, in the long term, against us.'

Kevin's cyborg antics have had another transformative effect. He has become famous. And it's clear he enjoys this. His website – www.kevin warwick.com – shows him staring wistfully at a tiny chip, as if he wishes it were back inside him, giving him special powers. It looks like the cover of an eighties electronica album. When I ask him for some further reading material, he modestly recommends his own book, *I, Cyborg*.

Mutant Sundis

Kevin is entirely positive about physical and electronic change. The smartening (up) of bodies. His experiments emerge from the same urges that drive so many young Britons. While he is working towards actual change, much of young Britain is working on a more symbolic level, reaching into the world of science fiction, of computer games and films, and bringing those behaviours and appearances, the dreams of a more exciting, stronger body, back into the present.

One group of kids who do this call themselves cybers. They wear fluorescent clothing and make-up, sometimes sporting circuit boards or robot-esque costumes. They love ketamine, partly because it transforms the way you feel inside your body, the way you see the world, and I find a club full of them over Easter.

Sundissential kicks off in a cavernous club in Birmingham. It's part one of the Easter Sundissential celebrations, and the website advertising the event had set up the challenge: 'Can you do the Triple? … three events, three locations and thirty DJs' … running from 10pm on Easter Saturday to midnight on Easter Sunday.

The club we're in bears the signs of previous functions. A row of organ pipes fills the wall at the end. The red and gold colour scheme, the dragon images on the stairs make me think of a Chinese restaurant. But that's about right, because this whole night is about transformation. The clubbers here are playing about with their appearance and their psyche by as many means as possible, becoming more efficient party machines. The catalysts of transformation, the things that get you to another state: drugs, music, clothing. All worn or consumed with the intention of increasing pleasure, of having a better time.

There's a guy in a T-shirt with the word 'harder' on the front and 'faster' on the back, both words illustrated by stick figures having sex. Someone else with a 'Sleeping Sucks' message. A third with 'Sex, Drugs and Hardhouse' competing with the sweat on his back. A girl smiling and dancing with four words across her chest: 'Will fuck for coke'. The most revealing is 'The Harder Generation' T-shirt. A boast or an acknowledgement that this group of people, this generation are up for more than previous generations: louder, faster, tougher music, less sleep, more drugs, more abandonment. A greater distance from normal human existence. A new form.

Sundissential confirms my impression that for many young Britons, there is no debate on drugs. Or the only debate is a practical one. Which drugs you're going to take tonight, how much of each, where you're going to get them from, and when you're going to drop them. The majority of people here are wasted: pupils wide, feet tapping, faces glowing, jaws clenching, staring into space, talking shite, dancing for hours on end. And loving it.

Whatever successful clubs claim about their drugs policy, the majority depend on the fact that the people who attend them are going to get high. That way, the music sounds better, and they'll stay longer. Red Bull might stimulate the body and the mind, but it's not really going to keep you awake for twenty-four hours. And this club stops serving alcohol at 2am.

Sundissential has an enlightened and realistic approach to drugs. Without actually selling them, it does everything it can to make the consumption of them as easy and safe as possible, assisting a positive and temporary transformation. So it stops being a problem and just becomes part of the night. In one of the quieter bars, Emma Barrie is sitting behind a table covered with leaflets and mini magazines, covering everything from ecstasy and cocaine to ketamine and GHB. Several of the leaflets feature a cartoon character called Peanut Pete, who makes his way through a number of drug experiences, passing on wisdom as he does so. The tone is one of practical acceptance. People will continue to take drugs, so why not help them when they do?

During the week, Emma works for the NHS. Tonight her job is to advise people about the drugs they have taken or might be about to take. She is not there to stop people taking drugs, simply to ensure that they have a better time when they do take them. The Birmingham police are aware of and appreciate her role. Because she's not police or paramedics, people feel happier talking to her, and it also means that she gets a better picture of what's being taken: the good pills and the bad ones.

It's one in the morning and glowsticks, dummies and dayglo hair fill the floor. The music and the dancing are relentless. Non-stop sped-up beats with piano breaks, sirens and klaxons. Boys stripped to the waist and girls in tiny bras and skirts. There's an energy and style here that goes back to the late eighties, and large raves in hangars off motorways. Back then, this kind of behaviour was illegal, dangerous, rebellious. Now, it's just another legitimate Saturday night.

But it's still all about escape and getting to another place. An MC paces the stage, asking, 'Where's the whistles?' and telling the crowd how great they are: 'You're fucking hardcore. Forget all the bullshit in the week. This is where it's at.' And the crowd agrees with him. They jump, pace, do strange hand signs. Rhythmic repetition. Manic eyes. Red cheeks. They've been dancing this fast since the club opened at ten. And they're still going hours later.

Drugs plus music is standard fare across Britain. Where Sundissential goes further, what gives this night its beauty and mutant status, is the clothes. Or rather the costumes. They are the visual equivalent of the music. Bright, absurd, tough and childish. Most importantly they make you laugh. They stop you being just another regular UK citizen, out on a Friday or Saturday night.

There are three lifesize Tweenies. There are cyber chicks with blonde dreads to their waists. Girls dressed as tigers and PVC nurses. Guys as spaced cowboys and messy aliens. I can't count the number of women and men who have made their own red and yellow fluffy suits, emblazoned with the Sundissential logo: a stick girl and boy, hands raised together in rapture. A man with the same logo in fluoro orange on his head. Girls in white fluffy boots everywhere. One guy wears a cascading LCD display across his chest. Kevin Warwick would be proud.

The costumes are liberating. People behave differently. They go up to people they don't know to ask them where they got the idea, or simply to congratulate their ingenuity. The influences are multiple: kids' TV, sci-fi, Hawaii, medics, fetish, etc, etc. They are one more ingredient in a journey away from day-to-day mundanity.

This crowd take their transformations seriously. You can't buy most of this stuff in the stores. You have to make it. As Marian – one of the night's entertainment managers, in a red and yellow schoolgirl's outfit and being caned by a headmaster when I meet her – says, 'People come here who live, breathe, eat and sleep Sundissential.' Who spend the time between nights making costumes for those nights. And this homemade, individual creativity is everywhere.

As Bernadette (eighteen, wearing a nurse's outfit, multiple bangles and one red, one yellow knee-high fluffy boot) says: 'It's the only place you can get away with this sort of behaviour.'

Marian adds: 'It's an escape from their reality. You can't walk down Digbeth High Street dressed as a Tweeny, but you can walk into Sundissential and no one will say anything. Except to admire you.'

In a world where our obsession with appearance tends to be presented as a negative thing, encouraging insecurities, Sundissential offers a refreshing break. Marian talks about size-sixteen girls who happily flaunt their bodies, wearing micro skirts and tiny tops. She tells me about a guy in a wheelchair who says that Sundissential is the only place where no one treats him as different just because he looks different. Marian talks about everybody being comfortable with who they are. It's tending towards the evangelical, but I have to agree with her. When everyone looks weird (the costumes, the drugs, the dancing), normal aesthetic judgement counts for nothing.

And this difference is cherished. I get talking with Natalee and Mary, both students at Birmingham, who tell me about the pull of the transformed world.

'It's like a different world when you go in there. Everyone's friendly. It's like a whole new world.'

'You don't actually want to come out at the end of the night. You get out of the club and you think, oh God, back in the real world, it's grey and wet and we've got boring work and normal shit to get back to.'

'It hits you quite hard.'

'That's why a lot of people go to afterclubs, people just don't want to stop, because that means you get back into the real world. It's horrible.'

Suburban transformation

Nights like Sundis tell you several things about drugs: how normalised they have become, how radically they can transform mass behaviour, and how much fun they are for loads of people. I wanted to get a better idea of what they felt like, what kind of transformation they delivered, and

I found that talking to people when they were high wasn't very revealing. In August I head for Basingstoke to talk to a group of clubbers who I had originally met at Sundissential.

The contrast between home and club, between weekday and nights out, between normality and transformation couldn't be stronger. Hatch Warren, on the edge of Basingstoke, is as suburban as it gets. The essence of commuter belt. I drive through winding cul-de-sacs, past houses scarred with fake wattle and daub, neat gardens and trim new cars. Neither of the two people I ask have any idea where the road I'm looking for is, though when I eventually find it, it's two streets from where I spoke to them.

I pull up outside the address and am reassured by the rapid beats drifting out of the inappropriately large arched window. This is the second time I have tried to catch up with them. The previous meeting never happened because the phone wasn't answered for three days … the result of a lost weekend.

It's Tuesday, which I figure is about as safe a night as any. One of the girls tells me that she was up from Friday until 1.30am Tuesday morning, when she found herself sitting on a chair, legs twitching, and realised she should force herself to go to bed. I'm grateful for her responsibility, and this evening, she's bright-eyed, cheerful and cogent.

These are people who don't like sleeping, who think they are harder and faster than anyone else. Their lives are all about quantity, warped reality and staying up late. All of them see drugs as having expanded their experiences and defined their social lives. They are pale and very slim … almost skinny. The signs of nights stayed up and days missed. The hottest British summer in memory seems to have passed them by. They get their colour from elsewhere.

There are four of them in the house: Gemma, eighteen, with a pierced eyebrow and tongue, spending her time between Bournemouth and Hatch Warren, where her boyfriend Mouse lives. He's twenty, with his hair in a fin and two lines shaved into the side. He's smoking the butt of a joint when I arrive and stays quiet most of the time. Although he coughs a lot.

He lives with Mark, twenty-five, who's wearing a Deviant T-shirt. During the week they work for a furniture company. Mark's the office manager; Mouse delivers sofas. Mark tells me that last week he didn't make it into work until Thursday because of a large weekend.

Mark's girlfriend, Joanne, is twenty-one and studying business and marketing at Southampton.

Inside, the suburban ambience disappears. There's a pair of decks and records everywhere. Empty milkshake bottles and crisp packets. Ashtrays full of butts. Computer games piled up by the TV.

Gemma admits she doesn't remember much about the night we met, but knows she had a good time 'because you never have a bad night at Sundissential. It's not possible. It's like a family. Everyone knows everyone and even if you don't know someone you can sit down and talk to them. You feel at home. And you've got Afteressential afterwards which carries on till ten in the morning.'

I met her on Saturday night; she finally went to bed on Tuesday. She wants to be a DJ, and plays in Bournemouth most Saturdays at Hype. She tells me with excitement about a gig she's managed to get lined up in Lincoln over the internet.

Her outfit of choice is 'a PVC nurse's outfit with fluffy boots and pink-and-black striped tights with fishnets over the top', and she's clear about why she likes dressing up: 'It's like being a kid again.'

It's also about setting yourself apart from perceived normality. Despite their suburban setting, these four are keen to distance themselves from the rest of Britain. Their strategies of disconnection: bright clothes, furious music and bags of chemicals.

We sit on a couple of sagging sofas and talk. Quite often Mouse stares into the distance, following a very different train of thought. Mark is more hyper, jumping up to his computer to show me some of the hundreds of clubbing photos he has taken to illustrate various points. All of them talk about their mental and physical transformations in terms of individuality and difference.

'When you go into clubs,' says Joanne, 'that's why people dress the way they do is because it is just trying to find something that you're not following because of peer pressure. It's a time when you can do what you want to do and express it through the music.'

'When you go clubbing and dress cyber,' adds Gemma, 'people make their own clothes, like trying to do something different to everyone else. Not like in normal society.'

I gesture around at the flat, and also through the large windows to the quiet Mondeo-infested street.

'Do you think you're part of normal society?'

'Not what people who don't know about clubbing class as normal society. I class normal society as just our little family, our little group of friends. That's it.'

Mark tells me about a house party that lasted a week.

'How do you manage to stay up so long?' I ask with measured naivety.

'Take huge amounts of drugs.'

'Lots and lots of base,' grins Gemma. 'It's like speed. Before it was pills. But I got a liking for base. It's a different buzz. I get told I do too much. Like last night I was sat in front of that computer at two in the morning, my legs shaking, thinking, fucking hell I need to go to sleep. I forced myself to go to sleep because I knew you were coming.'

When I ask Gemma what base is, she tells me it's super speed – purer than your average wrap – but she doesn't seem too bothered about the specifics. Her preference for base is a very functional one: it lets you stay up for days, feeling talkative and lively and loving music. But the drug that really gets them excited and has a proper transformative effect is ketamine. Although Gemma's not into it.

'That is a weird drug. It makes you lose all reality. You don't know what's going on. You completely lose the plot.'

Mouse speaks for the first time. 'Some people do. It's a drug which … '

' … you can't control.'

'You can. When you're on it, you do sometimes forget that you're on K and that's when you go, oh, what's going on here?, but then all of a sudden you just think, I'm on K, and then it's fine. It's just like a whole, another like world really. K's the hardest thing to explain. You can't explain until someone's done it, because it is so immense. It sort of … '

'Broadens your horizons.'

'Opens your mind to a lot of things. Cos on K you can go into a K hole where you lose all sense of reality and you're in your own little world, and some of the things I've seen on K … ' This is too much for him and he breaks into a fit of coughing and laughing.

Gemma takes over: 'He did it on the beach … and I've never seen anyone so fucked in my life.'

More laughing follows this, until Mouse gets his breath back.

'It's just like a dream. You go into a dream world. You sort of live in the dream. When you're on K you've just got to ride it out.'

'If you freak out it becomes really scary. We had to literally carry him to the car, and he was like, this is weird.'

'It was wicked. Some of the things I was seeing, like I had one K hole, like I say you've just got to go with it, and it's hard to explain, I went into the K hole like a dream, I went through evolution if you see what I mean and just kept going, and when I got to death I was just like, so what happens after you die; that's when I let my mind go, and I went from like death to like … I ended up being at the centre of the universe. It's really hard to explain. When I came out I was like, woah … '

There's a bit of a pause and Mouse looks puzzled, not sure if he's made a clear and profound point or just sounded flaky. Mark adds his own experiences. 'You can't explain ketamine. I prefer doing it when I get back from a club because it makes you fucking sketchy. It's trippy but in a good way. It's never really freaked me out. I jumped out of the van the other day and I thought I was that high off the ground and I could see these pumps and I was like … ' He mimes trying to reach for a petrol pump that is way above his head.

'It's probably not best to drive on it … the first time I was on it, I went to wash in the bathroom and my arms were like seven feet long and my hands were tiny and I was like, I'm never going to be able to get enough water to wet my face, and I was in the bathroom for about twenty minutes. It was funny. It's just strange. It totally fucks up your perception of things, like distance and sizes and balance. You get an out-of-body experience sometimes. I followed myself down the stairs watching me walk. It does open your mind.'

Finally he gives up trying to explain. 'Fuck it, I'll rack you up a line.'

Everyone laughs. In the tradition of the best *News of the World* reporters, I politely decline, thinking of a journey back to London past giant petrol pumps.

For these four, drugs are a way of getting a different, improved sensory input. If Esme sees piercing and tats as a continuation of fashion and hair colouring, then Gemma and co. see drugs as a logical extension of all the other things they feed their heads with: TV, music, fashion, PlayStation. Drugs simply offer a more exclusive and immersive experience – more of a piratopia … a place where normal people don't go.

Despite the difficulty they have in describing the effects of K, they are unanimous in their approval of it. Not just because it feels good, but because of longer-term beneficial effects.

As Mark says, 'Anything that opens your mind and gives you some weird experiences definitely adds to your being alive.'

'It's like a split personality,' adds Joanne. 'That's what clubbing's all about. Being someone different at the weekend to what you are in a normal day.'

Drugs seem permanently accessible – from friends, in clubs – an unquestionable and essential ingredient in their weekends of transformation. I visit them in the week that Wayne Wood appears in court, following the youngest ecstasy death in the UK. Jade Slack, ten, died after taking five Ferrari pills hidden in a cigarette packet. Despite this horror story, Wood's solicitor presents the death as an unfortunate side effect of modern leisure pursuits. 'He is an ordinary lad, part of a modern culture which takes ecstasy. But there's no suggestion in this case that he is an evil young man. In my submission he is an ordinary, stupid, misguided young man.'

And Gemma points towards a similar casual attitude. 'It's only been a problem when I got searched at Sundissential North and got arrested. Cos they found my pills. I got a caution, but I had enough on me for them to do me for dealing, but it was a bank holiday and they wanted to go home so they gave me a caution.'

There are risks associated with chemical transformations – both legal and physical. But they are risks that these four are nonchalant about, and more significantly, risks that Britain seems happy to put up with. The scare stories that pop up frequently mean nothing to these people, because they are generated outside the transformed world.

'What do you think about the way drugs are talked about in the papers?' I ask.

'There's a lot of horror stories but it's mainly by people who haven't done it and don't really know what they're talking about.'

'As long as you know what you're doing it's fine,' agrees Gemma. 'So many people do it. It's very unlikely to die off one pill. I know people who do twenty in one night and still don't die.'

'There's sensible ways of doing things and then there's being stupid.'

As we talk about being stupid, they start chatting about the upcoming Tidy Weekender. It's not the first time I've heard the Tidy Boys, or their record label, Tidy Trax, mentioned. Gemma sells it with the line, 'Be prepared to see nothing you've seen before.'

'It's like visiting an asylum,' adds Mouse. 'It's three and a half thousand people on a Pontin's holiday camp. For one weekend it just gets turned into a lunatic asylum.'

If that's not enough, Mark runs around the room while shouting at me. 'Nobody who's not a totally mad up-for-it clubber goes. It's only proper committed people. It's like three days fucking straight. You don't get townie people who just want to go out and cause trouble. Everybody is just totally fucking rinsed.'

After the eighth or so recommendation, I feel obliged to check it out. '4 days of fun and frolics for the harder generation' promises the website.

As soon as I start to leave Mouse finally shows a bit of animation. He slopes over to the decks and starts playing records again.

The harder generation

The road to Prestatyn is dotted with power stations, great lumps of metal, smoke and lights … the things that keep Britain plugged in and turned on. I drive past pebbledash bungalows, used-car lots and spot a rusting ship moored off the coast. The remnants of an older industrial age. Exactly the kind of crappy, grey, unimaginative world that Natalee and fellow clubbers are so keen to leave behind. Just before I reach Prestatyn I turn off to Talacre to get a bit of nature in. The sign has the symbol for a sandcastle on it, but the beach is more of a mud flat. There are couple of amusement arcades and more bungalows … a vision of how they did holidays back in the twentieth century.

I take a drive round Prestatyn before hitting Pontin's. It's a normal town, pubs, chip shops, groups of teens hanging around. There's no sense of the energy and weirdness that's building up a couple of miles away. Here, kids hang outside the takeaway and it's another normal Saturday, while down the road, boys put on rubber nurses' outfits and snort long lines of ket. I eat a terrible red chicken kebab and head towards the holiday camp.

A tall metal spiked fence separates the two worlds. A security guard lifts the red and white striped gate. I don't know if I'm entering or leaving a prison.

Billy Butlin got his idea for affordable working-class holidays in 1936, after being locked out of a guesthouse. Fred Pontin opened his first one ten years later. They were pioneers, introducing a different and accessible type of holiday: a small village for getting away. In 2003, the urge is the same, it's just the means that have changed. I wonder what they'd think about how leisure has moved on, been transformed. How their village for honest hardworking families has been repurposed for a stream of teenage drug-taking hedonists, devoted to physical and mental transformation.

There is room for three thousand at this Pontin's, and every place is taken. The rows of chalets have posters for Lisa Lashes, Tidy Trax and the inevitable 'Harder Generation' symbol. Different stereos pump out a conflict of tracks at silly b.p.ms: 'You think I'm crazy, you're probably right, but I'm gonna have fun every motherfuckin night.'

For the next couple of hours, it's all about preparation. I hook up with Gemma. She looks pale and weary … hasn't had any sleep and it shows. We hang out in her chalet for a bit, then I go visit a few more. The story's the same for everyone. Out last night, and there are bodies and clothes strewn everywhere, as people try to catch a few hours of low-quality sleep. They watch stupid early evening TV, smoke spliffs, put on their make-up. A few can't wait and start nibbling at pills, splitting one between four. When I bump into Gemma a few hours later she's in her nurse's outfit and her pupils look like they're trying to escape from their sockets.

By 9.30pm the flow of people and costumes starts: two guys in red rubber nurses' dresses, three girls in grass skirts, a man covered in neon and circuitry. Two other boys stagger past in a cardboard box with the legend 'Fragile: handle with care' on the side. One kid would have looked at home in Pontin's when it originally opened. Beige slacks rolled up to the knee, a string vest, little moustache and round specs. Just like a character from one of those jokey holiday postcards. Only the fluoro handkerchief knotted round his head gives it away.

As I discovered at Homelands, interviewing people on pills and ketamine doesn't always get you that far. Conversations drift between gibberish and silence. I ask people about their clothes and their reasons for coming. Perhaps the most coherent and accurate answer comes from a girl called Lisa. She is wearing ties. Her friend, who can't speak, has contact lenses that give him milky pupils and a dazed expression. She sums it up neatly: 'It stops you being you.'

In the main room hundreds of kids dance madly. Not talking. Just getting into it. The scene is Roman in its excess. Amadaeus Mozart and

Pickle of the Tidy Boys take the stage to cheers and raised hands. On the stage a guy reclines in a deckchair as two techno dancers writhe over him. It's like Sundissential, except madder. Because there's nothing else. For four days, there is no outside, no real world to impinge on the hedonism, to dull the party. This is total transformation, by every possible means: using drugs, colour, sound, costumes … and seclusion to create a very different – if temporary – universe.

In a smaller room, happy hardcore plays on, crazy sped-up beats and kids standing on the spot. 'Raving crew, are you ready?' screams the MC. Fluoro sticks, dayglo hair, neon clothes. This is all about turning it up, making it visible. A neon overdose, a cacophony of individualism. By 1am it's so hot that everyone is dripping. Make-up runs and cheeks are flushed. There are men dressed as angels. Women in orange arm-bands. Five emus flap around wildly. And of course the T-shirts … celebrating quantity, intoxication and altered states: 'It's like a personal visit from God.'

As well as the abandoned intake of illegal drugs – the ecstasy and MDMA powder, the base, the ket – there is a more scientific, calculated side as well. In one corner of the main room, next to a woman selling all sorts of fluorescent goods, is the O2Go oxygen bar. The owner, Mark Baxter, explains oxygen's role in this centre of consumption and transformation.

'When you're fucked,' he tells me, 'you become deoxygenated.' He sells pure oxygen, filtered through aromatherapy oils with either stimulating (lemon and peppermint) or relaxing (lavender) properties. He tells me that a similar technology is used by athletes, and that many US gyms already pump aromatherapy oils through the air-conditioning systems. For the clubbers, as for athletes, it's all about improving performance. He goes on to tell me about beta and delta waves, about oxygen hoods that convert your carbon dioxide to oxygen. The stall is perhaps a sign of future, more legalised chemical intake. I imagine a stream of stalls, selling powders, liquids and gases, as thoughtfully prepared and explained as O2Go.

From midnight onwards, the stall has a constant stream of people coming up to put the plastic tubes up their nose and reoxygenate. I give the peppermint a go. It clears out my nasal passage and is vaguely pleasant. The guy sitting next to me, dressed in white, with a mechanical hand, smiles crazily: 'When you've had all sorts of shit up your nose, this really clears it up.'

Of course, the night isn't magic for everyone. I see a guy walking along outside shouting repetitively, 'I'm sorry, I'm sorry,' while his mate hits him around the head. I see a girl lying outside a chalet and soon the paramedics show.

At 5.30am when the music stops, the room is still crammed with dancers, moving mad and fast. People trail out, looking surprised by the faint dawn that's appearing, skin mottled and goosebumped in the cold air. The transformation's wearing off, but the party isn't over. Groups trail back to chalets and music starts up. I go back with a bunch of kids dressed as Hawaiian dancers. We've been talking for about half an hour, fairly nonsensically, and they invite me back for a smoke and some ket. Despite my permanent curiosity, after sitting around with them for about twenty minutes watching their heads loll and broken sentences jolt around the room, the manic giggles and repetitive beats do for me and I head back to my car. Four miserable hours' sleep in the back with only a coat for a cover.

The morning after: a cold, overcast Welsh Sunday. Techno and trance still blast out from chalets. A few bedraggled costumes wander round, but it's mainly back to hoodies and jeans. I overhear inane conversations. A guy runs past tweaking his nipples and asking people if they are selling prawns. Someone else is taken off by a paramedic, slumped sideways. His mates laugh hysterically and wave goodbye.

People are still dancing in their chalets. A few play on the adventure playground. Despite the slight listlessness of the girl on the swings, she won't stop moving back and forth. For her, as for hundreds of others here, the temporary transformation and hedonism is too temporary. They want it always harder faster non-stop, for ever.

Go forth and modify

If clubbers were one group who fascinated me because of the time and energy they put into their elaborate transformations, then boy racers were another. The next level up from the cruise at Thurrock, these are kids who spend thousands making their cars faster and more beautiful. Magazines like *Redline* and *Max Power* are fashion mags for motorists: pages of accessories and additions, double-page spreads of gleaming cars, with twisted proportions and unreal colours.

While clubbers get together at night in dark urban buildings, boy racers show their transformations off during daylight hours on race tracks across the UK. So, one sunny Saturday, I'm bombing up the M1 in my distinctly unmodified Saab. I've always been quite happy with it, because it has a small tailfin and the word 'turbo' on the back. But it's twelve years old, it's all one colour, and the wheels fit neatly into their arcs.

The first sign that I'm heading in the right direction for the Redline Rumble is the lowered, tinted-windowed Renault Clio on the hard shoulder of the M1. Behind it: a police car, lights flashing. As I get closer, driving through rolling English countryside, past horses in fields and clumps of sheep, the number of alloys, spoilers, fins and oversized exhausts builds up until there's a convoy. My car feels naked among all the yellow trim and fat wheels. Later on, someone refers to it as a classic car. I don't think it's a compliment.

The Redline Rumble is democratic drag-racing. It takes place at the Santa Pod race course in Northampton. Anyone can have a go. You bring your car up to the line and thrash it for a quarter of a mile. All morning, pairs of cars come to do their best. From scrappy Fiestas that scream and lurch to Bimmers that suddenly look bland among all the colours and strange shapes. Puntos race Pugs, Porsches race Escorts. A Maestro takes on a Renault. A Fiesta races past with no bonnet and a giant bloke crammed in. A flash silver Mazda gets whipped by a knackered-looking Astra. It's like a romp through the last twenty years of affordable British cars. And they don't stop. Each race lasts about fifteen seconds. They manage to squeeze in 488 runs by 1pm.

Up in the stands, I get talking to a group of lads. One of them explains how it works and who races, pointing a signet-ringed finger over the race course.

'Anybody can turn up. Ten pound entrance, ten pound for three runs and you just line up and whoever you're next to, you just have a boot. Anyone against anyone. Can get embarrassing sometimes. 'Specially with the Skylines and stuff. See the blue one over there and the red one over the back. They're Nissans. They got 2.6-litre engine, twin turbo, rear-wheel drive. You go to prove your car on the strip. Once you get on once, it's really addictive. You have to keep coming back. You think: what can I do to make it faster? And you come back again and again and again.'

Conversations float over between races, about dodging cops and doing log books.

'I got banned for six weeks doing 120 down the M1.'

'I got done for drink driving. I still drive though.'

'He pulled me over, started getting angry. So I decked him.'

Girls in short skirts and bikinis talk about other girls in a disparaging way.

'She bent down to get something out the car and her arse was hanging out her skirt.'

'What did you say her name was?' a guy asks, laughing.

There are a lot of fuck mes when a good result goes through, as the time is read out in a reverent tone. And just in case people aren't getting it, the MC keeps things lively, celebrating the noise, the power, the speed and the smell of the whole race. His one-liners as incessant as the stream of cars to the starting line.

'It now takes 700 brakes to be God of the Pod.'

'Feel the burn, ladies and gentlemen. Who said smoking was bad for you?' as a Red Skyline revs up.

'We're gonna let them cool down. You know what happens when you spank them that hard. They get a little bit red.'

Away from the track, with the sound of revving engines in the background, it's a contemporary beauty parade. Doors and boots open, stereos thumping. Kids sit in the front seats making spliffs, watching DVDs or having a go on the in-car PlayStations, while owners add the final polish to their already gleaming motors. One perfectionist unwraps the clingfilm from the front of his car – there to stop dead insect mess. People chat and point at each other's artwork. The comparisons being: engines, paint jobs, radials, bass bins, lowering techniques and so on.

For most cars, their reason for being is their motion. These freak motors, like delicate pets, are best appreciated still, with boot, bonnet and doors slung open, constantly tended by their loving owners. Arranged in semicircles as if they might get lonely. The tweaks and additions go from the awesome – swooping side fins, gaping vents – to the absurd – a numberplate with an additional message: 'Back off unless you've got tits.' The cars carry their own slogans and websites too: T-shirts for machines: speedculture, kustomworx, blitz, bigfuckoffrims.com.

These cars have been transformed. So much that it's hard to recognise the original. There are extra lights, spoilers that scrape the ground; images of goat's heads and Manga girls adorn the bonnets. Some of them look more like spaceships than cars. One of the design companies is called Virtual Reality Styling, hinting at an otherworldy, unreal influence.

I speak with Philip, nineteen, from Stratford. He has a shaved head and sportswear. He's spent five or six grand making his car special. Once it was a Ford Ka. Now it's a gleaming silver bubble. All extra curves and special lights. I ask him what he's done to it.

'I got a body kit, MCR body kit, had it fitted by Essex racing, took about three or four weeks; got air filter on it, sixteens, exhaust, nitrous.'

He slyly indicates a small red switch below the steering wheel.

'Nitrous makes the car go faster. It's pure oxygen. The bottle's in the boot, it's fed through into the engine. As soon as you put the throttle pedal down to the ground, it opens up, sprays the gas in, mixes with fuel. Explosion. Speed. Wicked.'

I ask him why he's made such extravagant changes to the car and the answer is simple: because it goes faster and looks better.

'It's just the buzz. Look good. Get attention. Got to have a little bit of speed as well. It's just respect on the road, innit?'

'Which is most important – speed, looks or sound?'

Philip pauses as if deliberating one of life's trickier questions.

'Sound's good when you're driving along but you don't need a lot of it to enjoy it. I've gone for looks mostly, but speed, you have to have a little bit of speed. You can't have something that just looks flash. Having a nice car with a 1-litre engine you ain't gonna go anywhere, man. It just makes a lotta noise and goes slow. But I try to do my best. I'm putting a little turbo on as well. Little T15 turbo. Get about 130 brake.'

Although modifying cars is all about getting attention, getting noticed, sometimes it can be from the wrong source.

'I've never been pulled over. Not since I've had the bodywork, but I have been pulled over for driving with nitrous. They didn't know what it was, so it was all right. It's illegal if you don't tell the insurance company.'

'Does it bump up the insurance?'

'I wouldn't know cos I ain't told em. The police didn't even know what it was. I think he thought it was a fire extinguisher.'

I ask people to show me the best car at the rumble, and everyone points me towards the same one: a blue Nissan Skyline GTR R34. It's driven by Andy Barnes; at twenty-seven, a hero to a car park full of teens, whose cars don't pack the same power as his.

We talk between races. Two fans are blowing cold air onto the engine. There's none of the playfulness that I encounter with the younger drivers. For Andy, this is strictly business.

'Tell me what you've done to your car.'

'It's more about what haven't I done to it. It's got a full blueprinted engine, using steel internals, makes it stronger to run more power. It's completely blueprinted, so every part of the engine has been changed. The original parts are the head and the block. To buy the car originally, they're £50,000 straight out of the box from Nissan. They only ever imported a hundred of them. To tune it up as it is, the bar engine is probably around £33,000. And then specialist gearbox, specialist diffs, special wheels, suspension, driveshafts, interior, you name it, it's got it.'

For Andy the original Skyline was simply a frame for stuffing in as much power and speed as possible.

'The standard's got 280-brake horsepower, and the first thing you do when you get them is you want more power. First stage was 500 horsepower. Then we wanted more. So we got 600 horsepower. Then we wanted even more. So now we got 720 horsepower at the fly wheel. At high power we built the engine to produce 890 horsepower. And then we're going to add direct port nitrous on top. But today it's running 720 horsepower.'

He presents the changes like an ascension, a growing-up of the car. But no plateau will ever be reached. Each new addition quickly feels normal, and more power is required.

'The performance is pretty good, but I can't wait to turn it up. It's pretty hard to say, but you get used to 700 horsepower. It does happen. And you just want more and more, you know. You're always looking for that extra bit that puts you in the back of the seat. And once you get used to that, you want to push it in there even more. But as it is, it pulls in over 1.2g in acceleration, and if you was a passenger, it's like someone holding their palm on your chest, pushing you in the seat. It's pretty immense.'

Andy makes it to the final. His Skyline takes on a menacing-looking black and white Mitsubishi. Despite the 720bhp and Andy's semi-pro approach to the whole thing, he comes in a close second.

Philip and Andy insist that you can't just go for looks, but for some of the kids, it's all about beauty. John, twenty-two, from Birmingham – this time pairing the shaved head with shades – has a 1992 Honda Civic VTI. It is black, but a black that sparkles, shooting out reds, greens and purples. A giant fin sweeps out from the roof, and a pink exhaust pipe curls along the rear spoiler.

He tells me about his transformation. 'I've lowered it about a hundred mil all round, seventeen-inch wheels on. I've repainted the car in hologrammatic flake … I work in a body shop, I just asked for the chips from the place where we buy all our paint from and he showed me these chips and I thought I've got to have that. I've changed the front and rear lights, the front indicators, the side indicators. I've changed the rear standard spoiler and put a rear alloy spoiler on as well. I've changed the exhaust system, air filter, front seats, steering wheel, gearknob, dials, colour coded bits of my engine bay. I've had it eighteen months and I've been doing it bit by bit. Most of the stuff I either do myself or I know people who can get it me really cheap.'

The list goes on. Everything that can be tweaked, enlarged, lowered, coloured has been. About making it different and personal. As John says when I ask him why he's put so much time and love into it: 'Individuality. Just to be individual really.'

'Could you see yourself driving a more normal car?'

'I could never own a car without wanting to modify it. To put my mark on it. But saying that, there's a chap by me and over the past eight or nine months, everything that I've done to my car, he's gone out and bought exactly the same and he's pissing me off. He ain't got the money for the paint. But if you just see a car go past – it's a black Civic the same as mine – and you see similar wheels and similar spoiler; a lot of people can't tell them apart.'

His indignation makes me think of a woman spotting someone else in an identical dress at a party. For the boys here, whose clothing is the townie uniform of cap, sneakers and sweat pants, their cars are their fashion, their make-up. The colours are unashamedly feminine and fancy: lilacs and pearlescent white, powder-blues and violets. While the cars might look outrageous the clothes are predictable: football tops and hoodies, Hackett shirts, gold necklaces, tattoos, white Reeboks, Air Maxes, Burberry caps and FCUK everything. Girls in strappy tops, wedge heels, short denim and scraped-back hair. One guy walks towards me. His T-shirt reads: 'If you don't believe in oral sex, keep your mouth shut.' As he walks away, the back encourages me to FCUK safely. At Sundissential, individuality and creativity scream out from the clothes; here, all the love and inventiveness has gone into the cars.

And they serve a similar purpose to fashion: communication and attraction. As nineteen-year-old Richard from Hayling Island tells me: 'I think they look good. The dog's bollocks. Just to look different, innit? I've done everything bodywork-wise. I've spent thousands, mate. New bumpers, skirts, bonnet vent, bad boy conversion – gives the evil look on the headlights – boot spoiler, DVD player, Alpine head unit, JBL active sub in the back, alloys. It's getting there.'

He's here for two reasons: 'Sexy cars, fit bitches. A day out with the boys'.

And he believes his car can help him with the fit bitches.

'My girlfriend notices other girls noticing my motor. My missus don't get too happy about that one.'

'Is she here today?'

'No, thank God.'

Whereas Sundissential was almost transsexual in its mixing of costumes, boys and girls both dressing up and getting high, the Redline Rumble is a male thing. They do the driving, and they do up the car. The bikinied (very), amateur models posing in front of the cars, flashing their breasts and playing Twister with a few overexcited fifteen-year-olds, are for them too.

But there are loads of girls here, with boyfriends and friends. I talk to a few and they seem to share the passion, if not the tech specs, of the boys. One tells me she'd only go out with a bloke with a nice car. But only one girl races the entire day: Michelle, twenty, from Northampton. She's driving a battered red Renault Turbo, transformed with the same degree of dedication as the men.

'What have you done to your car?'

'Everything that can be done, near enough. Apart from water injection. It's got steel liners, a bigger turbo, strapped and flowed intercooler, induction kit, HT leads, piper cam. It's all to make it faster. And I'm pushing out 200 brake. The standard on a Renault 5 is 121 brake.'

Michelle thinks she's probably spent £8,000 over six cars. When I ask her what she does when she's not racing or doing up her car, she pauses, as if I've suggested something ridiculous.

'I go out and get drunk,' she says, laughing. 'My life is the car. I'm the membership secretary and area rep for the Renault 5 Turbo owners' club, so I have a lot of involvement in the club. Arranging events, doing memberships, getting new members to join.'

She has no doubt what she's interested in.

'Speed definitely. You've got two kinds. The kind you see in the magazines. And then you've got the people who concentrate on the engine more. Stealth mode, everyone calls it. Looks shit on the outside but is really good on the inside.'

Michelle goes off to race. She wins easily. Afterwards, her cheeks are glowing with adrenaline. 'It's a big buzz when you win. You're a bit nervous when you're on the start line and everyone's looking at ya. But it is a big buzz to win.'

'How many other girls are there racing here today?'

'None. None. I think I'm the only one. It's mainly a blokes' thing. I don't know why that is. They should get more involved, but they don't. They just come up here with their boyfriends on a day out.'

Michelle is on her sixth Renault; Andy just wants more and more; Richard is getting there but never arriving. There is no endpoint. As with the endless software patches, car modification is a never-ending process of continual improvement via speed, sounds and style.

As I'm checking the cars on display, I spot a guy in a 'Go forth and Modify' T-shirt, bringing a Noah-like urgency to the process, suggesting that these cars are another species to be protected and urged to propagate. Another T-shirt reads, 'Praise the lowered'. This semi-religious language gives the cars the status of new beasts created from old forms. This is the closest you can get to the powersuit from Metroid Prime – these creatures have sound, speed and screens. And personality: some are black and moody, all tinted windows and snarly trim. Others are more cartoonish and exuberant; the four-wheel equivalent of an eager puppy, ears, eyes and tongue too big for its tiny frame. The only thing missing is any weapons.

I'm reminded of pierced Jake. The same attention to detail and desire for turning a mass-produced item (a car, a body) into something that is irrevocably yours. Improving it: making it more beautiful. Making it always different.

Version 2.0

The story is similar at Crail Airfield, on the east coast of Scotland. It's a vision of public mess and private beauty: a sprawl of derelict buildings with every window broken. Beyond the airfield buildings lies a tranquil scene: cylinders of straw sit facing the sea on golden fields. When I'd arrived before eight – petrol heads don't mind getting up early – the sun was fighting the dawn clouds and strangely enough, but appropriately for this rustic Sunday, the sound of choral music was drifting over the track and the fields from one of the stalls. A few hours later and this serenity has disappeared, erased by a mish-mash of bass bins, revving engines and the smell of burger stalls. I talk to a few people and watch the morning's races, but I've got a long drive ahead of me, so decide to quit while it's still light.

I leave the car park, where someone is doing doughnuts over and over again, and get onto the main road. A stream of Rolls-Royces and Mercedes drives past, heading towards the Crail Golf Club, a beautiful course half a mile down the road, overlooking the ocean. Compared to the Corsas, the Pugs, the XR2s that I've ODed on, the luxury motors look pompous and bland. And the exuberance of Crail and Redline has obviously proved too much for my Saab. It sounds clunky and out of date. And won't go into reverse.

Luckily, there's no need for three point turns: for the next eight hours, I'm heading south down A-roads and motorways. On the way to Crail, I'd visited Birmingham, Manchester, Newcastle, Edinburgh, Glasgow. This time, the only places I stop are service stations. The dull cars, relentless concrete and garish repetition of the Welcome Breaks and the Motos make me think about the desire for speed, for beauty, for a twisted perception and a unique look that emerges from sterile and ugly landscapes. From Gemma's south London estate to the semi-derelict sprawl that is east Glasgow, these often grim landscapes are breeding grounds for colour and energy.

I remember wandering through Glasgow the day before and thinking how well it symbolises the desire for mutation, for transformation, for improvement that is the drive behind so many of the people I spoke to. It's far from perfect, it's sometimes done on a budget, it's still got a way to go, but the will is there.

Physically, Glasgow represents the contradictions and flux at the heart of many city centres; and more broadly at the heart of British culture. Inside the scrappy, graffiti-covered old town is a vibrant 21st-century cityscape fighting to get out. The transformation is happening in front of your eyes. The shells of old buildings remain, waiting to be filled with aluminium kitchens and big windows. A sign announcing the arrival of Jigsaw hangs off an old church. Other signs abound – for new leisure spaces, for luxury apartments. Versace Couture is two minutes' away from the pound shop.

On a larger scale this is Britain. Halfway between throwing off the old and getting into the new. Adept at games, computers and texting but often without any credit. Computer literate, but struggling with basic grammar and spelling. Imitating the style of Posh and Becks but at a fraction of the price. This country wants to be smart, wired and gleaming. But much remains grimy, regional and uninspired. And I wonder if this tension forms the impetus for many of the transformations I come across.

Away from Glasgow's city centre it gets more messy. There are acres of housing – estates, tower blocks, etc – from shiny new to semi-derelict. And not much to look at. Town planning doesn't extend to beauty. Two minutes from the neon shine of the Forge retail park, behind two dark towers, is a row of boarded-up houses. The entire front of the building has been covered in plywood, except for the windows. Light shines out. A pram lies forlornly outside one. In the park, kids in green and white soccer shirts lob bottles at each other. The swings are all knotted. Even in the summer evening it looks desolate.

For millions of British kids this kind of urban exhaustion is a permanent backdrop. It's not just trash and graffiti. It's the whole thoughtlessness of it. The sprawl of derelict and budget shops, the expanse of retail parks, the cul-de-sacs (a posh way of saying dead end), the bus stops which often are the closest kids get to a private room. With so much of the landscape unchangeable, it's no surprise that they change what they can control: their clothes, their hair, their body, their cars. The inside of their heads. Their pharmacology. Or that the bright glow of TV, a magazine's sheen, the lush colours of games, the flash of clubs and electric vibrancy of music vids are so beguiling. This is practical escapism. Or not even escapism. Filling what is bland, dull and broken with something whole, bright and beautiful.

This willingness and hunger for personal transformation and the creation of new forms suggests an impatience with what we've got, and the increasing ability to bring an image from our mind into this world.

Whether the action's taking place in suburbia or beneath the surface of an alien planet, the drive is the same. It's about redesigning the human form so it can operate better, more pleasurably, or just differently. British youth displays a hunger for a stream of new identities ... both online and on its own skin. This is more than fashion. This is transformation: of appearance, of behaviour, and of the places where these transformations take place.

Alongside the spreads of mad cars and pneumatic women in *Redline* or *Max Power* magazine, it's the detail that really stands out. Pages and pages of accessories: snake-eye lights, radials, exhaust tips, alloy wiperblades, undercar lighting. All about additions. As one of the bikinied girls replies when asked if she has real or artificial breasts: 'Real, but I'm going for fake.'

If something looks better, feels better, works better, then go for it. Daft Punk's track *Harder, better, faster, stronger* says it all; 'If something looks better, feels better, works better, then go for it.'

The dream for version 2.0 plays out across every aspect of modern culture: from the remix to the relaunch. Kevin Warwick's hunger for a cyborg existence may seem extreme, but he is simply applying to the body an attitude that permeates every slice of contemporary culture: from cars to computers, phones to pop stars, software to soft furnishings. Upgrade now.

This is a time of patches and plug-ins, where the inevitable obsolescence of objects is no longer a problem. We buy things knowing that they are incomplete, will always remain incomplete, but this unfinishedness is just part of the way things work. As with Jake's body, which he sees as a work in progress, and where the destination might change, so with the stuff that surrounds us. Video game interfaces teach us to regard everything as equippable and updateable ... including ourselves. Whether it's a car, a spaceship or your on-screen persona. A world of incomplete possessions. Of permanent ongoing improvement. Chatting with kids for whom transformation was so important made me realise that this is not vain, stupid or worthless. It's human. Pragmatic evolution. These are the terms on which pop culture works now. Ford Capri Mk IV. Matrix

Reloaded. New Labour. Teenage Big Brother. Antiques Ghost Show. Mac 10 Jaguar. Mac 10 Panther. A 40gb iPod to replace the 5, 10 and 20gb model. There's always a better version out there.

Version 2.0 is the language of nerds, but the expression of everyone. Upgrade me: make me better, faster, stronger. Changing the things you can, the things that are personal and close to you, because most of the world is too distant and tough to be affected.

The personal, local nature of the transformation makes a telling comment about the way young people in Britain see themselves in regard to the broader country. Despite the enormous energy for modification, for improvement, for trying to make things work better, this is largely directed at oneself, or the immediate environment. There was little talk about how change could happen on a larger scale. Indeed, the places where the most extreme transformations took place and were on show were by their nature in secluded distant spots: Crail Airfield, Prestatyn … places where there was little chance that the behaviour might seep out into the bigger, unmutant world.

'Life's a game'

The papers' news reporters covered the stars both in their stage personas and in their 'real' lives, more or less without discrimination ... for millions of readers this material represents the bulk of their 'news' diet. Editors judge that stories about stars are of more interest than what anyone else in society is doing, and they must be right ... But in the process editors have allowed the boundaries between fact and fiction to become blurred and sometimes – to the inexpert eye – indistinguishable.

Nick Clarke, *Media Guardian*, May 2003

The greatest threat of all, in fact, may be our growing freedom to immerse ourselves in a world of illusion where the problems of distant reality don't exist.

Adbusters

The genius of Eminem has been for short-circuiting understanding. You cannot disentangle his words, life, or art from one another. Sometimes he really means what he says and sometimes he's playing a part, and woe be to the outsider who can't tell the difference.

R.J. Smith, Manhattan's *Village Voice*, November 2002

Escape from Milton Keynes

I'm driving through that most unreal of cities – Milton Keynes – on the way to the Eminem gig. On spacious roads, past ordered roundabouts, with cubic steel buildings glinting perfectly in the sun. It feels like you've entered a video game, although it's more Sim City than Vice City. Before I reach the Bowl, I stop off at the Xscape centre.

The dome rises from the concrete like the tip of a fat chrome pipe sunk deep in the ground. Inside you can follow the signs for real sno, past the fake fir trees, and the commissioned and untagged graffiti. The slip between real and artificial, between normal and enhanced is blurred and easy, unthinking. That's the message graffitied on the walls of Milton Keynes Xscape centre: 'Outside a landmark destination, inside another world. Don't just exist, escape.'

But tonight the real escape is on the edge of the city: 65,000 people gathered at the Bowl to see the master of fictions, of blurred identities and actions: Eminem. For an act that has caused so much controversy and debate about the negative effect of violent, misogynistic, homophobic, antisocial lyrics, the crowd seems benign and unthreatening. Among the hordes of teens and twentysomethings, there are loads of younger kids, holding their parents' hands as a stream of hip hop plays on. You can tell the potential danger by the number of police. A few dotted around the perimeter. Nothing compared to the black-shielded mobs on Mayday. Overhead one police chopper circles lazily.

Throughout the night there are the signs of the coarseness, excess and lawlessness that Eminem has come to represent: a kid in a 'Britney swallows' T-shirt; Muggs from Cypress Hill brandishing a spliff as long as your forearm as they play 'I want to get high'; the crowd responding dutifully as they are told to 'Put your muthafuckin middle fingers in the air'. The crowd enjoys and totally accepts all of this. As had the *Sun* the day before. Normally quick to attack the kind of performer who celebrates drug-taking and underage sex, it devotes a double page to praising the previous night's gig.

Eminem's main emotion might appear to be anger, but there's very little of it here. After an hour of waiting for him to come on, the crowd stands up, does Mexican waves and throws plastic bottles which look like Milton Keynes birds flying through the air. But it's all good-natured.

Finally, Eminem enters on a ferris wheel. Above him in huge fairground writing is the legend: 'The Eminem Show'. It's not like he's pretending any of this is real. This is pure entertainment, best summed up by the ten-year-old wearing a Jason mask. Like other fictional bogey-men, Eminem is naughty but harmless. He affects everything and nothing at all.

And he plays with this contradiction throughout the gig. His act starts with clips of American newscasters and politicians bemoaning his evil grasp on innocent American kids, how his songs are all about rape and murder. Later on, one of the stage animations dramatises his supposed influence. It shows images of school shootings, of drug abuse and revels in his role in making all of this happen.

There is a disconnection between meaning and emotion. Angry is the subject. But everyone is loving it. Eminem has turned his very real life into a show for the world. He shares the mess of his personal life and makes it funny, makes it offensive, makes it mean something.

He introduces 'Cleaning Out My Closet', perhaps the most shocking of his tracks, where he lays into his trashy mom for the terrible way she brought him up, with the question: 'Anyone ever had problems with their mom?' before shouting, 'Fuck you, Debbie' and getting on with it. The bleak lyrics to this song gain integrity from back stories about his mom suing him, from descriptions of her pill popping, gambling and general neglect. It's the story behind his success, the roots of his rapping, and it's also entertainment for millions.

It's no surprise when 'Lose Yourself' gets the biggest cheer of the night. The song comes from *8 Mile*, the movie that shows Eminem rising from his trailer-park existence and winning the world over with his rhymes. The 'lose yourself' is an entreaty to the audience and also a challenge. He wants them to get so swept up in his music that everything else is forgotten.

But this isn't about losing yourself in the way that Nick Clarke or Adbusters might suggest, where your boundaries and markers are unclear, where you don't know where you are. This is not loss of reason or perception, but loss of obstruction, of the things that make life tough. For Eminem and for the audience, the message is about passion. Go into this world of exaggeration and distortion, of play and illusion, and you can emerge stronger and wiser. Losing yourself in the music, in the unreality of created worlds, is a strategy for success.

As I walk up the hill, I see that everyone knows the words. Are lost in them. Have escaped from Milton Keynes far better than they ever could have done at the sno dome. When I'm at the top of the Bowl, looking back over the crowd, D12 asks everyone to light up and thousands of points of fire fill the Bowl. They're not angry; they're showing their love. This is what words do. Stories about taking ecstasy, shooting people, hating your mom, being bullied … told in a particular way to create this crowd of shining, adoring faces.

The contradictions are splendid: a white kid singing about White America backed up by a bunch of black hip hop stars that he has created. Singing about police brutality as the police look benignly on, rapping about how he hates his mother as seven-year-old kids sit on their parents' shoulders.

'Some things are just much too illegal to do in real life'

In the old days, you knew where the real world ended and the fake ones began. These days, though, it's all mixed up. And, if you believe the critics, hapless audiences are often confused and bewildered by this blur.

As with so many criticisms levelled at our modern ways of doing life, the ones aimed at the insubstantiality of so much of our world tend to come from people with a sense of a before and an after. Who have grown up in a world where the lines were more clearly laid out, and are perhaps extrapolating their own sense of confusion, rather than representing a universal anxiety. Coupled with this fear of confusion is the familiar worry, the one that started this book off: that what happens in the unreal world drifts into the real one … so that it's a short step from hip hop to packing a gun; from taking out pedestrians in GTA3 to doing the same on the A3.

The PlayStation Experience, running for four days over an August weekend, demonstrates just how far we've drifted. It is the perfect fusion of real and unreal … seamlessly moving between layers of physical and virtual stimulation, and representing the disappearance of entertainment genres and boundaries. In this world, there are an infinite number of routes, all leading to fun.

Fun is what the lo-tech, line-drawing ads promise. In one, a bird watches a robot dance and remarks drily: 'I don't know how it works, but it's good, innit?' This level of comprehension probably applies to 95-plus per cent of the attendees to the four-day extravaganza. Unlike the rest of the Game week, which has been trade focused, this is strictly for punters.

And fun is what the enormous poster just inside Earls Court promises as well. An arrow labelled 'boring' points out into the street, into the normal, basic, unmodified world, the real world. An arrow labelled 'fun' points towards the exhibition centre, where screens and joysticks promise to take you somewhere better. But for the 300-odd people in the overflow queue (every day sold out), it feels like they might be the wrong way round. As one joker remarks: 'This ain't no PlayStation Experience. I don't remember a game called waiting for fucking ever.'

The queuers might have underestimated the popularity and pull of PlayStation, but PlayStation haven't underestimated their visitors. They know what their players want. This is the future according to PlayStation. A future that is fast, bright, multiple, simultaneous, noisy, playful. And endlessly generative. A future that combines multiple levels of stimulation and simulation effortlessly. Fun is 360 degrees total entertainment. Fun is real and virtual, physical and screen-based, live and animated.

I have been to a number of expos at Earls Court – mobile phones to next season's fashions – and this is the liveliest I've ever seen it. The PlayStation Experience is about everything happening at once. Music and MCs collide. Screens are everywhere. Giant screens, multiplayer, personal, mobile. Out of the corner of the eye, there's always something else to move towards. The latest titles are almost a backdrop to the craziness of all the other activity that brings many of the games' subjects and elements to life.

If gaming takes activities and makes them playable on screen, then PlayStation Experience gives them back to the real world. Breakdancing demos, Konami dancers, kickboxers, sumo-wrestlers, a Mad skills workshop on the basketball court, an Acclaim NBA Jam competition. And of course, on the main stage, as at every event for young audiences: the music. Kila Kela, Lisa Maffia, Mel Blatt … semi-celebrities lining up to demonstrate their participation in this entertainment melee. None of it conflicting. Just mixed up and multiple.

Perhaps the purest example of this is Kila Kela. A slight figure, he takes to the stage in loose jeans that continually slide over his hips, in battered Nikes and a mic. To start with, the crowd are unimpressed. They don't recognise this kid. He seems a bit scruffy, a bit lacking in visible star quality. And with nothing else but a mic and his mouth he produces fifteen minutes of impossible bass kicks and snare drums; hi hats and scratching. Mixing and falsettos. If you close your eyes you could be listening to a record. He sounds like a drum programme. By the end, the crowd are loving it, applauding this guy who has taken one step further towards a world where real and artificial, where man and machine, are merged.

The most successful entertainment is that which can touch all genres and bring them together. And computer games do this better than anything because they have a platform that lets all of these elements play out. Music, fashion, sport, fighting, competitions, even space-hopping. Anything you know from the world can make it into a game. Merging and blurring different genres until the boundaries don't exist.

PlayStation manages to appeal to a wide range of ages: from the three-year-olds up to their necks in coloured balls but still grasping joysticks, to thirtysomethings who were brought up on Commodores and Spectrums. But it's not all for everyone. The entrance to the boudoir is guarded by girls in bikinis, checking that no under-18s get through. Inside, people are playing games lying full length on plush red cushions. Playing games like Backyard Wrestling, Road Kill and Gladiator.

Nodding to the fact that these are just games, the sign at the entrance reads: 'Some things are just much too illegal to do in real life.' So you come and do them here. Whether it's driving too fast and wiping out other cars, taking on a variety of gladiators in a blood-drenched coliseum, or prowling through a moody, shadowy prison where death-row victims have been reincarnated as the methods of execution that befell them.

The point here is not that games let you do things that are illegal in real life, but that they let you do things that you can't do in real life. Whether it's driving too fast, skipping through a psychedelic landscape, or commanding a Second World War tank. They expand your reach and ability … they give you a set of experiences that you couldn't get elsewhere. Which is why dedicated gamers will place gaming above cinema or literature in terms of immersion and involvement. With other forms of entertainment, you are only ever reading or watching the hero. In gaming you become the hero.

I play violent games but I'm not violent

I ask the same question again and again of the gamers and music fans I speak to … about the correlation between what they play and listen to, and their behaviour and attitudes. The responses are revealing because of the similarities. Most people I speak to are very conscious of the arguments surrounding immersive entertainment and its effect on the player. But nobody credits it with affecting them. They all claim to understand the rules. The real and the unreal may be more mixed up in today's world, but there is a growing sensitivity to the different levels.

Sean, aka Shaolin, sixteen, plays games for at least six hours a night. We get talking at the qualifying rounds for Ultimate Gamer, a national games championship set up by the Sci-Fi Channel to make gaming in general more visible, and specifically to show off the new Hulk game. He has short, tousled hair, pale skin and seems nervous. His friend Nick won't talk with us. He says he doesn't like interviews.

Sean likes fighting games and shooting games – Streetfighter, Half-Life. He has a PC, Xbox and a PS2. He like PS2 better because there are more games. He plays a lot online. Shoot-'em-ups, RPGs. He's played against people from the States, from the Philippines, from Poland. He sees gaming as an intuitive activity, where you're not learning just how to play a single game, but where your gaming appreciation and ability increases the more games you play.

'You don't need skills to play, but you get better the more you play. You learn what to do. You learn tactics as you go on.'

Like any area of culture, the experts are the people who are immersed in it, who can read the nuances and references within games. Just as understanding the structure of a five-act tragedy can help you better appreciate *Hamlet* (or *Gladiator*), so understanding the dynamics of gaming makes the gaming more fun. From the outside what might look like a fairly mindless succession of screens and weapons has its own beauty and logic. As with other entertainment genres, there are structural rules and conventions that transcend individual games.

Sean gives a familiar reply when I ask if he thinks that computer games have a bad influence.

'No, none. I seen lots of criticisms about games but it's not everyone goes round stealing cars after playing the game. People don't understand the games. They just look at it and see what it's about and then they make assumptions.'

From comments like these, it becomes clear that modern entertainment fans have little respect or time for people who don't understand something making comments about the effect that it has on the people who do understand it.

The noisiest group at the qualifying rounds is watching Samuel wipe out soldiers with bulldozers, crates and the Hulk's oversized fists. He's here with his homies. They wear oversize denim or tracksuits and gold. Unlike Sean and Nick, they look nothing like the stereotype of social misfit gamers. More like your average hip hop fan or sports kids. Athletic, big, confident. Nothing bedroom about them. It's clear from the whoops for high scores and humorous cussing when the game gets the better of one of them that gaming is a social activity. High scores are traded in loud voices, and there's a huddle as one of Samuel's mates, Devene, looks unbeatable.

When I ask Samuel if he minds that his friend beat his score, he says of course not. They're all part of the same clique, and as long as some of them get through, that's what counts.

Samuel is twenty-two and has been playing games since he was six. His favourite games at the moment are Halo, Splinter Cell ('the graphics and gameplay just out of this world'), Dead or Alive 3 and Zelda. So three fairly macho 3-D adventure games, and one about pirates and girls with pointy ears.

He plays four to five hours a day. 'Mainly I play at night, but that often ends up going into the morning. When you get sucked in.'

Like Sean, he alludes to the fact that over time you build up a games knowledge, an understanding of how games in general work.

'I call myself a skilful games player. Because I'm multi-platform, so I can play all genres of games. If you're a proper gamer, most games you'll be able to pick up and play. You learn from previous play. For someone who doesn't play much, they're better off reading the manual.'

And gives a similar response to the question about violence.

'I play violent games but I'm not violent. I know the media try to portray that violent games produce violence in the street but I don't think it's connected. You might say a tiny portion is connected but in the mainstream, it's not really. Instead of taking your anger out on other people, you take it out on the video game. You just play a fighting game.'

Samuel's comments recall those of Sue Clark from the BBFC about violent films playing a cathartic role. In this sense, games perhaps perform a similar purpose to sport: conflict and aggression, representing actual battles, but in a controlled, safe environment. Gaming is just closer visually to the activities it represents.

As for Samuel's vision for games in the future, he's hoping for a time when they are more embedded in this world, so that there is less of a barrier between your physical being and the gameplay.

'Where I'd like to see them go would be more 3-D, more like holographic, so when you move, you move in the game. Less of a joystick, more of you doing stuff. Also real-life graphics is going to excel. The better quality it is, it makes it more real, so it makes it feel like it's actually happening so it does draw you into the game a lot more.'

The desire here is clearly one way: more immersion in unreal worlds, getting to the point where your whole body can be submerged in a stream of data and gameplay. Where your overall movements correspond to action in a game. So the intermediary (the joystick) disappears and you literally inhabit a created environment.

Ben, twelve, from Hemel Hempstead, has been playing since he was five. He started with a Sega, currently has a PS2, but is looking to upgrade.

'I'm getting a Gamecube, I hope,' he says as he looks over at his dad. His passion for gaming is clear: 'If I didn't have homework I'd be on there all day.'

His favourites are shooting games, like Grand Theft Auto, because 'they're fun'. He is similarly dismissive of the claims about the influence of video games.

'I reckon that's just stupid. It's just a game, innit? Who's it gonna hurt?' I ask if his dad minds.

'He didn't like me getting Grand Theft Auto. Vice City. But it's really cool.'

This clear understanding that Sean or Samuel demonstrate is echoed in a report by the ITC and BBFC, entitled 'How Children Interpret Screen Violence'.

Children are able to distinguish between fictional violence and violence that is 'real'. This research found no evidence of a conflation in participants' minds between violence in fiction and violence in real life ... Of all the images of violence presented to this sample, those events that were real (i.e. on the news) were the most affecting ... Dramas and soap operas are recognised as fictional representations of the real world, while the news is known to be the real world ... there are clear distinctions made between cartoon-like film violence, even if the characters are played by actors rather than animated, and film violence that shows human emotion and pain, even though set within a fantastical storyline.

And yet the way this is reported in the press is aimed at bemoaning an emotional insensitivity, rather than celebrating the depth and clarity of their understanding. 'Kids "numb" to violence on TV' claims the *Express* in a double-page spread. Surprisingly, the *Sun* gets closer by stating, 'News worse for children'. But they only give the story a few lines.

There seems to be unwillingness to accept that younger Britons can bring the necessary level of discernment to the entertainment that surrounds them. This is despite the fact that they are better equipped to do so, having only known these levels of immersion and stimulation. The games and the movies and the gigs – these are their forms, much more than their critics'.

For many games, their success is dependent on how successful the level of blur has been. While games clearly create a different space to this world, at the same time they attempt to get as much of the real world into that space as they can. So in Fable you play a warrior who ages in the course of the game, and whose appearance depends on what has happened to him. The sequel to Half Life boasts about introducing real-world physics into the gameplay, so if you shoot a gas canister it spins as a result of escaping gas.

At the same time, of course, games offer an improvement on this world. Midnight Club 2 lets you race illegally through intricately detailed copies of the streets of Los Angeles, Paris and Tokyo. It promises Shinjuku's hectic metropolitan maze, Kabuki-Cho's narrow back alleys, and advises you that because of heavily regulated jaywalking, roads are free of pedestrians. But while the streets may look very similar to the cities they represent – except glossier – your experience of them is far more exciting. You drive a car you could never afford, more dangerously and skilfully than any F1 ace, and you see your car, and others', at impossible, exceptional angles, as one flies over your head so closely that you can see the exhaust pipe and another screams past you millimetres away. And with the online version, you're no longer just pitched against a computer. The game promises, 'This time, it's flesh and blood opponents.'

The point here is that the real and the unreal flow between each other. They are not two distinct states, colliding with and opposing each other, but simply points on a continuum.

Def Jam Vendetta demonstrates this fluidity while bringing together many of the different elements that are criticised about today's youth cultures. Underground gangs, hip hop and illegal fighting – including girl-on-girl action – are combined in one glossy record-label and games-publisher collaboration. This indicates a far broader theme: the blurring of boundaries between different forms of entertainment, the way they slide into each other to defy categorisation. So slippage occurs not just between this world and a generalised unreal one, but between different unreal worlds too. Electronic Arts' partnership with Def Jam Vendetta allows both brands – favourites with young males – to borrow from each other's credibility and skills and produce something that neither could have made on their own.

The game is set in a familiar urban wasteland: wrecked cars, pitbulls, graffiti and bonfires. And the fighters in the game wear the standard street gear: vests, tats, gold chains, goatees. But as well as the truly fictional characters, you've got the option of playing a number of artists from the Def Jam stable. Their association with the game brings its sonic benefits as well, featuring artists like Scarface, Public Enemy and Ghostface Killah and titles like 'in cold blood', 'throw your gunz', 'bring the pain'.

It works both ways: the game gets a high-quality soundtrack, the record label gets its acts and albums featured, but more importantly the artists get a chance to appear dangerous without risking a criminal record. Because it's not just their music in the game, but their voices and their style. And their style includes head butts, low kicks and a heap of special moves. Hip hop is all about fighting your way up from the streets, but successful artists don't want to get their knuckles grazed any more. It pays better and is safer just to rap about it. This is a logical extension from rapping about life on the streets, and starring in videos with guns and gangstas. Just another level of immersion.

The game can go further in terms of image fluidity than either music or videos can. Because it introduces another element: the playa. That's you. In Def Jam Vendetta, you can take on not only a raft of fictitious players, but also assume the character of any of the hip hop artists who appear in the game.

So Dennis Coles aka Ghostface Killah is one member of the Wu Tang Clan as well as a solo artist. His name and his music exist both in this world and in the world of Def Jam Vendetta, where you the player can fight as a pixelated version of Ghostface. And bust a load of moves that Dennis could never pull off. And bringing it back into the real again, he leads the Def Jam Vendetta Tour, a month-long, twenty-one-state event across the US.

Creating a persona, a larger-than-life version of yourself for public consumption, is pretty much de rigueur in the world of hip hop, and more broadly within popular music. Most rap artists have given themselves names. Their persona is more than a band name, it becomes a real part of their personality.

This used to be star behaviour. But like everything else, if celebrities are on to it, we want a piece too. During meeting and talking with kids, I picked up a bunch of their e-mails. The addresses give clues as to their personalities, their online identities.

vodkajesus@
adorndbyheaven@
Squashed frog80@
Sycomaniac187@
Cyber_babe_52@
microbaby@
Unsafe666@
Miss_2_cute@
Princess_of_fiends@

Of course, most people don't just have one online identity. They have several virtual personalities floating alongside their regular ones. These are ways of complementing and expanding their personalities, passports to different behaviours.

This fluidity is best expressed by two favourite phrases that surface again and again when I speak to kids, often incidentally, irrelevantly, almost invisibly. 'Like' and 'sort of' acknowledge the impossibility of knowing completely or getting any closer than an approximation. Everything is a metaphor. Nothing is real.

Ultimate Gamer

The finals for Ultimate Gamer take place in Leicester Square. Thirty people make it; down from one thousand in the heats.

The competitors are playing on pods in the foyer. A modern matinee, it's a mix of teens and twentysomethings, all male: homies, grungers and geeks, although a few girls have come to watch. One man looks like he hasn't seen the sun in months. A dad counts his son, Wesley, down on a stopwatch and when he's done offers him a Lucozade Sport. With its slogan – 'replaces lost energy' – Lucozade seems a real-world equivalent to the health packs or energy bars you pick up in games.

This is where I first met Kiel, who has come down from Newcastle on the coach. He's just finished playing, and is talking fast, eyes flashing. He tells me that he thinks he can win. When I explain what I'm doing there, he slams his Walkman phones on my head.

'This is a tape we did,' he tells me excitedly. 'That's us MCing.'

I listen for a few moments, but it's hard to hear what's going on with the sounds of the Hulk in the background.

'If you come up to Newcastle, I'll show you round,' he tells me. 'Show you the clubs we go to, where we do graffiti, all that.'

The heats conclude without anyone really noticing, except for the officials who time it separately. The last ten get to play on the big screen. Kiel isn't one of them, but with the rest of the competitors and mates, we stroll into the cinema. It's only a quarter full but noisier than for any film I've ever seen.

In the centre of the room, overlooking the first block of seats, is a grey alienesque chair, with a gamepad attached. Next to it is a six-foot green thumb, representing both the Hulk's gigantism and the gamer's most important digit. This is where the showdown takes place.

One by one, the competitors take to the stage. Compared to their slick on-screen moves and tactics for multiple kills, their real-world bodies are less fluid. Most of the time it's just about the hands, rapid thumb movements, desperate finger-stabbing. The mouth contorts, and when things get tough the whole body starts jerking.

With the four-minute bursts, it's hard to see it as a spectator sport. Or a sports competition, because everyone is playing against the computer. And as the show's presenter, Emily, says, it's not easy to commentate when it's the same game over again. But it's certainly entertainment. And entertainment that lets you participate – both the players who get their five minutes perched above the audience orchestrating the action on a giant screen, and the audience, who bring the whole thing to life. Emily invites the audience up to take turns commentating, to take the pressure off her, and because they love it. The style goes from nervous to shouty. Emily doesn't look too concerned for her job. There are flashes of brilliance: 'It's a Hulk smash, a Hulk crash.' One boy is Shakespearean in his passion. Raising his hands to the sky. Shaking the mic. 'Carnage. We want carnage.' Over and over. The antithesis of the stereotypical pale player at home in his bedroom. Whistles, cries, green glowsticks, the whole place getting into it. Once again the real and unreal are mixed up as the crowd cheer both the contestants and the green freak on-screen.

There's no immediate winner: Stuart and Julian have killed 117 soldiers in four minutes. They are summoned up to the chair again, where they stand, greenlit, as they decide who goes first. Both of them have brought a good-sized bunch of mates and the whole cinema wants a winner, so there's more noise, and they look half excited, half embarrassed at the attention. Round two, and it's another draw: twenty soldiers in thirty-nine seconds. Finally Stuart pulls clear and finishes off thirty soldiers in fifty-two seconds. He climbs down from the chair, body shaking, wearing a dazed grin, and salutes the area of the cinema where his mates are calling his name.

Watching the awards ceremony – Stuart picks up a cheque for fifteen grand – I realise that this is one more arena where people can feel valued, skilful; where they have power. As with Eminem, losing yourself in the excitement of an unreal world feeds back to the real one. Contestants return from the alien chair with bright, glowing eyes to a complimentary crowd. The game might be unreal, but the power they had temporarily as Hulk becomes more solid as they are whooped by friends, competitors, and by a TV channel called Sci-Fi.

Dirtual reality

A few weeks later I go to visit Kiel in Newcastle. I'm keen to understand the mentality and experience of someone who spends hours and hours gaming. And is good enough to get to the final thirty in Britain. I go to learn about immersion in a virtual world, but talking to Kiel it soon becomes clear things aren't that straightforward. His virtuality is a lot dirtier, taking place in and always tinged by the real world. I arrive at his small terraced house in Gateshead and am shown up to his room by his mum.

Four boys await me – Ray, sixteen, Chris, fourteen, Andrew, fourteen, and Kiel, seventeen – in Air Maxes, jeans and collared shirts. Wearing fake gold and Lynx. They describe their style as charva, a Geordie take on townie. The room is crammed with a PlayStation, decks, CDs, records, a TV, pages of homegrown lyrics. There are fliers for a club called Hangar 13. The single bed has a South Park headboard. And above it there's a poster of a tin with the ubiquitous cannabis leaf and the message: 'Cannabliss. Warning: may expand your mind.'

It's a long summer and not much is going on. Except tag, drink, smoke, play computer games, write lines for their MCing. So for a couple of hours, I get the full force of their energy, a hectic non-stop tour through their world. Their conversations are pure stream of consciousness, flowing and jerking from *Jackass* to drugs to fights they've had to friends who are injecting heroin, to sneakers.

Emerging from the fast, often dislocated sentences and tangential subjects is an exhilaration at the amount of unreal stimulation that exists, coupled by an acute understanding of how entertainment works. There is no sense of confusion but instead a sharp awareness that the rules of behaviour within the virtual and the real world are different. And a firm belief in the inability of the unreal to impinge on human actions. At least not without that person's consent.

Nick Clarke, Adbusters and co. might believe that naive audiences struggle to make sense of the many layers of entertainment subterfuge that surround them. Speaking to someone like Kiel, though, I realise how patronising it is to imagine that they are duped or even confused. These boys can see exactly what's going on, as clearly, if not more so, as these media pundits, who might have the education and a few twentieth-century lit. crit. terms but are living it from outside and from a time of passive audiences.

We start by talking about gaming, and it's clear that these boys like to play. They reel off the names when I ask them what their favourites are: Metal Gear Solid, Final Fantasy, Soul Caliber, Vice City. There is also universal accord about the amount of time you have to put in to get good.

'You buy a new game,' states Kiel.

'And you play on it for hours.'

'Ages. Ages. When I bought Final Fantasy 10, I didn't come home for four days. When I bought Final Fantasy 8, I used to knock about with this kid called Scott, and I used to sit in his house, and he used to be going, howay, come out, and I'd be: no, I'm playing on this, I'm playing on this. One more hour. One more hour. One more hour. And he'd be sitting there, watching it, bored.'

Somehow the conversation skids over to school and beyond. Kiel has just left school, and is keen to do something more real: 'I did a science course, and I probably passed that. But I don't want to be a scientist. I want to be a fireman, or join the army. If you join the army, you get paid while you're away and you can learn a trade and then come back to the real world and get a job.'

'What would you think if you were called up to go to Iraq?'

'I'd love that. My sister's lad's in Iraq. He killed someone the other day. He actually shot someone. Like they come close so he had to shoot them, and he was saving people's lives but it was his bullet. Each bullet they've got is recognised so you can tell who shot someone and it was him.'

'So, would you fight for your country?'

'I could take it. I'd fight for my country. I'd die for the Queen.'

But Ray and Andrew are less convinced.

'She's done nowt for me.'

'I'd rather die for my family, like, than the Queen.'

From loyalty to the mechanics of capture and torture. Kiel's worried about what happens if they get hold of you, while Chris is not convinced that he could dish it out.

'And if you get caught, they might proper sit you in the room, and put electric wires and proper torture you. That's sick, that. They're nutters.'

'I couldn't do that, though, if I caught someone. I couldn't torture someone.'

And then back to the video games. I ask them what kind of things they get up to in Vice City. They answer in unison.

'Steal cars, shoot people, smash people's heads in, take people hostage, rob shops, blow cars up.'

There's no hesitation when I ask what the difference is between enjoying the violence in Vice City and doing it in real life. No confusion, or lack of understanding that the rules of video games are completely different from those in real life. The boundaries between fiction and reality may be blurred, and it might be easy to slip between the two. But this physical movement is not inevitably accompanied by a moral or behavioural slide. Chris sums it up neatly in one short sentence.

'There are consequences in this world.'

'It's stupid,' Kiel adds. 'You've got to be warped in the first place if you play a game and then say, oooh, I'm robbing a shop; you'd rob a shop anyway.'

'That could just be someone's excuse, like if they got caught. They'd just say, it's the game.'

Like a scholar drawing on academic sources for back-up, Kiel turns to the foremost authority on the influence of entertainment on young minds and starts rapping Eminem at me, in a Geordie-meets-West Coast accent.

'"They say music can talk to you, but can it load a gun and cock it too? Well, if it can, the next time you assault a dude, say it was me and I'll get sued." It doesn't influence me. You just got to be headstrong. But I bet there are some people who are already nutcases who just want an excuse. You can tell that Eminem is just getting money for it. It's just a laugh. It doesn't offend me. You know when it doesn't mean anything. I might say, Ray, shut up or I'll shag your da.'

Andrew chips in. 'Or I shagged your mother.'

Leaving Kiel's room, Ray and Chris take me on a tour of the local graf, eagerly pointing out their own tags, as well as those of local heroes. After running around wastelands and onto train sidings, we walk into Windmill Park and it's a great view. Kiel tells me how he came here one morning after taking a pill, him and his Walkman, looking over the city and pretending he was in *Titanic*, hanging off the prow of the ship, surfing the altered reality of a dawn Newcastle.

The unreal world provides a connection that is lost in the real world. I talk to Kiel and friends about the same games, artists and activities that I talk with loads of other kids about. They are common ground, universal topics. The rules are simple and clearly understood. But like the kids I speak with in Birmingham, the Gateshead kids feel disconnected from other parts of the city, and certainly other bits of Britain.

'It's good living in Gateshead,' Ray tells me, 'because I've been living here all my life, but say someone from down south come up they wouldn't like it. Like I wouldn't like to live down London. Here you feel safe and that. If you go somewhere else you feel like an outcast. You didn't feel right, walking about. Putting your head low and that. Here you walk with your head high.'

There's a more local disconnection as well. When we talk about dangerous areas in Gateshead, they mention 'south of the road', and then go into a long anecdote about a wifey who got killed after doing crack in a phone box.

'Doesn't affect us, we keep away, but it's still there. It's not gonna happen to us. We're not going to get killed.'

'The guy that killed her is still walking about.'

They tell me who did it. One of them calls Chris a grass. I'm not sure how serious they are, but I promise not to put it in the book.

As I drive away, I reflect on the energy of the last hour I'd spent in Kiel's hyperactive bedroom. The excitement with which they talk about their music, their graffiti, the computer games. And compare it with where they live. Which is a clean-ish but rundown estate in Gateshead. Identical shabby houses, bare scraggy bits of lawn, a few knackered cars. Not a shitty estate, but hardly a model town. And compared to the vibrant, sensation-bending colour and noise of gaming, music, clubs and graffiti, there is little comparison. Where would you rather spend your time?

Kiel and his friends manage to overlay their physical and somewhat dull world with multiple strands of dirty virtuality. Graffiti, music, lyrics, drugs, computer games are all means of playing with what you've got and making it look better or mean more, or feel extra. So graffiti makes a wall more interesting, not just because of the look, but because there's always an anecdote connected to it. Likewise Kiel's enthusiasm for lyrics that are meant to mess with your head is all about taking that head to another place. He shows me a couple of pages labelled 'Khoons n rymes', telling me as he does so: 'There ain't no copyright.'

'"Red kite, yella balloon. That's a headfuck. Blue, green or red, take the choice that's in your head. As those colours illuminate. That in your mind imaginate. I'm standing here, painting pictures in your brain. I'm playing with your mind once again."'

Ready for the
Steady for the
Ready for the action
It's in your brain
Start a chain reaction
As those chemicals start mix
Your brain starts playing trix
Flip the switch
The trip switcha
A brand new picture
The dreams so clear
So wake up wake up enjoy the atmosphere

Take the red pill

The Matrix is Hollywood's glossy and beautifully choreographed take on reality blur. Machines control the world and the majority of humans spend their whole lives plugged into a lifelong virtual reality experience, providing a power source for the machines. In *The Matrix*, our real world is their fake one. And the characters' real world is a fantastic sci-fi construct. The remaining human freedom fighters who are conscious in the threatened, drab real world of *The Matrix* can upload themselves into a computerised version of Earth in the late nineties, but an Earth where physical laws can be distorted if you have the talent.

At the end of *Matrix: Reloaded* – the second of the three films – it starts raining in the virtual world, signalling the disintegration of the constructed universe, and possibly a return to reality. It feels like that at the film's premiere in Leicester Square. The crowds are there, the big screens showing a mixture of clips and behind-the-scenes sequences; a lively presenter quizzes competition winners, and people line the entrance to the cinema. Before the first celebs arrive, though, dismal drizzle becomes a more solid downpour, and scantily dressed VIPs scurry through the puddles, their vision of a perfect entrance to the year's most awaited film short-circuited.

I go to the premiere not to see the movie but to talk to the fans, and try to understand why this tale of parasite machines and a virtual world that resembled our real one had caught so many people's attention. Most of the people I speak with are fans of *The Matrix*, but fans in the traditional sense: trying to catch a glimpse of Keanu and crew: a quick celeb hit. They talk happily about the special effects, the fight scenes, the bullet time, but for a film that claims to have sparked a following because of its philosophy, because of its central concept, the answers seem simplistic.

As I later discover, the real fans are elsewhere, too smart to venture into a world where rain can really ruin the fun. The real fans are in the closest thing we have to the matrix: the internet.

On cinemascreen.co.uk's discussion boards, the debate is all about the different levels of world we inhabit.

```
I'm glad to see that other people have grabbed onto this
concept of a 'meta-matrix' that the 'real world' is a part
of. If you watch the monitors behind Neo when they are
showing different scenes that Neo has been through, it shows
some things that have happened to him in the 'real world'.
How could the Matrix be showing scenes of things that
happened in the 'real world' unless that too was a part of
the matrix?
```
                                   Reviewed: Mike Vacca, 19 May 2003
```
Humans are living within a matrix of a matrix. No one is
free from the Meta Matrix yet … but in the 3rd movie … Neo
and Agent smith will work together to break free …
```
                                   Anthony Cambeiro, 17 May 2003

The appeal of *The Matrix* works on several levels. Most obviously, it presents the level of total immersion – most humans never wake from their virtual existence – that Samuel hankered after. Total immersion in a world so physical, so tangible that you cannot tell it's a construct. More broadly, it acts as a metaphor for today, by presenting a version of our real world as a fake one, while also suggesting that the real world in the film is a mess, with humans facing destruction ... and the only way to fix it is by entering the virtual world of the Matrix. Outside the Matrix, humans are powerless, at the mercy of machines. Within it, anything is possible.

But interestingly, despite the original premise, the final message is not anti-tech. Keanu – the One – sacrifices himself so that humans and machines can live in harmony. And of course the behind-the-scenes story of the movie is about as pro-tech as you can get. Technology to produce pleasure and entertainment. It revels in the modern, the new, the never done before. But also the paradoxes that technology brings with it, acknowledging the fear that it causes within us. 'These machines are helping us, while others are coming to kill us.'

Like most successful contemporary entertainment, *The Matrix* is not confined to one genre. Beyond the film, a collection of stories, told across different media, offer deeper involvement for those who seek it. There is a computer game and a series of animations commissioned by the Wachowski brothers – the trilogy's directors – to complement the films. One by Yoshiaki Kawajiri features two samurai characters riding in the snow, considering whether ignorance and happiness is better than knowledge of the Matrix.

'Maybe you regret taking the red pill?' the black samurai asks. 'It crosses everyone's mind at least once. The wish to return to an ordinary life. A carefree life. The life we had before knowing all this.'

'Even if that life was just an illusion?'

'It's ironic that one could be more at peace in the virtual world.'

'I took the red pill because I wanted to know the truth.'

I e-mail Jess, a 21-year-old student and one of the site's experts on the film. He replies with a lengthy explanation of *The Matrix* story as well as some broader thoughts about *The Matrix*'s appeal.

```
I think that people of my generation, X, Y, whatever you
want to call it, are kind of disenchanted with reality in
general. We've been bombarded with so much violence and mass
culture via television and the internet, we aren't affected
```

by the hardships other folks face. Thus I think it's easy to feel like our world is something pulled over our eyes to protect and control us. That, in conjunction with human desire to seek the truth, makes The Matrix a perfect escapist fantasy for those of us that don't necessarily like society's growing dependence on technology and corporations for what to think and feel.

He also sees it as an ideal film for a generation who slip through identities.

It's the perfect metaphor for the levels of reality we all experience on a day to day basis. For example, on any given day, I move from a sleep/dreaming reality into the 'real' world, then navigate the internet, for example, which is IMHO another reality. We become a digital signature, an e-mail address, for the time we spend online. Instead of walking and picking up a book, to compare the internet to a library, we simply navigate to our destination by tapping a few keys.

Later, when I sit down at my Xbox to play some halo, I switch from the real world where walking forward requires the use of my legs, arms, balance centers, etc, to a videogame, where walking forward only requires the press of a button. I feel like my generation is the first to take technology for granted.

At no other time in human history has man had so many choices for a particular reality, and never have we taken it so lightly. Escaping reality through these simulated experiences is second nature to us. It is only natural that a film depicting the same struggle would have mass appeal to my generation.

Is fiction more fun than reality?

absolutely. ;)

Un/real tournament

What dawns on me as I watch hundreds of kids run round the PlayStation Experience, as I see lighters raised to Eminem, when I'm talking to Kiel or hearing Samuel's dreams for physically immersive gaming, is that the so-called battle between reality and artificiality is over. For most under-twenties, there is little awareness that a battle has even been fought. Or even that two sides existed to take part. The binary definitions of real and virtual or fake or artificial are too clumsy and inaccurate to be helpful these days. To find a purely real experience, a moment that is not overlaid with some form of 'unreal' information, is nearly impossible in today's world.

Each day millions of British kids and young adults have their reality enhanced by minidiscs, iPods and mp3 players; TVs, radios and computer screens; cinemas and arcades; cashpoints and mobile phones. That's an awful lot of extra worlds and fresh stimulation tacked on to the normal world. Apple's iPod is lighter than two CDs and can hold 10,000 songs. Sony's PSP gives you PlayStation-quality games on the move, and lets you listen to CDs or watch DVDs if you don't fancy gaming. They provide a permanent and near endless soundtrack or accompaniment to the world as you move through it. This is how our contact with the real world works … plugged in, switched on, moving around through a myriad of sources, often several at the same time. TV in the background, sound down while playing Xbox, playing video games with the stereo on, texting while watching TV, in fact texting while doing anything else. Living through Windows. And this is just the start.

For the kids I speak with, this is an enriching rather than a polluting experience. They don't play games to escape reality; nor do they reject anything inorganic in a quest for authenticity; rather they skilfully and multiply combine and move through different levels of enhanced reality. Sometimes this is as simple as walking home while on the phone; other times it involves spending hours in an entirely fictional world, created by the imaginations of thousands over months and months. This is so normal, so embedded in our daily experience of life that the idea that each is a trip outside of our body's limits seems over-academic and faintly ridiculous.

There is no real any more; it's all tinged and overlaid with the unreal, the enhanced, the improved. To try and make the distinction between a real experience and a non-real experience is impossible. But to believe – as Nick Clarke seems to – that this is a confusing condition for the inhabitants of this blurred world is naive and patronising. The younger you are, the more easily, swiftly and fluidly do you move through the layers of different reality that make up our daily experience.

I spoke to games players at competitions, at exhibitions, at home. When I asked the majority of them why they enjoyed playing so much, the answers were simplistic. Because it's fun. Because I enjoy racing cars/shooting people/fighting/killing aliens/getting a hole in one … getting a high score.

Originally, I'd guessed that the development of computer games offered role play, escapism, the ability to change your character and behaviour, to acquire new skills, to solve problems. These are without doubt true. But what I didn't understand is that they are also almost invisible. Nobody talked about them. The transition between your human body and the screen figures is so frequent, so familiar that it is hardly noticed. It just becomes another way of being. Another possible personality. People move easily and naturally through a myriad of overlaid worlds, and each of these have elements of reality and virtuality in them. The adjustment is automatic … like when you hold your breath as you jump into water.

The overlaid world is already here; the transition is just becoming smoother. Whether it's technology like Bluetooth, which lets different pieces of nearby kit talk to each other without wires, or Shazam, which lets you point your phone at the radio and discover the title and artist of the song that's playing, or Eyetoy, a camera that sits above your screen filming you and then putting that image into a game that you are playing, our world is a mist of other information and stimulation, and it's getting mistier all the time.

Whether something is good or not is determined just as it always has been. Do I like this; does it make me laugh; do I want to tell someone else about it? Whether you're comparing a squat party or a computer game; a mobile ringtone, a music video or a cruise, it all comes back to the same thing. Did it make me feel different? Did I experience something new? Did it make me wiser/happier/stronger/more popular? Does it help me grow?

Disconnect/zones

Perhaps it's naive to believe in the real world. Our experience is always mediated, enhanced. Kids are just better at moving through different layers of reality. Understanding and responding to the different levels. Existing simultaneously in several. It's the so-called real world – that world of tax and wars, of politics and companies, of geographies and histories – that seems most unreal because it is most distant. If you cannot affect the existing world, if it feels so untuned to your desires and values, why not make and inhabit worlds where you can have some effect, some recognition?

Xbox's 'Play More', Nintendo's 'Life's a Game', PlayStation 2's 'The Third Place' all allude to the infection of this world by the gaming world, or the collapsing of the two to form a different combined space, somewhere that hovers eternally between the real and the unreal, and is both at the same time. For teenagers, games offer a very different model of response from the real world, where, largely, you can put a great deal of effort in (a badly paid job, two years of coursework) for unsatisfactory results. I wonder if this is broadly true for many of the activities that young Britain finds valuable. From drugs to modified cars to fashion, the rewards are out of proportion to what you have to do to get them. You could call this lazy. Or you could call it smart. Identifying the places where you can get the best result for the least effort.

Many of the people I spoke with spent a great deal of time in unreal environments – from the heightened atmosphere of clubs and festivals to the spacecraft-like controls of their cars, or the immersive worlds of video games – but I never got the sense that they had any trouble understanding that there were different rules for each place. Or any confusion about where one place ended and the other began.

Games, clubs, cars are beguiling. They offer places where people have influence, where their actions are rewarded. They are beautiful, shiny and fresh. Digital perfection beats real-world imperfection, beats real world imperfection, beats the lack of influence over events in this real, geo-political world.

This urge for creation, for influence, for status, for meaning has led to a situation where more and more of these places, these disconnect/zones, are being formed. They have always existed, but British youth is getting better at making them and finding them, even if they only last for a few hours. Sometimes these are fully virtual, as in video games, but more often they are a combination of sounds, music, images and graphics. Physical locations that are separate from the humdrum world they usually occupy: whether it's Pontin's in Prestatyn, or a Tesco's car park.

The growing amount of time spent in unreal environments impinges and directs real-world behaviour and attitudes. But perhaps not in the simplistic way that many critics imagine. The kids I spoke to seemed dismissive of the possibility that violent computer games or angry lyrics lead to corresponding real-world behaviour. However, there are more subtle and deeper-reaching effects … on a value system, on how people see their reach in the real world compared to the virtual one. Perhaps the biggest lesson that unreal worlds teach young Britons is that there are places they can go where they do have influence, where output is greater than input. The physical laws of the unreal universe are less fixed, more responsive, more fun. In the unreal world, you mean more.

Disconnection and hope

Chaotic from the outside, beautiful within

The most significant disconnection that I discovered over 2003 was that between young Britons and the media that claims to represent them. Any misunderstood system looks chaotic from the outside, so perhaps mainstream media portrays British youth as amoral, superficial, wasted and dumb because their behaviour seems inexplicable.

Many of the accusations levelled at young Britons are correct: they take a lot of drugs, they play violent computer games, surf porn, listen to furious lyrics, have little respect for the government, think fashion is vitally important, and look to distant unreal celebrities for life advice.

But the more people I spoke to, the more disconnect/zones I visited, the more unfair these accusations appeared. The public portrayals of this thing called youth culture – whether they are attention-seeking headlines, sales-seeking slick ads or award-seeking gloomy documentaries – bear little resemblance to most of the experiences of young people in Britain. They are elements of truth that have been distorted to serve a different purpose.

I felt cheated by the portraits of the depressed, the disturbed and the dangerous and felt that looking at these without searching for the positives is at best irresponsible, at worst contributing towards the very situation it claims to describe. Much of the information we receive about this generation is mediated. And the mediator has its own agenda. The purpose of newspapers is to sell copies, so they will present the world in a way that is most likely to do this. The purpose of TV documentaries is to get viewers. In a massively crowded mediaplace, where hundreds of channels vie for attention, it's the extreme, the disturbing, the new that will get attention. The representations of our world that media give us conform to the same rules and pressures as all other entertainment and communication in today's world.

Kids can read, watch TV, listen to politicians. They recognise that their forms of entertainment, their loyalties and behaviour are criticised. That many people in authority seem to have given up on them. Is it any wonder that they feel disconnected?

Life in Britain in 2003 is far from rosy for many of the kids who live it. As always for this age group, there is violence, prejudice, poverty, depression, insecurity, etc. But the strategies of disconnection – from the past, from mainstream politics, from traditional forms of education, from taboos and shame, from duty, and most importantly from reality – are not those of a stupid, uncaring, vacuous bunch. They are practical, sociable and often enjoyable responses to a world that is difficult for everyone, and within which a new code of existence is still being created.

Rather than finding this degree of disconnection discouraging or upsetting, by the beginning of 2004, my impression of British youth had become more positive. I felt cheered by my contact with boy racers, with drug users and graffiti artists. Within these frowned-on activities I had found beauty and humour. Friendliness and energy. The kind of things that make living worthwhile. At the same time, there were few signs of moral ambiguity or destructiveness. The majority of people I spoke with were more conservative than I had expected. They had decided on a set of personal moral codes, and were judgemental of people who acted differently.

Kim Howells suggested the politics of culture is as important as any type of politics, and this understanding lies at the heart of young Britain. Is this the first truly existential generation? One that recognises and almost accepts the impossibility and implausibility of changing or influencing anything on a national or political level? That would explain their complete immersion in the immediate, the visceral and entertaining. Choosing between lack of control and personal influence. Between limits and infinite possibility. This is why there are so many disconnect/zones in existence: places where the rules are different from normal Britain.

Rather than gated communities for the rich, these places act as gated entertainment communities: for fetish, drugs, booze, speed, absurdity. The excess and difference are all ways of keeping people out and legitimising a particular type of behaviour. Means to make space in a crowded country.

While some of the forms may seem familiar, there is a very different dynamic to previous bursts of countercultural youth energy. Unlike the free party scene in the late eighties, or the sixties' mission to bring acid to the world, the energy and intent of our 21st-century disconnect/zones is hardly ever directed outwards, beyond their own sphere of influence. It's about local influence over national or global impotence. There is a tacit understanding – one that has gone beyond cynicism or hope – that change does not happen on a national or political level. But that doesn't mean it can't happen on a local, personal level. What is being done in these zones, some of which is legal, some of which isn't – but all of which works better when it is self-contained and uncontaminated by the tedium and dirt of Britain – is driven by passion and pleasure.

Douglas Coupland's *Generation X* in the late eighties identified a Western generation whose response to an uncaring, unfair, materialistic world was to not give a fuck, to descend into apathy and parody. In contrast, Britain today shows many signs of a more active, practical and positive response to a world that continues to be unfair and unappreciative.

The active disconnection from many of the things that contemporary society continues to try and attach importance to – politics, business, history – has not led to apathy, but instead to passion, creativity and influence. It's not the skaters or the clubbers or the vid game addicts or even the tokers that you should be worrying about. Nor the fame-obsessed or the sneaker collectors. It's the ones without the interests and the passion. The 'I don't know' or 'I don't care' kids. It's the aimless kids, the unhyperactive, the ones who cannot see the plethora of options that exist for them.

When you are part of a particular scene, talking to people who are immersed in it, there is little strangeness – whether it's watching a fifteen-year-old snort lines of ketamine off a food-chopping board, or watching two people fuck as a crowd looks on. Perhaps some of the tensions we see occur when these behaviours slip out of their zones and come into contact with other parts of Britain. And with their frequency and the numbers involved this happens more and more often.

Pretty cars and pink hair

Throughout my journeys across Britain, two groups of young people stood out. These were the psychedelic clubbers and the modified-car kids. One made up mainly of students; the others more likely to be kids who left school at sixteen, often still living at home with their parents, and whose first jobs were providing them with a relatively high disposable income. They don't constitute a huge proportion of British youth, although neither are they niche groups. My interest in them was not because I felt that they represent the future of British youth. I don't think that all young people tend towards souped-up motors or cyber style. But these people seemed to embody deeper beliefs and desires.

Between them, they stand for most elements of behaviour and attitude that are transforming the way that British youth acts, how they think about themselves and where their aspirations lie. By looking towards these groups and understanding them, you can get a broader sense of priorities for the wider young British population. Leaving the pretty cars and pink hair behind to arrive at some more general truths.

Both groups create a distinct look and behaviour, which in turn leads to a tight-knit social group. It is immediately obvious from your clothing, from your car, whether you belong. Their events take place in secluded or cut-off locations, ensuring as little interference as possible. This means that for a few hours, at least, they can determine their own laws, their own parameters of conduct. This is important, because the majority of members are involved in low-level illegality: dealing and taking drugs, writing on walls, driving too fast in places you're not meant to, driving under the influence of drugs.

Both activities are marked by a restless desire for self-transformation and improvement. Aesthetic and physical. And a hunger for increased stimulation: speed and quantity. Whether it's music, drugs, acceleration or costumes, the refrain is consistent: louder, brighter, faster, harder. More.

Beyond the events themselves, there is ongoing contact between members, via websites, chatrooms and mobiles, offering a fluid and almost permanent means of staying in touch, organising the next events. And connected to this is the possibility of visibility within your community, of local fame – via outlets like *Redline* magazine or the Sundissential website.

The qualities that struck me about both groups – and which spread across most of the young people I talked with – were the passion and personal creativity that they put into their interests. No passive recipients of a bland entertainment diet, these kids created their own: spending time, money and love to make something beautiful and individual.

While it is easy to argue that every young generation seeks to distance itself from the activities and beliefs of the culture that it is inheriting, today's disconnect/zones are different from previous ones because they tend to ignore, rather than reject, the laws and morality that they feel are irrelevant, and replace them with their own. They find places where they can behave as they please, where they have influence and recognition.

Through computer games, through the internet, through graffiti, through the secluded events that take place across Britain every week, the learning is simple. If you don't like where you're at, if you feel insignificant or irrelevant, then there are places you can go where you do count, where you do have a voice.

This generation is not content to be ignored, to inherit outmoded ways of doing things; to conform to old-fashioned belief systems. But rather than pushing against a system, they create places beyond that system's influence. They choose which part of public Britain they like, and when it doesn't satisfy, they make their own versions.

They are not content to wait until someone else decides they are grown up. They want self-determination now. And increasingly they don't need an older generation to legitimise it.

And this stubbornness indicates a broader truth about contemporary Britain. We are in a transitory stage, moving to an age of far greater personal responsibility and self-sufficiency. The model of a nation united by laws, religion, a particular orthodoxy is outdated. Instead you choose from a constellation of possibilities. As with any period of transition, it is a time when boundaries are tested, when new belief systems rub up against old ones.

In the end, what I took from my journeys round Britain, the hundreds of conversations I got into, the thousands of kids I watched entertaining themselves, was almost entirely positive. Sitting with Gemma in her tiny south London flat and hearing her ambitions to be a singer. Letting Saru show me his profusion of photos, stickers, drawings, tags. Seeing Esme parade above a crowd of fetish fans. Hearing some of the Baseline Ladiez' tracks. Reading Kiel's lyrics. Clambering around with Chris and Ray to discover hidden graffiti. Flicking through Natalie's meticulous documentation of parties and protests. Watching a hall of psycho-activated kids go nuts. Seeing mutant cars tear after one another down a race track.

I found much of Britain ugly, repressive, judgemental. But I was constantly surprised and enlivened by the range and energy of the responses to such an environment. Within every disconnection is a powerful attraction to a set of values and behaviour, and one which points towards a new social dynamic. This generation of young Britons is simultaneously used to being ignored and criticised by the British establishment, and nevertheless getting exactly what it wants. British society is loose enough for this to take place, for personal responsibility to expand, for unquestioning inheritance to be replaced by practical curiosity.

Going back to the numerous criticisms that were being made of young people in Britain, it seemed that the *characteristics* of young modern culture – novelty, velocity, volume, choice, stimulation, hedonism, sexual and violent imagery, fashion, computer games, music, celebrity – were often mistaken for the *problems* of youth culture.

Most people I spoke with embraced the very scenarios and situations that were being criticised – drug-taking, celebrity culture, graffiti, promiscuity. Embraced them wholeheartedly, with passion and creativity. Not because they were dupes, corrupt or evil; but because these things bring pleasure and self-esteem. Kids are much more capable of understanding the importance and significance of their activities and environments than we are.

So my final question: why is the diversity that young Britain displays and loves treated so critically? Britain is not a melting pot, but a mishmash of cultures and beliefs, whose distinct identities contribute to a powerful if permanently disconnected country. As the rate of cultural change and the volume of new phenomena continues to rise, so it is likely

that more disconnections will occur within generations and that previous generations will be left behind more quickly. Disconnection happens in creative cultures; it is a sign of human potential. The more disconnections that a country can hold, the more cultures it can contain that are at odds with each other, the healthier that nation is. History shows us that there are always generational disconnections, that we hate what is new – Henry Miller, Elvis, the pill, flares, Sex Pistols, etc, etc – even as it gives us something fresh.

Surely it's more useful to welcome this diversity? Rather than knocking it, we should be asking what we can learn from it. We might not like every element of difference, but it is an inevitable and constructive process. Why get upset by it? Britain should not be seeking to erase difference but to embrace it. Instead of trying to label and contain this generation we should see where it takes us.

Because this generation – if such a loose term is correct for the range of ages I spoke with – doesn't need another name, another cute set of typographies, or some extra laws to keep it in check. It needs a break.

We should be proud of our disconnected generation.